Islamophobia

TRANSGRESSIONS: CULTURAL STUDIES AND EDUCATION

Cultural studies provides an analytical toolbox for both making sense of educational practice and extending the insights of educational professionals into their labors. In this context *Transgressions: Cultural Studies and Education* provides a collection of books in the domain that specify this assertion. Crafted for an audience of teachers, teacher educators, scholars and students of cultural studies and others interested in cultural studies and pedagogy, the series documents both the possibilities of and the controversies surrounding the intersection of cultural studies and education. The editors and the authors of this series do not assume that the interaction of cultural studies and education devalues other types of knowledge and analytical forms. Rather the intersection of these knowledge disciplines offers a rejuvenating, optimistic, and positive perspective on education and educational institutions. Some might describe its contribution as democratic, emancipatory, and transformative. The editors and authors maintain that cultural studies helps free educators from sterile, monolithic analyses that have for too long undermined efforts to think of educational practices by providing other words, new languages, and fresh metaphors. Operating in an interdisciplinary cosmos, *Transgressions: Cultural Studies and Education* is dedicated to exploring the ways cultural studies enhances the study and practice of education. With this in mind the series focuses in a non-exclusive way on popular culture as well as other dimensions of cultural studies including social theory, social justice and positionality, cultural dimensions of technological innovation, new media and media literacy, new forms of oppression emerging in an electronic hyperreality, and postcolonial global concerns. With these concerns in mind cultural studies scholars often argue that the realm of popular culture is the most powerful educational force in contemporary culture. Indeed, in the twenty-first century this pedagogical dynamic is sweeping through the entire world. Educators, they believe, must understand these emerging realities in order to gain an important voice in the pedagogical conversation.

Without an understanding of cultural pedagogy's (education that takes place outside of formal schooling) role in the shaping of individual identity – youth identity in particular – the role educators play in the lives of their students will continue to fade. Why do so many of our students feel that life is incomprehensible and devoid of meaning? What does it mean, teachers wonder, when young people are unable to describe their moods, their affective affiliation to the society around them. Meanings provided young people by mainstream institutions often do little to help them deal with their affective complexity, their difficulty negotiating the rift between meaning and affect. School knowledge and educational expectations seem as anachronistic as a ditto machine, not that learning ways of rational thought and making sense of the world are unimportant.

But school knowledge and educational expectations often have little to offer students about making sense of the way they feel, the way their affective lives are shaped. In no way do we argue that analysis of the production of youth in an electronic mediated world demands some "touchy-feely" educational superficiality. What is needed in this context is a rigorous analysis of the interrelationship between pedagogy, popular culture, meaning making, and youth subjectivity. In an era marked by youth depression, violence, and suicide such insights become extremely important, even life saving. Pessimism about the future is the common sense of many contemporary youth with its concomitant feeling that no one can make a difference.

If affective production can be shaped to reflect these perspectives, then it can be reshaped to lay the groundwork for optimism, passionate commitment, and transformative educational and political activity. In these ways cultural studies adds a dimension to the work of education unfilled by any other sub-discipline. This is what *Transgressions: Cultural Studies and Education* seeks to produce – literature on these issues that makes a difference. It seeks to publish studies that help those who work with young people, those individuals involved in the disciplines that study children and youth, and young people themselves improve their lives in these bizarre times.

Islamophobia

Understanding Anti-Muslim Racism through the Lived Experiences of Muslim Youth

Naved Bakali
McGill University, Canada

SENSE PUBLISHERS
ROTTERDAM/BOSTON/TAIPEI

A C.I.P. record for this book is available from the Library of Congress.

ISBN: 978-94-6300-777-1 (paperback)
ISBN: 978-94-6300-778-8 (hardback)
ISBN: 978-94-6300-779-5 (e-book)

Published by: Sense Publishers,
P.O. Box 21858,
3001 AW Rotterdam,
The Netherlands
https://www.sensepublishers.com/

Printed on acid-free paper

TABLE OF CONTENTS

ACKNOWLEDGMENTS

This work has been a culmination of the efforts of a number of individuals who have helped to bring this work to fruition. For their dedication and commitment I would like to thank them and acknowledge their contributions. Firstly, I am profoundly grateful to Shirley Steinberg for her invitation to write this book and for her support in seeing it through with discussion and editorial input. I would like to thank my family Rauf, Nasima, and Naushine Bakali, Ara, Sofia, Shan, and Adam for always supporting me in my academic pursuits throughout my life. They have truly been a constant source of inspiration and comfort. I would also like to thank Dr. Aziz Choudry, for his diligence, insight, and his tireless efforts in my graduate training. I am grateful to Dr. Ronald Morris and Dr. Anila Asghar for their help and advice. They provided thoughtful insights in support of this work. Additionally, I would like to thank the Fonds de Recherche Société et Culture (FQRSC), for their financial support in facilitating my research. My dear friends Mahmoon, Manzir, Farzad, Hamaad, Sher, Kotter, Bundy, Mirza, and Ali, have always been a source of encouragement over the years while putting this work together. My colleagues, Nadeem, Megan, Haidee, Ryan, Jenn, and Zia provided me with mentorship, advice, and thoughtful insights. I am indebted to them for their help. Finally, I would like to thank my wife, Sadia Virk, and children. Sadia has been an unwavering pillar of love and support for the past ten years and has always encouraged me to pursue my dreams. Had it not been for her patience and sacrifices I would not have been able to complete this work. I have written this book with my dear children in mind. It is my hope that my research will one day contribute to a better world for my family. Thank you all for your help, support, sacrifice, and love.

INTRODUCTION

Islamophobia: Meta-Narratives and Localized
Discourses of the Muslim 'Other' Post-9/11

A TYPICAL DAY FOR MUSLIMS IN CANADA?

Monday, November 16, 2015. It was an ordinary day in Toronto, Ontario; Canada's largest city and one of the most culturally diverse cities in North America. A young mother is on her way to pick up her children from Grenoble public school. As the streets are filled with a beautiful mélange of leaves with beaming hues of red, orange and yellow, she decides to walk to the school, while enjoying the cool Canadian Fall weather. However, today, despite its mundane routines would be different for this mother. On this day she was brutally attacked by two young men. The youth viciously assaulted her, delivering blows to her abdomen and face. The ordeal ended when they took her cellphone and whatever money she had. On the surface, it would seem that this unfortunate incident was simply a robbery by a couple of street thugs looking for some loot from an easy target, however that was not the case. This mother was a young Muslim woman, who wore a *hijab* and she was targeted by these youth because of her appearance. As she was being assaulted, the young men were yelling racial slurs at her, calling her a 'terrorist' and telling her to 'go back home'. The attack culminated with the pulling of the woman's *hijab* signifying the impetus of their hatred and violence towards the young mother. This incident was one of a number of hate crimes, including a mosque being set ablaze, instances of verbal and physical assault, and vandalism, across Canada in the wake of the Paris attacks on November 13, 2015, where Muslim terrorists orchestrated three suicide attacks killing 130 and injuring 368 people.

Another similar incident took place in London, Ontario, on June 21, 2016. A young Muslim woman was at a supermarket with her four-month-old son when she was verbally harassed, punched multiple times, spat on, and had her *hijab* and hair pulled by another woman whose only apparent motive for targeting her was that she was Muslim. Incidentally, the perpetrator was wearing a bright red t-shirt that had the word 'Canada' sprawled across the chest, emblazoned with the iconic Canadian maple leaf below. Two days prior to this incident, a Quebec City mosque had a pig's head wrapped up in a decorative bouquet left on its doorstep accompanied with a note saying 'Bon appétit'. These incidents came shortly after a mass shooting at an Orlando gay nightclub in the US at the hands of Omar Mateen, a 29-year-old mentally unstable gay Muslim man. Mateen allegedly pledged fealty to the terrorist organization the Islamic State of Iraq and Syria (ISIS) over the phone while engaging in his gruesome massacre killing 49 people and wounding 53 others. These instances of racial violence and abuse, as well as others like them across Canada, the United

States, and Europe are a somber glimpse into the lived experiences of a number of Muslim minorities in Western nations in the context of the War on Terror.

The September 11, 2001 attack (9/11) in which Muslim terrorists targeted the New York City World Trade Centre and the ensuing War on Terror have fundamentally affected the lives of Muslims, not only in Muslim-majority countries, but also in European and North American nations. Anti-Muslim racism and discrimination has seen a consistent growth in Canada throughout the period following 9/11. In recent polls conducted across Canada, which asked Canadians if they had a generally favourable or unfavourable opinion of Islam, Christianity, Judaism, Sikhism, Hinduism, and Buddhism, it was found that Canadians have a greater dislike towards Islam than the other faiths. 54 per cent of Canadians had a negative opinion of Islam, while 69 per cent of Quebecers had unfavourable perceptions of the faith (Angus Reid, 2013). Hate crimes against Canadian Muslims more than doubled from 2012 to 2014 going from 45 to 99 (Paperny, 2016). In Quebec, various mosques have been vandalized (CBC, 2009, 2013; CJC, 2008; CTV, 2006), and legislation such as Bill 94 and Bill 60[1] have been passed or proposed restricting Muslim women's dress in Quebec. Many of the biases and discriminatory practices towards Muslims in Western nations both prior to 9/11 and its aftermath have been referred to as a phenomenon called Islamophobia.

MUSLIMS AND THE 'TERRORIST' DIALECTIC

Much of the anti-Muslim sentiment in the post-9/11 context has revolved around the notion of Muslims being violent and threatening to Western nations. Words such as 'terrorism' and 'terrorist' in political and media discourses have increasingly become subjective terms to disproportionately highlight violence committed by Arabs or Muslims over violence committed by other religious and ethnic groups. For example, on February 18, 2010 Joseph Stack, a software consultant, purposely flew a light aircraft into a government building in Austin Texas. Stack engaged in this hostile and violent act due to grievances he had with the US government, which he articulated in a suicide-manifesto. Stack was responsible for the death and injury of over a dozen people, yet despite the similarity to the 9/11 terrorist attacks, news agencies made concerted efforts not to label this act as terrorism (Greenwald, 2010). In stark contrast to the media coverage of this event, Muslims who planned similar attacks such as Umar Farouk Abdulmutallab (a.k.a. the Underwear Bomber), Faisal Shahzad (a.k.a. the Times Square Bomber), the alleged Canadian terror cell labeled "the Toronto 18", and Michael Zehaf-Bibeau, the man responsible for the 2014 Parliament Hill shootings in Ottawa, were all featured prominently in news media as terrorists.

These examples highlight how in the context of the War on Terror, terrorism is increasingly being defined by the cultural and religious affiliations of the people committing the acts and not necessarily by the acts themselves. In other words, the labeling of an individual as 'Muslim' determines if such acts fall under the definition of terrorism or just random acts of violence. As Karim Karim (2002) observes, 'Islam' has become a term "that is manipulated according to the needs of the particular source discussing it. Among other things it has come variously to refer to a religion, a culture, a civilization, a community, a religious revival, a militant cult, an ideology…" (pp. 108–109). Therefore, in the post-9/11 context, 'Islam' in public discourse has become synonymous with an 'Otherness' affiliated with terror and violence. This has become increasingly pronounced in the Canadian context with the growing number of 'radicalized' Canadian Muslim youth going overseas to join ISIS. For example, when questioned by a reporter concerning the anti-terror legislation, Bill C-51,[2] on January 30, 2015, Prime Minister Stephen Harper clearly associated the monitoring of terrorist activities with mosques. When asked how this legislation would differentiate between radicalized individuals and teenagers just messing around in a basement, Mr. Harper responded that terrorism is a serious offence "no matter what the age of the person is, or whether they're in a basement, or whether they're in a mosque or somewhere else" (reported by Mastracci, 2015). In another incident, the Canadian Justice Minister, Peter McKay, claimed that an attempted Valentine's Day shooting spree in February 2015 was clearly *not* a terrorist activity, because the attempted plotters did not have any "cultural affiliations". Mr. McKay did not specify 'Muslim' cultures. However, he made specific reference to groups like ISIS when discussing how such an action could have been classified as an act of terrorism (Auld & Tutton, 2015).

It is clear from the above discussion that anti-Muslim bias and racism in the context of the War on Terror is ideologically driven, as terms such as 'terror' and 'terrorism' are defined and propagated through unequal power relations and are seemingly exclusively affiliated with Islam and 'Muslimness'. Stephen Sheehi (2011) further elaborates on this point, as he describes anti-Muslim racism, or Islamophobia as an ideological formation. For Sheehi, an ideological formation is created by a culture that employs a fixed set of tropes, analyses, and beliefs, which inform governmental policy, political and media discourses, and social beliefs and practices. This is not to say that Islamophobia originates from a fixed group of media outlets, government bodies, or political organizations. Rather, these actors are collectively involved in the dissemination and normalization of anti-Muslim bias in Western contexts. It is my belief, as will be demonstrated throughout this book, that anti-Muslim racism as an ideological formation has been fundamental in shaping and influencing the experiences of Muslims in Canada and in other Western nations in their daily interactions as well as their participation in institutional structures such as schools. Viewing anti-Muslim racism as an ideological formation helps to locate Islamophobia within a broader global context, as well as its construction, dissemination, and practice at localized levels. In other words, Islamophobia occurs within the context of a global meta-narrative and is also specific within localized discourses and practices. Therefore, this book will examine how Islamophobia manifests through a global meta-narrative relating to global conflicts, the War on Terror, dichotomizing cultural groupings such as the Orient and Occident, and the 'clash of civilizations' thesis. However, this book will also demonstrate how Islamophobia is constructed and utilized at localized national and provincial levels.

EXAMINING MUSLIM EXPERIENCES IN CANADIAN SCHOOLS

In this book I set out to learn about Muslim youth experiences in Canadian schools in the context of the War on Terror. I specifically looked at the experiences of young Muslim women and men who currently attend or had attended secondary schools in the Canadian province of Quebec since 9/11. Additionally, I interviewed Muslim and non-Muslim teachers for their anecdotal comments about Islamophobia in Canadian secondary schools. In conducting interviews with participants, I employed a critical ethnographic approach, which can be understood as a "research methodology through which social, cultural, political, and economic issues can be interpreted and represented to illustrate the processes of oppression and engage people in addressing them" (Cook, 2008, p. 148). Therefore, this methodological approach can be particularly useful when examining oppressed or racialized groups. Critical ethnography involves interviewing subjects and creating a record of observation, collecting field notes, observing participants in social sites, as well as analyzing the social structures with which participants interact with and which impact or influence the social surroundings of participants.

My objectives in doing this study were three fold. First, I wanted to explore whether or not these youths felt they experienced discrimination in their secondary schools in the post-9/11 context and if so, what factors may have facilitated this. Second, I wanted to determine if there was a discernable connexion between the types of representations of Muslims in popular cultural media and how Muslims felt they were perceived in their secondary schools. It was paramount for me to understand if there was a relationship between Muslim representations in the media and the experiences of Muslims in schools and if so, were Muslim students cognizant of how that relationship was defined. My final objective was to provide Muslim students with the opportunity and a platform to reflect upon and express biases and prejudices they may have experienced as Muslims in Canadian schools in the post-9/11 era. It was my hope that this could be an empowering experience for these young people who have rarely had an opportunity to be heard in relation to their experiences with race and racism in their schools.

This was a qualitative study. Much of my analysis and understanding of the issues presented in this work were constructed from a critical race perspective. To collect data on the experiences of my participants I engaged in audiotaped interviews and group discussions. In some instances, this involved engaging in multiple interviews for clarification purposes. Interviews took place over a span of twelve months from May 2013 to May 2014. Interviews were semi-structured, posing open-ended questions relating to how Muslims were perceived in society; if perceptions of Muslims were shaped by media representations; and if they had encountered racism against Muslims within educational contexts. As I am a Muslim teacher, my research required me to engage in a self-reflexive process, which can be described as the researcher's engagement of continuous self-examination and exploration of how their personal biases influenced their research and findings.

ORGANIZATION OF THIS BOOK

I have divided the book into two parts. I refer to Part One as 'understanding Islamophobia', which is composed of Chapters One to Four. Part Two, comprised of chapters Five and Six, discusses 'experiencing Islamophobia'. Given the argument that I advance, that Islamophobia is an ideological formation which can be delineated into global meta-narratives and localized narratives, Part One of the book elucidates the global and localized narratives and practices of Islamophobia, while Part Two of the book examines how both forms exist within the experiences of Canadian Muslim youth. Chapter One will introduce and historicize the phenomenon of Islamophobia by examining Muslim-Western relations throughout the crusades, colonialism, and the War on Terror. This historical analysis will demonstrate how the Muslim 'Other' has been perceived at various junctures in Muslim-Western relations, thus illustrating some of the complexities and the evolutionary nature of anti-Muslim prejudice. Furthermore, Chapter One will compare and contrast manifestations of Islamophobia in North America and Europe to better understand how Islamophobia differs in varying contexts, as well as how some of the similarities contribute towards a larger meta-narrative of anti-Muslim bias. The chapter will conclude by briefly discussing the theoretical tradition of critical race theory to clarify how I have positioned myself in my analysis of anti-Muslim racism.

Chapter Two will discuss how Islamophobia is enacted through the social relations of race, gender, and class. The central focus of the chapter will examine how the 9/11 attacks and the War on Terror have impacted Muslim communities in North America and have influenced and informed perceptions of Muslims. This chapter will demonstrate how in the post-9/11 context, Islamophobia is mediated and manufactured by the War on Terror through these social relations. The emergence of Islamophobia through the social construction of race entails espousing negatively evaluated meanings of a group by virtue of assumed biological qualities. In other words, the conception of Muslims as an inferior 'race', who fundamentally differ from the 'Westerner'. Examining Islamophobia through a gender lens involves attending to the construction of Muslim women as abused and oppressed at the hands of dangerous Muslim men. The narratives of victimhood of Muslim women have been coopted by liberals, conservatives, as well as feminists for justifying empire and Western intervention in Muslim majority nations. Islamophobia through class relations entails addressing the vulnerability of Muslim underclasses and targeted laws which have affected Muslim immigrant working-classes in the context of the War on Terror. Examining Islamophobia through these social relations will help contextualize participants' comments and experiences discussed in chapters Five and Six.

Chapter Three will look specifically at Quebec society, as my study examines Islamophobia through the experiences Canadian students residing and going to school in the province of Quebec. Here, I will briefly examine Quebec's history including the cultural shift in the 1960s which redefined Quebecois identity, referred to as the 'Quiet Revolution'. As I will show, these changes brought about a reinvigoration of linguistic and nationalist sentiments, which resulted in a turbulent relationship with the 'Other', the brunt of which, I will argue, has been borne by Muslims in the post-9/11 context. Ultimately, chapter Three will demonstrate how Islamophobia in Quebec, though impacted and influenced by the meta-narrative of Islamophobia in the North American context, also emerges as a result of historical, political, and social influences specific to Quebec and Canadian society. In other words, Islamophobia in Quebec is a textured and multifaceted phenomenon interacting with a number of local and global influences.

Chapter Four will examine popular cultural mediums, which have influenced knowledge production of Muslims in the North American context. This will include analysis of selected films, news media coverage of terror attacks committed by both Muslims and non-Muslims in Canada and the US, as well as Muslim portrayals in television programs. The purpose of this chapter is to further develop and understand the global and localized narratives of anti-Muslim racism and how popular cultural media are central to reinforcing them. The dominant media framing of Muslim women discussed in this chapter relate to victimhood. Stories about Muslim women as victims reproduce the notion of Muslim woman as imperilled and in need of saving. The dominant frame of Muslim men in the media relate to dangerous and violent figures singularly depicted as the archetypal 'Muslim terrorist'. This chapter will argue that negative representations of Muslims in the media legitimize certain actions and inactions as well as authorize particular ways of seeing the world, which reinforce dominant understandings of Muslims.

Chapters Five and Six will examine the lived experiences of Canadian Muslim youth in their secondary schools. These chapters will analyze the participants' comments and how they relate to discussions of Islamophobia in previous chapters. Chapter Five discusses Muslim female student participants' experiences and Chapter Six examines the experiences of Muslim male students, as well as teacher participants' experiences. I combined the categories of Muslim male students and teacher participants in Chapter Six because my analysis of these two categories was shorter in length than the Muslim female student category. Chapters Five and Six will draw from the experiences of current, former, female and male Muslim students, as well as Muslim and non-Muslim teacher participants to help paint a portrait of the lived realities of Muslims in Canadian secondary schools and their experiences with race and racism.

The book will conclude with a discussion of the similarities and differences between the different categories of participants, as well as analyze the causes of Islamophobia experienced by participants. This Chapter will also briefly highlight some of the struggles for social justice undertaken by Canadian educators towards social justice and anti-racism education as a way forward.

NOTES

[1] Bill 94 passed in 2010 and required individuals who wore face coverings to remove them if they wanted to work for the Quebec government or receive governmental services. Bill 60 was a proposed Bill for state secularism and religious neutrality which would have restricted government employees, or people working for government funded institutions from wearing religious attire. Both Bills were primarily directed towards and affected Muslim women, as well as members of other religious communities.

[2] This legislation broadens the mandate of Canadian security agencies and enhances their powers. Critics of the Act argue that the legislation gives Canadian security agencies too much power, as some aspects of it contravene the Canadian Charter of Rights.

PART 1

UNDERSTANDING ISLAMOPHOBIA

History and Context

HISTORICIZING AND THEORIZING ISLAMOPHOBIA AND ANTI-MUSLIM RACISM

What is Islamophobia? Where did it originate from? Do we even know what the term means and refers to? Any type of informed discussion about Islamophobia needs to examine the historical processes, events, and personalities fundamental to its formation. Failure to do so can result in reductionist shortcomings, which view Islamophobia solely as a product of the present day political climate and the War on Terror. Islamophobia runs much deeper than that. As I will demonstrate throughout Chapters One and Two, Islamophobia since 9/11 has been mediated by the War on Terror, however anti-Muslim racism in Western contexts has an enduring legacy, resulting from historical power relations and imbalances, which have positioned Muslims as a diametrically opposed 'Other'.

The first half of this chapter will engage in a discussion to clarify the phenomenon of Islamophobia. In providing a functional definition for such a complex term, this chapter will first engage in a historical analysis of anti-Muslim racism as well as discuss how it emerges in various Western contexts. Thereafter, this chapter will trace the history of the usage of the term 'Islamophobia' and provide a comprehensive definition that will be used throughout the rest of the book. The second half of the chapter will provide a theoretical grounding of my analysis of Islamophobia which is informed by a critical race theory perspective. This entails discussing the basic principles of this body of scholarship, why I have adopted this perspective, and some of the contributions of critical race theory in the field of education.

HISTORICIZING ISLAMOPHOBIA

Islamophobia is a relatively new term which draws its etymological roots from Europe in the early 20th century. However, fear and mistrust towards Muslims and being perceived as a diametrically opposed 'Other' have deeper roots in Europe. As Paul Weller (2001) has observed, "Islamophobia is undeniably rooted in the historical inheritance of a conflictual relationship that has developed over many centuries involving the overlap of religion, politics and warfare" (p. 8). Western perceptions of Muslims and Islam began to form as early as the 7th century, when the Islamic faith began to make inroads into the Byzantine Empire. As Muslim armies conquered vast territories and key cultural sites including Egypt, Damascus, and the venerated holy city of Jerusalem, Islam was perceived as a threat, particularly by the

Church in Western Europe. Europe, in large part due to the influence of the Roman Catholic Church, saw Islam as a

> three-pronged challenge to its stronghold and wellbeing. First, Islam was both a religious and social ideology, one perceived to be able to challenge Europe's relative stability. Second, it was a proselytic religion, one that had the ability to challenge the ascendency of the Roman Church as well as the expansion of Christianity and third...not only might it be argued theologically that it had superseded Christianity, but through conversion and any social foothold gained within Europe's borders, so it might have had the potential to confine Christianity to the spiritual, theological and social wildernesses. (Allen, 2010, p. 26)

Muslim armies managed to make advances within some Western European territories, including the Iberian Peninsula and parts of Southern France. However, for the most part Islam was known to Europe in the absence of a physical presence. Eventually, by the turn of the 11th century, perceptions of this threatening 'Other' would be used as a tool to gain political authority and ascendency by the Catholic Church through the Crusades. Defense of Christendom and Jerusalem through the Crusades provided the papal authority with an opportunity to gain recognition as the legitimate temporal ruler of the Christian faith with the ambition of reuniting the Eastern (Greek) and Western (Latin) Churches. The Crusades, a call to arms by Pope Urban II that led to the fall of Jerusalem from Muslim hands in 1099, was propagated as a militaristic pilgrimage to reconquer and liberate the holy lands of Jerusalem from the perceived heathens of Islam. Christians who returned to Europe from the Crusades told tales of idolatrous pagans possessing extravagant wealth and luxuries living sensual and lecherous lifestyles. These stories of the near East fueled misconceptions in European societies and fomented a narrative which justified a civilizing project in light of shifting power dynamics between Europe and the Orient. Attempts to civilize the 'Other' ensued through colonial expansion over the course of the next few centuries. Thus began another chapter in Europe's interaction with the Orient—colonialism.

Postcolonial theorists have examined the impacts of colonialism on both the colonized and colonizers, who have benefited from the violence and promotion of racist ideology resulting from colonization. One of the foundational works, which has examined the colonization of Muslim majority nations, the ideologies which provided moral justifications for it, and its continuity in constructing Muslims as 'Other' was Edward Said's (1979) *Orientalism*. This work was a critique of Orientalist scholarship, and has informed many of the current day critiques of anti-Muslim racism. According to Said, Orientalism is "a style of thought based upon an ontological and epistemological distinction made between the 'Orient' and (most of the time) 'the Occident'" (p. 2). Said noted the presence of Orientalist thought in the works of European scholars, artists and academics throughout the 19th and

20th centuries. Through analyzing canonical European literary works from this era, Said observed the existence of misrepresentations, over-simplifications and binaries which constructed the West as being diametrically opposed to the East. Said argued that Orientalists viewed the East or the "Orient" as being overly sensual, primitive, and violently opposed to the West. According to Said, these views of the Orient perpetuated a constant ensemble of images and stereotypes that completely ignored the diversity across the Orient.

Said contended that Orientalism was a tool that was used by Western academics, scholars, and artists to assert dominance over the East. As he stated,

> Orientalism can be discussed and analyzed as the corporate institution for dealing with the Orient—dealing with it by making statements about it, authorizing views of it, describing it, by teaching it, settling it, ruling over it: in short, Orientalism [is] a Western style for dominating, restructuring, and having authority over the Orient. (p. 3)

The ideas of control and domination discussed by Said in *Orientalism* originated from the history that European nations have had in dominating Arab and Muslim-majority nations throughout the period of imperialism in the 16th and 17th centuries. In another one of his works, *Culture and Imperialism* (1993), Said discussed how the practices of imperialism persisted throughout the post-colonial era. Said noted, "In our time, direct colonialism has largely ended; imperialism...lingers where it has always been in a kind of general cultural sphere as well as in specific political, ideological, economic, and social practices" (p. 9). This mindset of superiority is believed by Said to have laid the foundations for Orientalist thought throughout the 19th and 20th centuries, and which in turn constructed the "Orient" as inferior and subordinate to Europe.

Said's work, though predating a number of other studies examining anti-Muslim racism continues to be foundational. As Kumar (2012) notes, a number of lingering Orientalist myths continue to endure in dominant Western discourse about Islam. These include the notion that Islam is a monolithic religion that perpetuates gender-based discrimination, that Muslims are incapable of reason and rationality or democracy and self-rule, and that Islam is an inherently violent religion. Building from the insights of this scholarship, which argues the homogenization of Muslim cultures, I contend that Orientalism has influenced our present day understanding of Islamophobia. However; Islamophobia is distinct from Orientalism and the two should not be conflated or understood to be the same.

Though colonialism was not exclusive to Muslim-majority lands, due to Europe's historical interactions with Muslims it took on a unique form of expression. As Akbar Ahmed (1999) notes, colonial powers perceived Islam as "a civilization doomed to barbarism and backwardness forever" (p. 60). Thus, the colonization of Muslim-majority lands was construed as being an act of magnanimity as they were civilizing the antithetical 'Other'. It is clear that anti-Muslim perceptions have been deeply rooted in the European context. However, the question arises whether there are similarities in how anti-Muslim bias and racism manifests in North American societies.

ISLAMOPHOBIC TRENDS IN NORTH AMERICA AND EUROPE

When examining negative views and perceptions of Muslims and Islam, a number of similarities emerge within the North American and European contexts. The reason for briefly examining how Islamophobia manifests similarly in varying Western nations is to demonstrate that anti-Muslim racism falls within a meta-narrative, in which there are general trends that transcend local contexts. Many of these commonalities, though rooted in white supremacy, have manifested in specific and textured ways in the context of the global War on Terror. The most glaring of these similarities occurs in the way Muslims have been represented in the media, more specifically the narratives that are produced in news media. Muslims have been repeatedly presented as violent, misogynistic, and inclined towards terrorism. One such example would include the recent controversy in the case of the French satirical magazine *Charlie Hebdo*. The magazine produced a number of trope laden and satirical depictions of Prophet Muhammad in 2012, similar to cartoons produced by the Danish newspaper *Jyllands Posten* in 2005. Prior to their publication it was obvious that such images would infuriate a substantial number of Muslims worldwide. The images were printed by the media outlets, which argued that the discontent of a segment of society should not trump the principles of freedom of expression. Yet, in 2003 *Jyllands Posten* rejected the printing of similar cartoons depicting Jesus, as the editor at the time believed it may cause offence and provoke public outcry. Similarly, in the North American context, Peter Gottschalk and Gabriel Greenberg (2008) have documented a series of caricatures insulting and negatively depicting Muslims and central figures in Islam as early as the Suez Crisis in the 1950s to the present War on Terror. Other examples of tensions exacerbated through the media in both Europe and North America include the negative focus on the construction of Islamic buildings and structures. In 2009 Switzerland held a referendum to ban the construction of minarets on mosques. Media coverage of this issue included inflammatory rhetoric arguing that minarets were a symbol of Muslim dominance in Switzerland, despite the fact that there were only four minarets in the country at the time of the referendum. Similar points of contention arose in the US during the opposition to the construction of Park 51, a Muslim community centre located approximately two blocks north of the former site of the New York City World Trade Centre. Media reports about the proposed centre remained relatively tamed at its inception. However, by the summer of 2010 a barrage of news analysists and conservative pundits aggressively condemned the construction of the centre, labelling it the 'Ground Zero Mosque'.

Another similarity can be seen in the types of fears and tensions towards local Muslim populations that have arisen in the context of the War on Terror. Both North

American and European nations have fostered increased anxieties towards its Muslim inhabitants and Islam in light of terrorist attacks and terror plots in these regions. In North America there has been the 9/11 attacks and the ensuing al-Qaeda inspired attempted terror plots of the Times Square Bomber, the Underwear Bomber, and the Fort Hood Shooting. More recently there have been a number of ISIS inspired 'lone wolf' attacks in Canada and the US committed by extremist Muslims. In Canada there was a shooting on Parliament Hill and a targeted hit-and-run attack in Ottawa and St-Jean-sur-Richelieu respectively in 2014. Additionally, in the US, there was a mass shooting in San Bernardino in 2015 and Orlando in 2016 by Muslim perpetrators. Given the absurd amount of mass shootings in the US, media coverage disproportionately focused attention on these two attacks because they highlighted the threat that Islamic extremism poses to the US. However, the overwhelming number of homegrown terrorist attacks in the US since 9/11 have been committed by non-Muslim white right-wing extremists (Plucinska, 2015). Similarly, Europe has experienced the July 7, 2005, suicide bombings which targeted civilians taking public transportation in central London, as well as a series of attacks in France by ISIS operatives in 2015 and 2016. Media coverage of the 'ISIS inspired' attacks in North America and Europe fixated on how the perpetrators of these acts were in some way affiliated with or inspired by Muslim terrorist groups abroad. With the exception of the attacks in France, none of these men trained with or were given direct orders from terrorist organizations. Conversely, a number of the assailants had histories with mental illness, violence, and drug abuse. These along with other sociological influences may have provided a more complete picture to explain why these men engaged in such actions.

Class-based discrimination has also targeted European and North American Muslims. Cesari (2011) observes that Muslims in European societies are mostly immigrants and are socioeconomically marginalized, as the immigrant unemployment rates are twice that of natives. This has brought about many instances of class-based discrimination for European Muslims. Similarly, Junaid Rana (2011) has documented how the War on Terror has brought about the policing of immigrant Muslims in North American societies, which have selectively applied laws against working-class Muslim immigrants. Another similarity between anti-Muslim racism in North American societies and European contexts is that anti-Muslim sentiment often arises from apprehensions towards cultural erosion. As Nathan Lean (2012) mentions, "[a]nti-Muslim sentiment [is] not just a feeling among certain segments of the population. It [is] state-sponsored praxis that aim[s]...to reinstate the heyday of white Christian Europe" (p. 171). Preservationist discourses of white Christian Europe have fueled fears of the impending Islamization of Europe. Islamization is an ideology which asserts that Muslim populations are threatening to numerically and culturally submerge all of Europe. Despite the lack of substantive evidence of a 'Muslim demographic boom', this ideology has gained popularity in the public sphere and has been widely expressed by politicians, popular authors and media pundits. Similar fears of cultural erosion permeate a number of North American contexts, particularly in several Canadian provinces as noted by Bilge (2013), Haque (2012), and Thobani (2007). As will be seen in Chapter Three, much of the anti-Muslim racism and the existence of Islamophobia in the Canadian province of Quebec revolves around fears of Muslims fomenting the cultural erosion of the French white Quebecois majority.

Anti-Muslim bias and racism has also been intensified in North American and European nations as a result of right-wing politicians and political figures. In 2011, Canadian Prime Minister Stephen Harper stated in an interview with CBC News that the greatest threat to Canada's national security is "Islamicism". It is unclear exactly what this term means, as it is not an actual word, however, the implied sentiment was that violence inspired by Muslim extremists occupied the primary focus of the national security apparatus. A number of Republican politicians in the US have also used Islamophobia as a political tool to gain prominence as defenders of American freedom and values. In 2011, Presidential Nominee, Herman Cain, described how Muslims were a fifth column in the US making "creeping" attempts to ease *Sharia* law into the US legal system (Green, 2015). Donald Trump, the Republican Nominee for the 2016 US Presidential election, has openly used anti-Muslim rhetoric as a rallying cry for his campaign, proposing an open ban on all Muslims from immigrating to the US if elected. Europe has also seen a rise in radical right politics. Todd Green (2015) notes that extreme right-wing parties constitute the second or third largest parties in the parliaments of Netherlands, Norway, and Denmark, and has the largest representation in the Swiss parliament. The most outspoken of these European Islamophobe politicians is Geert Wilders, the founder and leader of the Party for Freedom in the Netherlands. Wilders's anti-Muslim vitriol was most prominent in a short film that he produced called *Fitna* (2008), which explicitly linked texts from the Quran with violence and terrorism. Wilders was eventually charged with hate speech under Dutch law in 2009 for the film, however he was acquitted. The media frenzy surrounding the trial served to bolster his reputation as a staunch defender of European values and culture in face of the Islamization tidal wave confronting Europe. Having analyzed some of the historical causes and ideologies which have fostered and promoted anti-Muslim sentiments, and briefly viewing similarities in anti-Muslim racism in Europe and North America, I will now define how 'Islamophobia' as a concept and phenomenon will be understood throughout the rest of this inquiry.

DEFINING ISLAMOPHOBIA

To better understand the phenomenon of Islamophobia and thus be able to use an operational definition for it in this book, let us first look at the term's origins. The earliest found usage of the term 'Islamophobia' can be traced back to France in 1925 by authors Etienne Dinet and Slima Ben Ibrahim where they wrote 'accès de délire Islamophobe' ('Islamophobic delirium'), referring to Western perceptions of Muslims. In another instance Caroline Fourest and Fiammetta Venner (2003) claimed that the term was used during the Iranian revolution by religious conservatives to describe Muslim women who refused to wear the *hijab*. However, neither of the instances noted above describe how it has come into usage in contemporary times. Arguably the most influential work from which the term 'Islamophobia' acquired the greatest currency and usage that relates to present understandings arose from a report entitled *Islamophobia: a challenge for us all* by the Runnymede Trust in 1997. The Runnymede Trust is a British think tank that was created in 1968 to challenge racism, to help influence anti-racist legislation, and to promote a cohesive multi-ethnic Britain. The report described Islamophobia as the "shorthand way of referring to dread or hatred of Islam—and therefore, to fear or dislike of all or most Muslims" (Runnymede Trust, 1997, p. 1). The report argued that Islamophobia produced 'closed views' of Islam, which could be understood as viewing Islam monolithically, and as an ideological adversary which needed combating and disciplining.

The Runnymede Trust report was greeted with mixed reactions. There was both praise and criticism from Muslim and non-Muslim groups and organizations. One critique suggested that in the process of condemning biases and racism towards Muslims, the report simultaneously reproduced derogatory narratives of Muslims by consistently linking Muslims with terrorism. Another criticism of the report was that it often conflated racism specifically directed towards ethnic groups with prejudices against Muslims and Islam in general. Despite some of its shortcomings, the report and its model of Islamophobia laid the foundations for the most common and widespread definitions and conceptualizations about Islamophobia.

A number of academics and intellectuals have further attempted to define Islamophobia, referring to it as intolerance towards Muslims' religious and cultural beliefs (Esposito & Mogahed, 2007). Some have argued, however, that the term "Islamophobia" is somewhat problematic in and of itself as it is latent with the assumption that negative views towards Islam and Muslims arise from psychological traumas synonymous with other phobias such as agoraphobia and arachnophobia rather than arising from social anxieties towards a distant 'Other'. As such, the term 'Islamophobia' may be imprecisely used to describe a "diverse phenomenon, ranging from xenophobia to antiterrorism...[grouping] together all kinds of different forms of discourse, speech, and acts by suggesting that they all emanate from an identical ideological core, which is an irrational fear (a phobia) of Islam" (Cesari, 2011, p. 21). Some theorists have broadened the ideas implicit in the term Islamophobia to include "the practice of prejudice against Islam and the demonization and dehumanization of Muslims...generally manifested in negative attitudes, discrimination, physical harassment and vilification in the media" (Mohideen & Mohideen, 2008, p. 73). These definitions, though useful in many respects, fall short of a comprehensive understanding of the phenomenon of Islamophobia.

Defining such a term can pose a number of challenges. If an overly broad definition is employed, then instances of anti-Muslim racism could escape censure because ultimately the term becomes meaningless and does not describe a phenomenon that can tangibly be grasped or observed. Conversely, if an overly

17

simplistic definition is used, then inadequate solutions lacking the depth and complexity required in addressing anti-Muslim racism will abound. That being said, I am drawn to the following comprehensive definition by Allen (2010) for use throughout the book:

> Islamophobia is an ideology, similar in theory, function and purpose to racism and other similar phenomena, that sustains and perpetuates negatively evaluated meaning about Muslims and Islam in the contemporary setting in similar ways to that which it has historically…that inform and construct thinking about Muslims and Islam as Other. Neither restricted to explicit nor direct relationships of power and domination but instead, and possibly even more importantly, in the less explicit and everyday relationships of power that we contemporarily encounter, identified both in that which is real and that which is clearly not. (p. 190)

The above definition recognizes the historical roots of Islamophobia predating the 20th century and explains that it is a phenomenon which has been influenced over the centuries by various strains of thought and ideologies that viewed Muslims and the Orient as the 'Other'. This definition also acknowledges the varying spheres in which Islamophobia exists (i.e. social, economic, and political) and that these views result from both explicit and implicit power relations. Explicit power relations include enacting discriminatory political policies and legislation, as well as biased media discourses, while implicit power relations entail encounters with the non-Muslim majority attempting to maintain cultural dominance. Additionally, couched in this definition is the notion that Islamophobic messages, ideas, and actions can at times be subtle. Hence, although terms such as 'Muslim' and 'Islamic' may not be explicitly used, there may be implied meanings within messages, ideas, and actions that discriminate against Muslims. Now that Islamophobia has been defined in a comprehensive manner, I turn to discuss the theoretical approaches I have employed to inform my critique of anti-Muslim racism in North American contexts.

CRITICAL RACE THEORY

Critical race theory has been historically understood to have developed as a subdivision of critical legal studies (CLS) on the basis of racialized social and economic oppression. CLS argues that "the reasoning and logic of the law [is] in fact based on arbitrary categorizations and decisions that both reflect and advance established power relationships in society by covering injustices with a mask of legitimacy" (Taylor, 2009, p. 2). In other words, CLS advocates that the law is a power-inscribed tool that serves the interests of some in society while perpetuating injustices towards others under the guise of being fair. One of the shortcomings of their critiques has been the failure to acknowledge the pervasiveness of racism within the legal system. Hence, critical race theory developed because of these deficiencies.

Critical race theory arose in part because of a perceived failure in the strategies employed during the civil rights movement, as influential critical race theorists "argued that the traditional approaches of filing *amicus* briefs, conducting protests and marches, and appealing to the moral sensibilities of decent citizens produced smaller and fewer gains than in previous times" (Delgado, 1995, p. xiii). Key legal scholars that influenced the field of critical race theory in its formative years include Derrick Bell, Allen Freeman, Charles Lawrence, Richard Delgado, Lani Guinier, and Kimberle Crenshaw. Critical race theory at its foundation has two primary interests. The first is to understand how the regime of white supremacy as well as its subordination of peoples of colour came into being and has been able to persist in society. The second is understanding the relationship between law and racial power and working towards changing the status quo. Within this paradigm race is not perceived as biological, but rather as socially constructed. In other words, terms such as 'white' and 'black' do not refer to individual or group identity. Rather, they indicate "a particular political and legal structure rooted in the ideology of White European supremacy and the global impact of colonialism" (Taylor, 2009, p. 4). Critical race theory is a theoretical approach in which race and racism is a starting point for analysis. From this perspective, racism is a structure embedded in society that systematically advantages whites and disadvantages people of color. It is considered a 'normal' condition and not something anomalous. The overall goal of critical race theory is to dismantle systemic inequalities in society through problematizing and focusing on dominant ideologies associated with race.

There are a number of fundamental concepts that inform this theoretical perspective which include: *racism being embedded in society, racism being a persistent feature of society, critiques of liberalism, the notion of interest convergence, property rights in whiteness, storytelling,* and the overall goal of *dismantling racism.* Critical race theory argues that because *racism is embedded in society* it appears normal to those in positions of power and privilege and it is not perceived as something that is abnormal or aberrant. Hence, assumptions of white superiority are so rooted in the political, legal, and educational cultures of society that they are almost unrecognizable. According to this perspective racism exhibits in "the racial makeup of those in power and those who are disempowered as well as in the frequent absence of people of color in everything from political leadership to school curriculum to popular media" (Marx, 2008, p. 164). Given that white supremacy is understood to be the *de facto* political and ideological backdrop to society, racism is undetectable to the privileged members of society. Therefore, ironically, whites are unable to understand the world that they have created. Their advantages in politics, economics, and in education are imperceptible to them and therefore they are unable to comprehend non-white experiences and perspectives that have been shaped by white privilege. Critical race theorists hold that peoples of colour, on the other hand, have first-hand knowledge as well as multigenerational experiences which confirm the disadvantages that arise from being non-white. An example of *racism being embedded in society* could be seen in Canadian responses to Omar Khadr's capture and imprisonment. Omar Khadr was a Canadian citizen who was captured as a child soldier by US forces in Afghanistan in July of 2002. When news leaked out about his repeated torture and the Canadian government's indifference in protecting his rights, Canadians on the whole expressed little outrage, some polls indicating that the vast majority of Canadians were unhappy when he was remitted to Canadian state custody. Khadr's remittance to Canadian state custody only occurred after spending over a third of his life in a foreign prison. This instance is somewhat troubling as Canada has used humanitarianism and the cause of child soldiers to promote and sanitize its image as a benevolent and enlightened Western nation.

The second characteristic of *racism being a persistent feature of society* maintains that because racism is embedded in society it cannot simply be removed. This characteristic of critical race theory problematizes 'progresses' in racial equality through the notion of 'racial realism'. This term was coined by Derrick Bell (1990), and it implied that racism is a problem influencing law and society because it is a problem afflicting the human condition. Therefore, attempts to resolve racial inequalities must always be viewed with skepticism because of its ingrained nature in society. The *persistence of racism* can also be viewed from the perspective of victims of racism and racialized violence, as their experiences can be traumatic and have lingering effects. For example, in Robina Thomas' (2014) study of Canadian residential schooling policies, she notes that not only did these schools contribute to the cultural genocide of Indigenous communities, but also inflicted sexual, physical, mental, and spiritual abuse on Indigenous children, which have affected generations.

Additionally, critical race theory is *critical of liberalism* because entrenched in notions of liberalism is the view that jurisprudence is, or at least should be, colour-blind. Critical race theorists would argue that colour-blindness in reality masks the influence of race and racism in routine forms of inequality, which in turn prevents it from being recognized as entrenched in the justice system. The idea of colour-blindness subverts the lived reality of people of colour. Through the persistence of colour-blindness, not only is there a denial of racism, but it enables the continuance of and inability to critique white privilege. This concept has been noted by Sherene Razack (1998), in her examination of domestic violence cases among Aboriginal and women of colour in Canada. As she notes, violence in these communities is discriminatorily viewed as a cultural trait rather than a product of male domination. These instances highlight how the legal system has helped facilitate injustices for racialized communities. When women of colour come forward with domestic violence cases their communities are besmirched and looked down upon, while if they do not report these instances, violence against women in these communities persists.

Another concept key to critical race theory is that of *interest convergence*. This was also developed by Bell (1980), who argued that legislation that favours racial equality is permitted only when it benefits dominant groups or groups occupying positions of privilege in society. In relation to this point, Bell cites the example of *Brown v. Board of Education* in which the decision to desegregate schools was made on the basis of recognizing the economic and political benefits that it entailed rather than ending the racist nature of the status quo. According to Mary Dudziak (1988) the ruling for *Brown v. Board of Education* came at the height of the Cold War. When images of lynchings and the Klu Klux Klan being part and parcel of US society abounded in the Soviet Union, China, and India, the US Justice Department felt the desegregation of schools was necessary to serve the nation's foreign policy interests. This would portray the image of a benevolent progressive US society. A more recent example of this concept manifesting in Canadian society can be seen in the Truth and Reconciliation Commission in which Prime Minister Stephen Harper issued an apology to former residential school students on June 11, 2008. The commission was mandated by the Federal government with the intent of facilitating a reconciliatory relationship between Indigenous and non-Indigenous Canadians. However, as Chris Anderson and Claude Denis (2011) observe, the Canadian government's intents in creating this commission were disingenuous, patronizing, and were used as a tool to demonstrate the nation's willingness to engage in fair and respectful dialogue with Canada's First Nations communities.

The notion of *property rights in whiteness* could be understood as the belief that by virtue of being white come certain entitlements to land, property, or resources. This view was paramount in the ideologies which justified slavery and developments in free-market capitalism. Based on my interpretation of this characteristic, *property rights in whiteness* could also be seen in more contemporary examples such as the food for oil program in Iraq during the period of sanctions in the 1990s, International Monetary Fund (IMF) and World Bank loans which require indebted countries to exchange their natural resources for interest owed on their debts, as well as the occupations of Afghanistan and Iraq since the onset of the War on Terror. Additionally, *property rights in whiteness* may assume that whiteness in and of itself is a form of property, which has resulted in the practice of 'passing.' Passing occurred when people of colour, usually blacks, were able to pass as being white. The process of passing gave black people economic access as well as social mobility that was otherwise unattainable. According to Bell (2009), passing was based on an economic logic that was "related to the historical and continuing pattern of white racial domination and economic exploitation" and provided a "whole set of public and private privileges that materially and permanently guaranteed basic needs and, therefore, survival" (p. 45). Passing is a useful concept that provides insights into some of the tensions experienced by marginalized members of society who are able to blend into the majoritarian culture, as will be discussed in Chapter Five of the book.

Storytelling is central to critical race theory because seldom are the voices of the racially marginalized and oppressed heard in place of the narratives of the dominant groups in society. One of the main purposes of *storytelling* or narrative is to "redirect the dominant gaze, to make it see from a new point of view what has

21

been there all along" (Taylor, 2009, p. 8). As critical race theory has been influenced by postmodernism, embedded within this approach is the idea that 'truth' is socially constructed and that there are multiple 'truths' and 'realities.' Therefore, narratives of racially marginalized peoples and groups provide insights into their 'truths' and 'realities' as a result of their lived experiences. Incorporating the voice of the oppressed is utilized in critical race theory for three reasons. Firstly, it is employed because much of 'reality' is socially constructed; second, stories provide members of the socially marginalized a vehicle for psychic self-preservation—a remedy for the psychological pain caused by racial oppression; and finally, the exchange of stories from teller to listener can facilitate prevailing ethnocentrism and the tendency to view the world in a singular fashion (Delgado, 1989).

It may be argued that the use of narrative lacks objectivity and scholarly rigour. However as Bell (2009) observes, narrative speaks for and legitimizes itself. It is employed to record experience and insight of those who are rarely heard. Some have suggested that *storytelling*, though an important and useful tool, should never be used uncritically. In her examination of oppressed groups in courtrooms and classrooms, Razack (1998) suggests that the use of narrative and *storytelling* needs to be coupled with a deep understanding of our multiple identities and how they are constructed and intersect in a given time and context. Hence she argues that we need to probe beneath the surface and not simply question what we know, but rather how we know it. In other words, we need to engage in a reflexive process to better understand how we perceive our experiences.

Dismantling racism describes the overall purpose of critical race theory. This signifies a commitment to work towards societal change and improve the lived realities of racially marginalized people. As Bell (1990) states, "We must realize, as our slave forebears did, that the struggle for freedom is, at bottom, a manifestation of our humanity which survives and grows stronger through resistance to oppression, even if that oppression is never overcome" (p. 397). Hence, social justice and the pursuit of freedom are at the heart of critical race theory.

CRITICAL RACE THEORY AND ISLAMOPHOBIA

A number of critical race scholars have framed their analysis and discussion surrounding the racist treatment of Muslims in Western nations around laws which have been enacted to unjustly target Muslims. Critical race theory is therefore a logical framework to employ in this work because part of my critique of anti-Muslim racism in Chapter Two will demonstrate how the law is being used as a means to perpetuate racial subordination. Critical race theory provides a framework, as discussed above, for theorizing and understanding why and how racism occurs. It elucidates subtle and explicit forms of racism and articulates how they can be prevalent in society, yet disguised and masked in such a way that they continue to exist unimpeded. This is indispensable for analyzing participants' responses in Chapters Five and Six, as it clarifies if they have experienced racist treatment and explains why they may have been perceived in a discriminatory manner. Furthermore, I have adopted this framework because scholarship from this perspective describes anti-Muslim racism as systemic racism which pervades society. Anti-Muslim racism, from this perspective, is not simply an outgrowth of the 9/11 terror attacks, but rather is symptomatic of a long enduring tradition of racism that has existed and is engrained in Western societies. In other words, the racist treatment Muslims have experienced in the post-9/11 context is the result of pre-existing racism towards racialized 'Others'. This manifests through numerous social structures including educational institutions. Critical race theory is a theoretical approach that helps explicate the ideological constructs that are prevalent in social structures and embedded in society, which I contend have cast Muslims out from the nationalist space.

Additionally, it is my belief that through this theoretical framework, policies and legislations policing Muslims, as well as the War on Terror can be properly understood. Critical race theory provides a framework for understanding anti-Muslim racism holistically, which is not simply limited to hate crimes, bullying, and instances of racialized violence. Rather, state policies and practices, political and media discourses, and political conflicts are all entrenched in the practice of 'Islamophobia'. Theorizing anti-Muslim racism from this perspective demonstrates how the law is a power-inscribed tool that can be used to perpetuate injustices.

CRITICAL RACE THEORY IN EDUCATION

As discussed previously in the chapter, critical race theory initially developed through the field of law. Increasingly, academics from other fields have employed this theoretical perspective in analyzing social and racial inequities in different spheres. For example, a number of the seminal critical race works and theorists have examined cases related to education seeking to explain the social construction and existence of racism in educational institutions. Indeed, a major milestone which formalized and influenced the critical race theory movement took place in an educational setting when Harvard Law Professor, Derrick Bell, protested and eventually left his position at the school because of its refusal to hire women of colour. This sparked other student led protests over the hiring practices of minorities and people of colour at schools across the US in the 1980s. Critical race theory in education, as in the field of law, arose because of a perceived failure with traditional civil rights movements strategies. Critical race theory in educational settings includes criticisms of school curricula being used as a means of maintaining white supremacy through the process of 'master scripting'. Master scripting refers to the omission of narratives of people of colour because they challenge the dominant culture's authority and power. As Swartz (1992) observes,

> [m]aster scripting silences multiple voices and perspectives, primarily legitimizing dominant, white, upper-class, male voicings as the "standard" knowledge students need to know. All other accounts and perspectives are

omitted from the master script unless they can be disempowered through misrepresentation. Thus, content that does not reflect the dominant voice must be brought under control, *mastered,* and then reshaped before it can become a part of the master script. (p. 341)

Swartz's use of the term 'master scripting' was primarily focused towards African American experiences with schooling. However, similar arguments can be made for other peoples of colour, as narratives of most cultural groups, with the exceptions of Europeans, rarely form a meaningful portion of North American educational curricula. Therefore, critical race theory in the field of education provides a theoretical basis for critiquing Eurocentric educational curricula, which privileges the experiences, narratives, and interpretations of whites over other races and cultures. Utilizing critical race theory as a framework for critiquing traditional educational curricula may be a daunting task given the existence of master scripting in curricula that is embedded with racist notions of white supremacy. Yet, it is a necessary task, and as this book will demonstrate, is especially needed when examining racism towards Muslims in educational settings in hyper-nationalistic contexts.

CONCLUSION

This chapter provided a historical trajectory of anti-Muslim racism in Western contexts. Muslims have been perceived as a threatening 'Other' as early as the 7th century, when the faith began to grow and spread into the Byzantine Empire through militaristic expansionism. For the most part, Islam was known in absentia throughout most of Western Europe. Only glimpses of Muslims and Muslim cultures were experienced in the 'Dark Ages' of Western European society through the Crusades. As tales of the exotic, lecherous, and overly sexualized antithetical Muslim 'Other' fomented, the process of 'civilizing' the Muslim 'Other' took on the form of a colonial project. This marked an important shift in Muslim/Western relations. Throughout this period, Orientalist views of Muslims and Muslim cultures dominated the civilizing project. Lingering Orientalist myths helped to lay the foundation for more contemporary forms of anti-Muslim bias and discrimination, which this book refers to as Islamophobia.

Islamophobia is an ideology, which traces its genealogy to early interactions between Muslim and Western cultures, however it has been influenced over the centuries by various strains of thought and ideologies that viewed Muslims as 'Other'. Islamophobia exists in varying spheres (social, economic, political, etc.) and is the result of implicit and explicit power relations. This includes discriminatory political policies and legislation, biased media discourses, as well as encounters with members of the non-Muslim majoritarian culture attempting to assert their cultural dominance. Islamophobia can exist in subtle forms through media and political discourses, and can also take on more aberrant manifestations such as hate speech, hate crimes, and other discriminatory and abusive practices.

Any informed discussion about Islamophobia requires a thorough theoretical grounding to help situate anti-Muslim bias and discrimination within a broader historical discussion of racism and white supremacy in Western contexts. I have discussed critical race theory as a lens for interpreting Islamophobia to facilitate my analysis of anti-Muslim racism in the following chapter. Chapter Two examines the social relations of race, gender, and class and how anti-Muslim sentiment in the post-9/11 context is inextricably linked to the War on Terror.

VIEWING ISLAMOPHOBIA THROUGH THE SOCIALLY CONSTRUCTED POWER RELATIONS OF RACE, GENDER, AND CLASS

INTRODUCTION

This chapter will examine the phenomenon of Islamophobia through the social relations of race, gender, and class. As the first half of the previous chapter set out to define *what* Islamophobia is, this chapter will spell out *why* and *how* Islamophobia emerges in the post-9/11 context from a critical race perspective. In doing this analysis, I will be discussing the relations of race, gender, and class separately. However, that is not to imply that these exist independently of one another. Rather all of these social relations exist all together and all at once (Bannerji, 2005). The overall aim of this chapter is to demonstrate how Islamophobia is socially organized through race, gender, and class relations to shed light on how Muslims have experienced it in North America. In the post-9/11 context, Islamophobia which manifests through race, gender, and class, has been mediated through the War on Terror. Hence, my discussion of these social relations will be connected to analysis of the War on Terror. I begin my discussion of Islamophobia from a critical race perspective by examining the social relation of race.

RACE

Islamophobia emerges through the concept of 'race' when Muslims are perceived negatively by virtue of assumed biologically based qualities inherent within them; *they* are different from *us*. Embedded within these beliefs is the notion of white supremacy. As Kumar (2012) observes, "Enlightenment philosophers divided human beings into various races or "species" with distinct characteristics...[this] led white Europeans to conclude they were superior to other "darker, colored peoples," who were both "ugly" and at best "semi-civilized" (p. 29). These notions that developed in the enlightenment period endured to form the theoretical foundations on which imperialism and colonialism were built. Razack (1998) contends that the epistemological cornerstone of imperialism viewed the colonized as possessing "a series of knowable characteristics [that] can be studied, known, and managed accordingly by the colonizers" (p. 10). These 'known characteristics' painted the native as a barbaric savage that represented the antithesis of the colonizer. More recent theorists have described a number of ways in which Muslims have been understood as culturally inferior in light of existing political realities.

Politicizing Islamopohobia: Culture talk, 'good Muslims'/'bad Muslims', and race thinking. A number of critical race theorists have drawn from Mahmood Mamdani's (2004) work relating to *culture talk*. According to Mamdani, culture talk "assumes that every culture has a tangible essence that defines it, and it then explains politics as a consequence of that essence. Culture talk after 9/11, for example, qualified and explained the practice of 'terrorism' as 'Islamic'" (p. 17). This conceptualization of Muslims creates a discourse in which they are understood to possess certain essential characteristics and features. These features include predispositions to violence and aggression, barbarism, and misogyny. Conversely, Western cultures are deemed to be inherently civil, progressive, and liberal. It is through this notion of culture talk that arguments can be formulated suggesting that Muslims are not only incapable of modernity, but also resistant to it. Culture talk has been employed by critical race theorists because it theorizes how anti-Muslim racism can become politicized. The most common and pervasive usage of this has occurred through the notion of a 'clash of civilizations' first asserted by Bernard Lewis and further developed by Samuel Huntington. Their basic thesis argued that the opposing nature and essences of Western and Eastern cultures will result in an inevitable conflict. This simplistic narrative is often at the heart of media and political discourse surrounding the present day conflicts between Western nations and the Middle East. Completely ignored by the clash of civilizations thesis is an in-depth analysis of historical and political factors which have influenced conflicts between Western and Eastern nations.

The notion of culture talk cannot be understood independently of issues relating to politics, and gender. For example, both Lewis and Huntington served as policy advisors to the US government prior to and throughout the current War on Terror. The Bush administration, as well as the conservative media drew their ideological justifications from the logic embedded in the clash of civilizational discourse when justifying the wars on Afghanistan and Iraq. One of the central arguments justifying these wars was the assertion of bringing freedom and democracy, especially to the women living in these countries. As Razack (2008) mentions, "three allegorical figures have come to dominate the social landscape of the 'war on terror' and its ideological underpinning of a clash of civilizations: the dangerous Muslim man, the imperilled Muslim woman, and the civilized European" (p. 5). Hence, through the notion of culture talk one can understand how Muslims were portrayed and conceptualized in order to justify the War on Terror. The discourse of Muslim men was that of a violent and misogynistic threat; Muslim women were understood as lacking agency and in need of rescue from their inferior and oppressive cultures; and Western nations were perceived as potential saviours as they embodied the ideals that Muslim cultures were incapable of possessing. These allegorical figures or archetypes, as I will refer to them throughout the book, are essential to understanding Islamophobia in the post-9/11 context.

Another dominant frame in politics which is frequently employed in relation to racism towards Muslims in the context of the War on Terror is that of the 'good Muslim' and 'bad Muslim.' According to Mamdani (2004), political and media discourses dichotomize Muslims into two camps. 'Good Muslims' are "modern, secular, and Westernized" and 'bad Muslims' are "doctrinal, antimodern, and virulent" (p. 24). These political and media discourses advocate that good Muslims can be modernized and adapt to a globalized world. Bad Muslims, conversely, are anti-modern and destructive. They require policing and need to be put into place through military action. It is through this logic that the War on Terror gains credibility, as it is being waged against the 'bad Muslims'. Local Muslim populations are assumed to be 'bad Muslims' unless they are able to prove themselves to be 'good Muslims'. Within this political formulation, 'good Muslims' are supportive of the wars in Iraq and Afghanistan as they fall within the group that is 'with us' as proclaimed by George W. Bush when he heralded the War on Terror. 'Good Muslims' cannot be critical of the War on Terror and must unquestionably support US and Canadian foreign policy. 'Bad Muslims' may not necessarily be violently opposed to the West, but simply choose not to adopt a Westernized identity. Nowhere was the separation of 'good Muslims' and 'bad Muslims' more apparent than in the rounding up of thousands of innocent Muslims and Arabs in the US after the 9/11 attacks simply because of religious affiliations and acquaintances.

One may presume that culture talk and 'good Muslim', 'bad Muslim' discourses during the War on Terror emanated from those on the political right, since the Bush administration—with overwhelming support from neoconservative politicians, think tanks, and pundits—spearheaded the war. However, as some scholars have noted, Islamophobic rhetoric was not limited to the right. Rather, there were liberals who also embraced Islamophobic views and policies. Liberal strands of Islamophobia reject the 'clash of civilizations' thesis and recognize that there are 'good Muslims' with whom there can be diplomatic relations. This was demonstrated by Democratic US President Barack Obama when visiting Cairo in 2009, giving his 'A New Beginning' address. His address was an attempt to mend relations between the US and Muslim majority nations in the wake of George Bush's presidency and the War on Terror. However, throughout Obama's presidency it became clear that he was not only perpetuating the War on Terror but had taken measures to increase its breadth and depth. During his first term he increased punitive sanctions against Iran for its supposed nuclear weapons program—a claim which has yet to be substantiated with credible evidence; escalated the wars in Iraq and Afghanistan by increasing the number of US troops and civilian deaths in this conflict; authorized the use of drones in Pakistan which have resulted in numerous civilian casualties; continued legitimizing extraordinary renditions; continued the operation of the Guantanamo Bay prison; prosecuted 'enemy combatants' held at Guantanamo, including Canadian Omar Khadr, who, according to the Geneva Convention, was an illegal prisoner of war and a child soldier at the time of his capture; and has authorized the assassination of Anwar Al-Awlaki, a US citizen who was never tried or found guilty of any crimes. Hence, conservative Islamophobia initiated and justified the War on Terror, while liberal Islamophobia sustained and sanitized it. For Democrats or Republicans, liberals or conservatives, in Canada, the US, and abroad, it is clear that Islamophobia has been used as a political tool to orchestrate fear of Muslims locally and abroad to legitimize and win support for an imperial agenda through notions of racial inferiority. It is for this reason that the War on Terror is instrumental in understanding Islamophobia in the post-9/11 context. These differences in liberal and conservative expressions of Islamophobia, or as Kundnani (2014) has framed it, culturalist and reformist approaches to understanding the Muslim 'Other', are useful as they describe how racist perceptions of Muslims are fomented and experienced by Muslims within broader society. As this book examines experiences of racism of Muslims in secondary schools, culture talk, liberal and conservative expressions of Islamophobia, as well as other concepts, provide a theoretical basis for understanding these experiences.

Another concept which helps shed light on how Islamophobia operates through the social relation of race is that of *race thinking*, which is "a structure of thought that divides up the world between the deserving and undeserving according to descent" (Razack, 2008, p. 8). Hannah Arendt (1944) views race thinking as an ideology which "interprets history as a natural fight of races" (p. 39). Hence, it is a perspective that constructs privilege through race. Deserving races are entitled to control and dominate less deserving races. Like culture talk, race thinking is also used as a political tool to exercise power. In the context of the War on Terror, race thinking has been used to garner support for laws that have suspended due process and violated fundamental rights particularly for Muslims. This has been accomplished through legislation such as the USA PATRIOT ACT and the Anti-Terrorism Act that have been legislated in both the US and Canada respectively. Provisions within the PATRIOT ACT authorize the state to: monitor ethnic and religious groups; permit the indefinite detention of non-citizens whom are suspected of having ties to terrorism; search and wiretap without probable cause; arrest and hold a person as a "material witness" whose testimony might assist in a case; use secret evidence, without granting the accused access to the evidence; put to trial those designated as "enemy combatants" in military tribunals instead of civilian courts; and deport non-citizens based on guilt by association. As a result of these provisions, thousands of Muslims in the US have been rounded up and detained unjustly, have had their fingerprints taken, been deported, and racially profiled. A number of charitable organizations were closed or unable to continue operating because Muslims feared being investigated if found donating funds to these charities (Alsultany, 2012).

In the Canadian context similar laws have been enacted through the Anti-Terrorism Act (2001 and 2015) and the Immigration and Refugee Protection Act. Measures within the Anti-Terrorism Act (2001) include:

the strengthening of state powers of surveillance and detention; the imposition of greater restrictions on immigration and refugee policies; the increased scrutiny of immigrants and refugees (both at the borders and within the country) and a strengthening of the powers of deportation; a commitment to fighting the war against terrorism under the leadership of the Bush administration, most specifically to participate in the war on Afghanistan; and the intensification of intelligence, security, and military alliances with the United States. (Thobani, 2007, p. 348)

Although not as many Muslims have been affected by this law in Canada as in the US, a number have been racially profiled, intimidated by Canadian Security Intelligence Services (CSIS), and most notably, provisions within this law allowed for the illegal detention, extraordinary rendition, and torture of Maher Arar, a Canadian citizen of Syrian descent in 2002. Additionally, the Immigration and Refugee Protection Act authorizes the Minister of Citizenship and Immigration in conjunction with the Solicitor General to issue a security certificate. Security certificates, like the provisions mentioned above, suspend rights and due process for non-citizens residing within Canada. Critics contend that they are an example of pre-emptive punishment in which people are being punished before they have committed any crime or wrong-doing. Race is central to pre-emptive punishment as it is embedded with the belief that *they* are not like *us*. *Their* culture is uncivilized and violent and it is just a matter of time before *they* harm *us*. These provisions in US and Canadian laws have stripped away basic fundamental rights of Muslim men. Such a situation, where the suspension of the law (i.e. stripping away fundamental basic human rights) becomes the law, can be described as one where there is a proliferation of 'camps' (Arendt, 1973). These are spaces that legally authorize the "suspension of law and the creation of communities of people without 'the right to have rights'…camps are places where the rules of the world cease to apply" (Razack, 2008, p. 7). The danger of camps and the logic that underlies these spaces is that they normalize the violence enacted by the state as actions associated with the law and therefore legitimize and sanitize them. The basis for which camps operate in contemporary times is through race and how race is perceived.

Racializing Muslims: Pre-emptive prosecution, exaltation, and legislating Islamophobia. Increasingly, Muslims have been categorized as a race. Rana (2007) contends that in the American context this dates back to the civil rights movement in the 1960s. During this period, Islam was a liberatory identification for African Americans through the Black Nationalist movement of Nation of Islam. This posed a threat to the white supremacist social hierarchy of the US and eventually "the figure of the Muslim became racialized through social and cultural signifiers across national, racial, and ethnic boundaries" (Rana, 2007, p. 150). If Islam has been categorized as a 'race', it is clear that Muslims—members of this 'race'—have been marginalized, surveilled, denied their full citizenship rights, and detained in camps. This has occurred through pre-emptive prosecution.

The presence of pre-emptive punishment, discussed above, invariably results in pre-emptive prosecution, which involves

targeting innocent people that haven't actually done anything wrong. It includes a range of tactics such as the use of *agent provocateurs* to incite people to do things they otherwise would not to the charge of "material support" for terrorists, which can be applied to something as innocuous as giving money to a charitable foundation. (Kumar, 2012, p. 147)

As is the case with pre-emptive punishment, the underlying logic of pre-emptive prosecution is that those being prosecuted, in this instance Muslims, have a predisposition towards violence and committing violent crimes. As Downs (2011) observes, "to prove disposition, the government claims that routine, normal behavior of the defendants—dress, religious observances…etc.—indicates a 'predisposition' to commit terrorism, based on the false stereotype that *all* Muslims are predisposed to commit terrorism" (p. 17). As such, the logic goes that "if they are sufficiently 'Muslims' they are sufficiently 'predisposed'" (Downs, 2011, p. 17). Pre-emptive prosecution has been virulent both in the US and in Canada in the post 9/11 context in which 'terror plots' and the notion of 'providing material support to terrorists' have been used as a means to manufacture fear and apply laws selectively against Muslims. A number of these manufactured terror plots employed *agent provocateurs* and informants, to try and fish out terrorists where they would not otherwise exist.

A report published by New York University's Center for Human Rights and Global Justice entitled *Targeted and Entrapped* (2011) found that the government often resorted to a dangerous incentive structure by offering informants reduced criminal charges or changes in immigration status. The report goes on to mention that the "government's informants introduced and aggressively pushed ideas about violent jihad and moreover, actually *encouraged* the defendants to believe that it was their duty to take action against the United States" (p. 2). This has been the case with a number of informants and *agent provocateurs* in the US and Canada including Shahed Hussain in the case of the Newburgh Four; Craig Monteilh who infiltrated a Southern California mosque for the FBI;[1] Shamiur Rahman, who was paid US $1,000 a month by the NYPD to 'bait' Muslims into making incriminating statements; as well as Mubin Sheikh and Shaher Elsohemy, the informants who provided a fire-arm, three tonnes of ammonium nitrate, and were paid $300,000 and $4.1 million, respectively, in the Toronto 18 case. A British Colombia couple, John Nuttall and Amanda Korody were also lured into a terror plot by Royal Canadian Mounted Police (RCMP) *agent provocateurs.* The attempted attack involved planting bombs at the British Colombia Legislature in a 'Canada Day Bomb Plot'. The mentally unstable methadone addicts were found guilty on three terrorism related charges in 2013, despite the fact that Nuttall repeatedly expressed concerns about the legitimacy of the plot and desperately sought spiritual advice from a religious scholar or family members about engaging in such actions. Every time Nuttall expressed such concerns the undercover RCMP officer prevented him from seeking such guidance. Furthermore, the RCMP officer convinced the couple that he was a member of a powerful international terrorist organization that would probably kill them if they did not go through with the plot. Eventually, in 2016 a British Colombia judge stayed the charges against Nuttall and Korody stating the police used trickery and subterfuge to manipulate the couple, effectively creating a terrorist threat instead of foiling one (Trumpener, 2016). The practice of pre-emptive punishment and the use of agent provocateurs is indicative of how a constant cloud of suspicion is cast over Muslims in North American societies and demonstrates how Muslims have experienced Islamophobia in the post-9/11 context. The enactment of racist and biased laws as seen in the discussion of pre-emptive punishment and prosecution in the Canadian and American contexts is not a recent phenomenon.

The US has had a long and enduring history of racism, which started long before its encounters with Muslims and the Muslim world. From as early as the conquests of the Americas and the extermination and subjugation of Indigenous Peoples, to the slave trade which built America's economic prowess on the backs of slaves, and the internment of the local Japanese diaspora during World War II, the US has had an unimpressive record of violating human rights and freedoms of racialized groups. A similar pattern can be seen within the Canadian context as documented by Sunera Thobani (2007), through selective immigration policies of 'preferred races', laws regulating native populations, and other legislation which has unjustly targeted racialized communities.

Thobani's (2007) analysis argues that in the case of Canada it is "not that the law was discriminatory and that racism can be found in its rulings. It is that the Canadian legal system *is* a regime of racial power" (p. 54). According to Thobani, these deviations when applying laws to racialized groups can be understood as the practice of *exaltation*. Exaltation is the process of attributing certain qualities which characterize the nationality of a people. Those who do not embody these qualities are considered strangers to the national community. As Thobani mentions, "national subjects who fail to live up to the exalted qualities are treated as aberrations...The failings of outsiders, however, are seen as reflective of the inadequacies of their community, of their culture, and, indeed, of their entire 'race' (p. 6). In other words, there are certain imagined qualities inherent within English/French white Canadians. Those qualities exalt them over others and in essence define who gets to be a 'real' Canadian. When a national subject is unable to live up to these exalted qualities they are perceived as exceptions to the rule. Those who do not fit within the mould of the Canadian national subject (i.e. members of immigrant communities and people of colour) are believed to be strangers who do not truly belong within the nation. Such a difference warrants a change in behaviour towards, and treatment of certain classes of citizens. The exalted national subject is able to forget their own violent treatment of others throughout their national history, while at the same time condemning other racialized groups for engaging in similar actions and explaining such behaviour as defective and inferior qualities which are said to form the essence of that group. The process of selectively forgetting one's national history of violence thus gives rise to the notion that the rights that exist for national subjects are a result of an inherent worthiness.

The concept of exaltation can also explain how certain cultures can be perceived as contaminants to the nation. National subjects who convert to Islam and engage in criminal activities can have their deviant behaviour explained through the adoption of a foreign religion, as they have lost their status of exalted national subjects. This logic was operational in the reactions to the hit and run attack by Martin Couture-Rouleau in St-Jean-sur-Richelieu, Quebec, as well as the Parliament Hill shootings by Michael Zehaf-Bibeau in Ottawa, Ontario, occurring in October 2014 within days of each other. Both of these murders were described as acts of terrorism by Prime Minister Stephen Harper in his address to the nation as well as media outlets on the days of and following the events (Maloney, 2015). Political and media discourses claimed these men were inspired by the Islamic terrorist organization ISIS. However, both men were prone to violence in the context of conditions preceding their adoption of radicalized views that included mental illness and drug abuse (Derfel, 2014). These men's violent actions cannot be understood independently of their lives and personalities prior to their acceptance of radicalized Islamic views. However, their acts according to dominant political and media narratives were a result of Islamic influences, which posed a threat to the nationalist space. In his address to the nation, the Prime Minister described how these events were a grim reminder of how violent acts of terrorism experienced in other nations can also occur in Canada, implying this type of violence was foreign to the nationalist space. He made these statements despite the fact that a similar act of violence was committed a few months prior, when Justin Bourque of New Brunswick murdered three and critically injured two RCMP officers in June 2014. Bourque, like Zehaf-Bibeau and Rouleau, had adopted radicalized anti-government ideologies prior to committing these murders. However, Bourque's crimes were not classified as acts of terrorism in media and political discourses (O'Toole, 2014). Additionally, Harper's condemnation of supposed acts of Islamic extremism in Canada did not warrant a similar condemnation of anti-Muslim backlash which surfaced in cities across Canada in the aftermath of these events.

The concept of exaltation helps illustrate how 'terrorism' is constructed as a foreign contaminant and infects the nation through Islam. Bourque's actions, being a white Canadian man, were incomprehensible, and were explained as an aberration. He was understood to be someone with mental health problems or socially abnormal. In contrast, Couture-Rouleau and Zehaf-Bibeau, also white Canadians, were held to be infected with 'Muslimness' and therefore classified as terrorists, which was the primary factor explaining their actions. As Islam is constructed as a racialized faith, Couture-Rouleau and Zehaf-Bibeau were perceived as no longer being nationalist subjects, but had degenerated into threatening Muslim 'Others' upon their conversions. Hence, in the case of Couture-Rouleau and Zehaf-Bibeau, narratives of Islamic terrorism were used to sanitize homegrown terror. The Prime Minister's national address in light of the tragic events committed by Couture-Rouleau and Zehaf-Bibeau, located their acts of violence and terror in the meta-narrative of global Islamic terrorism. This cast the actions of these white Canadians as originating outside of the nation, thus preserving Canada's exalted status.

One may argue that the notion of exaltation in present times has no place in Canada and other Western nations given that they pride themselves on fostering and encouraging multiculturalism. However, drawing from the criticisms of

Ahmed (2000), Bannerji (2000), and Hage (2000), nations adopting multiculturalism engage in a process of re-imagining their national image in such a way that they can co-exist with others, while using this difference to assert white citizens' cultural superiority. Societies such as Canada, Australia, the US, and those in Europe have had enduring histories of racialized discrimination and imperialist violence. These histories do not simply vanish by claims of 'multiculturalism'. Indeed, such claims serve to mask a nation's racist attitude or behaviours towards certain groups. When nations pass legislation locally such as the USA PATRIOT ACT, or the Anti-Terrorism Act (2001 and 2015), and engage in imperialist wars such as the occupation of Afghanistan and Iraq, the mistreatment of racialized 'Others' goes unacknowledged because of claims of being a multicultural nation. Within the multiculturalism framework it is understood that certain racialized 'Others' are inferior and incapable of modernizing and therefore engaging in the process of modernizing these 'Others' is a benevolent act. This masks the racialized violence towards groups that are believed to be locked in a pre-modern state when attempts are made to civilize them. The following sections will provide a deeper and more complete understanding of the phenomenon of Islamophobia by examining issues relating to gender and its intersection with race and class.

GENDER

In this discussion about gender, I will examine how Islamophobia has been used to reproduce discourses which construct Muslim women as abused and oppressed at the hands of Muslim men. The mistreatment of women is hardly a new phenomenon or one that is limited to only some communities. However, when women from Muslim communities are the victims of violence there is a tendency to explain this gendered-based violence through practices and beliefs inherent within their culture. This type of discourse which is stripped of the economic, social, and political contexts in which the violence is taking place, reinforces conceptions of Western superiority and the barbaric 'Otherness' of Muslims.

The plight of the 'imperilled Muslim woman'. After the 9/11 attacks, the Bush administration, along with its Canadian and European allies, began its War on Terror, invading and occupying Afghanistan and Iraq. There were a number of criticisms aimed at the Bush administration for waging wars on countries which did not conclusively prove to be direct threats against the US. Rather, both Afghanistan and Iraq were *potential* threats, as Afghanistan was giving asylum to Osama Bin Laden, who was believed to be behind the 9/11 attacks, and Iraq supposedly possessed weapons of mass destruction, a claim which later was found to be completely false. Many of the criticisms of the War on Terror were deflected by its advocates through coopting feminist discourses, framing the invasions as wars that would liberate Muslim women.

The Bush administration, despite an abysmal reputation for protecting women's rights domestically, advocated the necessity of the war on Afghanistan to rescue

Afghan women. The President's wife, Laura Bush, along with a number of female politicians reiterated the Republican Party line in advocating women's rights through the violence in the War on Terror. Even feminist groups like the Feminist Majority, which represented over 220 human rights and women's organizations in the US and worldwide, supported the War on Terror reproducing the tropes of the 'imperilled Muslim woman' who needed to be saved from the 'dangerous Muslim man' and her supposedly backwards violent culture. Thobani's (2010) examination of white feminist discourses in the US and Canada surrounding the War on Terror noted that "they have helped revitalize 'Western' feminism through a focus on the global that constitutes the West's gendered subject as the mark of the 'universal,' and the world of the Muslim gendered subject as that of death, violence, and misogyny" (p. 129). In other words, these discourses have perpetuated a hegemonic relationship of the West and its Islamic 'Other'. Portraying the War on Terror as a women's rights issue created a situation where countries like the US and Canada, spoke out on behalf of Muslim women against their oppressors. However, in the process, "the voice of the "Third World" woman herself [was] effectively silenced, evacuated from an argument that [was] about her but in which she [was] seldom invited to participate" (Morey & Yaqin, 2011, p. 179). Ultimately, framing the oppression of Muslim women as a cultural trait, as the War on Terror has done, inadequately accounts for the causes of suffering of women in Muslim countries. Similarly, a recurring theme that has appeared in Canadian political and media discourses of violence perpetrated against Muslim women at the hands of Muslim men has been that of 'honour-based violence' and 'honour killings.'

Honour-based violence; a uniquely Muslim phenomenon. Honour killings and honour-based violence are forms of violence enacted upon a family member or member of a cultural group who is believed to have brought dishonour to the family or community. Often this type of violence occurs within the context of marriage. The use of the term honour killings or honour-based violence can be problematic because such violence is not framed as a generic form of violence against women, but rather as a type of violence which originates within the perpetrator's culture. This creates a tendency to construct and explain similar acts of violence that are committed against women from Western cultures differently. These acts are usually referred to as instances of domestic violence or crimes of passion in which the actions of the assailant are not understood to originate from inherent qualities of violence and backwardness.

Honour killings and honour-based violence are believed to most often occur when a man kills or abuses a female member of his family because of 'immoral acts.' These acts include refusing an arranged marriage, flirting with or having relationships with men, marital infidelity, requesting a divorce, or being a victim of rape. However, with the exception of arranged marriages, a number of these issues are underlying causes for domestic violence cases in Western nations (Razack, 2008). Ultimately, the problem with constructing violence against Muslim women as being caused by having values contradictory to the West's creates the perception that being Muslim is irreconcilable with being a Westerner. As Morey and Yaqin (2011) observe, "The post-9/11 depiction of honor killings as a minority and often Muslim issue…is symptomatic of the way a certain kind of cultural practice can be held up as an example of the key difference between a civilized Self and an unenlightened Other" (p. 71). Media and political discourses of violence suffered by Muslim women locally and in Muslim-majority countries have created a space where 'native informants' have become prevalent in the post-9/11 context.

Native Informants. Jiwani (2010) discusses how there are two types of media stories about Muslim women; stories relating to victimhood and stories relating to escape. Stories about Muslim women as victims reproduce the 'imperilled Muslim woman' archetype and those framed around Muslim women escaping centre on narratives of Muslim women who attack Islam. Other stories surrounding Muslim women do not receive as much notoriety and are not seen as news-worthy. Hence, Muslim women are constructed in the media as victims of oppression needing to be saved, with the exception of those who have empowered themselves by turning against their faith. These women have been referred to by some as native informants. If *hijab* clad women with religious and cultural affiliations embody the 'bad Muslims' in the context of the War on Terror, native informants—their antithetical counterparts— have been constructed as 'good Muslims'. These women have provided narratives reaffirming archetypal depictions of 'bad Muslim' men and women from an insider perspective. The logic that follows is that if Muslim women themselves claim that Islam is oppressive towards women, then it must be true. Native informants in the US, Europe, and Canada include Ayaan Hirsi Ali, Irshad Manji, Nonie Darwish, Wafa Sultan, and Brigitte Gabriel. Most of these native informants do not have scholarly or academic credentials which qualify them to speak authoritatively about Islam, Muslims, or Muslim-majority countries. Yet these women have made successful careers based on their insider claims about Islam. After 9/11 and the ensuing War on Terror, a space was created where native informants were able to produce oppressive narratives of the backwards and misogynistic practices and cultures of Muslims and Arabs which were readily consumed by the political elite, media, and Western audiences. These narratives were not particularly powerful or well thought out. Rather, they were diatribes against Islam and Muslims heavily influenced by their limited personal experiences. Some native informants, as was the case of Hirsi Ali, were simply opportunists who used their vitriolic Islamophobic rhetoric to advance their political careers, as a number of her claims were later disproved.

The works of these native informants reached a wide audience because they satisfied the public's and their government's need for narratives that justified the war and destruction in Afghanistan and Iraq, in addition to the other militaristic operations undertaken by the US in its war against terror. Through their claims of being self-critical feminists, native informants have used their Islamophobic reproaches to advance racist neoliberal agendas. A common trend that binds their works is inattention to historical accuracy. Thus, the works of native informants examine problems in the Muslim world devoid of historical and political analysis.

Not only do their narratives support the archetype of the 'imperilled Muslim woman' but they also reinforce the notion that the key to salvation lies in the Westernization of their minds and bodies.

I turn now to discuss how class relations contribute to racist and discriminatory treatment of racialized groups and how the War on Terror has facilitated this for Muslims. Additionally, I will show how Islamophobia is employed to further the economic interests of Empire through free-market capitalism. This economic approach has aided in securing precious natural resources in Muslim-majority countries brought on by the War on Terror.

CLASS AND ECONOMICS

Colonized nations have histories of being exploited by the West, resulting in cultural and economic subordination. The end result of this exploitation is a wretched existence for the colonized. This point was eloquently made by Fanon (1963) when he described the lived realities of the settlers and the natives:

> The settlers' town is a strongly built town, all made of stone and steel. It is a brightly lit town; the streets are covered with asphalt, and the garbage cans swallow all the leavings, unseen, unknown and hardly thought about…The settler's town is a well-fed town, an easygoing town; its belly is always full of good things. The settlers' town is a town of white people, of foreigners. The town belonging to the colonized people, or at least the native town, the Negro village, the medina, the reservation, is a place of ill fame, peopled by men of evil repute. They are born there, it matters little where or how; they die there… The native town is a hungry town, starved of bread, of meat, of shows, of coal, of light. The native town is a crouching village, a town on its knees, a town wallowing in the mire. It is a town of niggers and dirty Arabs. (p. 39)

These realities described the native/settler experience during colonialism. However a similar situation exists in the post-colonial era, where the Third World is exploited not directly by a colonizing country but rather through international financial institutions, which impose political and economic regimes that ultimately serve to strip nations of their natural resources. Organizations such as the World Bank and International Monetary Fund (IMF) lend developing nations—overwhelmingly formerly colonized nations—funds which result in their perpetual indebtedness. To qualify for these loans, Third World governments are required to implement domestic policies coopting the well-being of their own populations in exchange for benefiting Western corporate enterprises. The use of international financial agencies such as the World Bank and the IMF to implement free-market economic reforms in developing nations has often been termed as a type of neocolonialism in which formally decolonized nations remain economically disadvantaged while Western countries profit enormously through corporate enterprises continually feeding off of these nations. The exploitation of developing countries through *laissez-faire* economic policies has negatively affected the vast majority of their citizens. These policies have affected Muslims and non-Muslims alike. However, the War on Terror created a situation where the impact of neoliberal exploitation on Muslim-majority nations were heightened, sometimes through militarization and occupation.

Framing Muslim women as imperilled and Muslim men as dangerous through the War on Terror provided moral justifications for a civilizing mission in which violence and occupation of Muslim lands was necessary. Central to these narratives was the notion of bringing these nations into modernity and advocating democratic reforms. Yet, in these narratives, modernity is conflated with globalization and democracy with neoliberalism. In other words, modernity and democracy in these nations has come to mean the legitimization of political leaders who allow other nations to become the primary beneficiaries of their country's natural resources. Thus, the repressive monarchies of Saudi Arabia, Bahrain, and Kuwait have been allies to the West, while being excluded from discussions of bringing modernity and democracy through the War on Terror. The War on Terror had little to do with the US and other nations bringing democratic reforms to Muslim-majority countries. Rather, a primary motivation in this war was controlling the oil resources of the region at any cost. Consequently, US foreign policy has prevented the emergence of any government that might threaten its influence in the region. Therefore, it is only when a nation adopts a *laissez-faire* economic system in which its natural resources become liberalized that its political system, democratic or not, will be acceptable in the eyes of US hegemony.

The economic incentives underpinning the War on Terror were not solely driven by a sense of greed and economic prosperity. Rather, these aspirations to possess racialized peoples' wealth and exploit their labour emanates from a sense of superiority. Economic abuse towards racialized and socially marginalized groups has a historical legacy in Western nations. Europe and the Americas benefited tremendously through the exploitation of African slaves. Similarly, throughout the periods of nation building in Canada there have been stark examples of racist attitudes. The early arrival of black and Asian migrants in Canada dates back to pre-Confederation Canada. There was tremendous opposition to this migration under the auspices of keeping Canada a white nation, however their labour was recognized as necessary. Thus, these migrants were reviled as a necessary evil and viewed as degenerate and inassimilable (Thobani, 2007).

The exploitation of racialized and socially marginalized groups is rooted in the belief that certain races of people are worthy of being exploited because of their inherent inferiority. This has been the case not only at the local level, but also through imperialist encounters like the War on Terror as Thobani (2007) observes,

> [f]acilitating the right of global mobility long enjoyed by white subjects, and of a global entitlement that allows them access to the best part of the planet's resources, has historically been central to the mission of this west. That mission is today finding expression in the new invasions and occupations. (p. 251)

In other words, white supremacy undergirds the economic motivations of the War on Terror, as has been the case with other imperialist endeavours throughout the colonial era. These notions of white supremacy have also facilitated class-based discrimination against Muslims in the aftermath of 9/11 through targeted legislations.

Targeting of Muslim Immigrant Working-Classes Through the War on Terror. Rana (2011), in his study of the Pakistani migrant worker diaspora has examined how the global economy's push for cheap labour in the context of the War on Terror has brought about the policing of immigrant working-class Muslims. Building on Nicholas De Genova's (2002) framework of illegality, Rana (2011) argues that in the post-9/11 context, Muslim migrant workers "are accepted into informal global labor migration markets that also deem them dispensable in times of crisis and thus disposable through deportation" (p. 139). This makes 'illegality' for Muslim migrant workers a political identity, which uses their status as migrant labourers as outside the law. What is meant by this is that if immigrant populations are deemed as posing a threat to national security, the rule of law no longer applies to them and they are stripped of their rights. This has manifested in legislations like the USA PATRIOT ACT, under which thousands of Muslim immigrants in the US have been detained and/or deported. Rana further argues that since 9/11, there has been increased surveillance and incarceration of Pakistani immigrants in the US. Through policing strategies such as detention and deportation, immigrants may be detained until the state deems they no longer pose a threat or have no useful information, at which point they are deported by force or voluntarily. According to Rana, "[t]he detention and deportation regime relies on selectively enforcing immigration laws among suspect immigrant populations…it is not probable cause but guilt by association with certain ideas, people, or organizations that guides the logic behind who becomes a suspect" (p. 150). In other words, a state of exception exists for these immigrant working-classes with regards to their rights of due process. Detention in the post-9/11 context has taken on the form of racial violence aimed at disciplining Muslim immigrant populations. This manifests through processes such as enhanced interrogation techniques, extraordinary rendition, and long-term detention. These measures that are applied against immigrant populations represent violence enacted on a class of people who are normalized as illegal and criminal. Hence, working-class Muslims have become targeted and are more vulnerable in the context of the War on Terror. Similar treatment of Muslim immigrants has taken place in the Canadian context.

As previously discussed, security certificates allow for the detention and expulsion of non-citizens who are deemed threats to national security, based on secret evidence. The overwhelming majority of security certificates in the post-9/11 context have targeted Muslim men of Middle Eastern origin. A security certificate permits:

the detention and expulsion of non-citizens who are considered to be a threat to national security. Detainees have no opportunity to be heard before a certificate is issued, and a designated judge of the federal court reviews most of the government's case against the detainee in a secret hearing at which neither the detainee nor his counsel is present. The detainee receives only a summary of the evidence against him. Detention is mandatory for non-permanent residents...and there is no possibility of release unless a person leaves Canada, or the certificate is struck down, or if 120 days have elapsed and deportation has still not taken place. (Razack, 2008, p. 26)

Additionally, detainees deported to their countries of origin as a result of a security certificate face the possibility of torture there. These provisions strip away basic and fundamental human rights. Muslims detained on the grounds of security certificates since 9/11 include, Hassan Almrei, Mohammed Mahjoub, Mohammed Jaballah, Mohamed Harkat, and Adil Charkaoui. All five men have spent time in prison and under house arrest with extremely strict conditions. Mohammed Mahjoub who was released from prison and placed under house arrest in 2007 complained that his conditions were humiliating for him and his family and deprived his children of the possibility of a normal life and therefore requested to be returned to the Kingston Immigration Holding Centre (Freeze, 2009). In other words, his house arrest conditions were so difficult that he preferred to return to prison. Both Adil Charkaoui and Hassan Almrei eventually had their security certificates quashed. Mahjoub sought to have his security certificate quashed, as a large portion of the evidence against him was obtained through torture, however his request was denied (Perkel, 2012). Security certificates have detained people indefinitely on the basis of secret evidence and have produced humiliating unlivable circumstances for these immigrant Muslim men.

CONCLUSION

Islamophobia in the post-9/11 context is structured and organized by the social relations of race, gender, and class, which are indispensable in understanding the emergence of the archetypes of 'dangerous Muslim men', 'imperilled Muslim women,' and 'civilizing Europeans'. These archetypes have sanitized and legitimized the violence of the War on Terror and have been instrumental in fomenting anti-Muslim racism and Islamophobia in Western nations. Through 'race', Islamophobia manifests itself in culture talk, race thinking, and 'good Muslim' 'bad Muslim' discourses. Additionally, examining Islamophobia from the perspective of race has revealed the proliferation of camps—spaces where the suspension of the law becomes the law.

Islamophobic views were also clearly demonstrated through 'gender' in 'imperilled Muslim woman' discourses which have advocated rescuing Muslim women from their backwards and misogynistic cultures. 'Imperilled Muslim women' narratives created a space where anti-Muslim rhetoric was masked under the guise of feminist discourses, justifying violence towards Muslims through the War on Terror. The most virulent of these came from native informants who legitimized imperialistic agendas. When looking at Islamophobia through a lens which attends to economic and class relations it is clear that anti-Muslim sentiments have been useful tools in generating support for imperialist wars through promoting the archetype of the 'civilizing European'. These wars have usurped natural resources from Muslim-majority countries. Expropriation of these resources was not solely motivated by financial and economic benefits, but also from a deep sense of entitlement to the resources of supposedly racially inferior peoples. The War on Terror has not only brought about an expropriation of resources from Muslim-majority nations but has also facilitated the application of laws in the US and Canada in targeted ways, which have descriminated against Muslim underclasses.

Islamophobia is organized and structured by race, gender, and class all together and all at once. Any examination of these relations independently of one another results in a partial and incomplete understanding of the phenomenon of Islamophobia. Islamophobic discourses surrounding race, gender, and class have been useful tools in garnering support for the War on Terror. The War on Terror has enabled biased treatment towards Muslims by justifying the selective application of repressive laws against Muslims locally and invading Muslim-majority countries like Afghanistan and Iraq. The following chapter will attempt to further examine Islamophobia by looking at anti-Muslim racism in Quebec, as this book examines the experiences of Canadian Muslims who attended Quebec secondary schools.

NOTE

[1] FBI even permitted Monteilh to have sex with the Muslim women in their investigation if it would lead to better intelligence. Monteilh himself later admitted that his work amounted to entrapment. So much so that the Muslim community he infiltrated reported him to the FBI because of the radical views he was disseminating.

HOW THE MUSLIM 'OTHER' HAS BEEN CONCEPTUALIZED IN THE QUEBEC CONTEXT

INTRODUCTION

With a total area spanning 1,542,056 square kilometres and a population of approximately 8 million, Quebec has the largest land mass and the second largest population of all the Canadian provinces.[1] Quebec possesses a unique status in relation to the rest of Canada, as the majority of its inhabitants are francophone. The official language of Quebec is therefore French, which differs from all the other provinces and territories in Canada that have adopted English only, or English and French as their official languages. The primacy of the French language in Quebec relates to its establishment as a French colony prior to Canadian confederation, as well as historical language rights struggles with the Canadian government. In this chapter, I will provide a brief overview of Quebec history, discussing traditional norms in Quebec society prior to the 1960s and the radical societal shift during the period referred to as the Quiet Revolution, which reinvigorated French language nationalism and shifted the social order of Quebec to become more secular in nature. I will discuss how Quebec identity was redefined during this period through employing identity politics—an approach to politics that seeks to secure political freedom of a marginalized group within a larger political body. Quebec identity politics, as I will use the term throughout the book, entails political processes aimed at mobilizing the white French Quebecois majority to seek greater political autonomy and having the rest of Canada acknowledge their minority status and the uniqueness of their cultural heritage. In the post-9/11 context, Quebec identity politics have framed Muslims as threatening to traditional Quebecois culture and society.

Furthermore, this chapter will discuss how secularism manifests uniquely in Quebec and how this has affected Quebec's integration policy of interculturalism. Understanding French secularism and interculturalism helps contextualize a number of nationalistic debates, which have occurred in Quebec framed around 'Us-talk' (Bilge, 2013), such as disputes over reasonable accommodation. This exclusionary 'Us-talk' has reinforced the 'civilizing European' trope. Additionally, this chapter will discuss how Quebec secular and liberal feminist discourses have framed Muslim women as oppressed, conforming to the archetype of 'imperilled Muslim women', which in turn have manufactured fears of the 'dangerous Muslim man'. It concludes with a discussion of how Muslims and Islam have been perceived in schools in Quebec which will help lay the foundation to build my analysis of lived Muslim experiences in Quebec secondary schools.

OVERVIEW OF QUEBEC HISTORY

Quebec society has traditionally been very influenced by the Catholic Church, whose presence dates back to the first arrival of the French in the Americas. When Quebec was 'discovered' by France in the 16th century, French fishermen and fur traders engaged in economic relations with Indigenous Peoples. The European market for furs developed and beaver furs became a lucrative market. Consequently, the French began to develop settlements and established a French colony with European political and religious institutions. By the 1650s, Indigenous Peoples had been decimated by war and disease. This presented an economic opportunity for French immigrants, since the Indigenous Peoples were no longer intermediaries in the fur trade. Hence, there was an influx of French immigrants. The growth of French settlements led to an eventual expansion in farming, which has been described as Quebec's pre-industrial phase in history. In this period, the Catholic Church along with the French monarchy exerted great influence on society. The role of the Catholic Church was to uphold social order. Judeo-Christian values were the basis for criminal codes and for education. The state used its power to give authority to religious officials. This was accomplished through establishing parishes and enforcing tithe collection. As Quebec, or New France as it was called in this period, was a colony of France, the French monarch was the ultimate head of state. Seventeenth-century France accepted the king's rule as divine right. Hence, the relationship between state power and the Catholic Church was one of reciprocity. The king gave authority and power to the Church. In return the Church legitimized the monarch's authority.

Tensions existed between France and Britain during the colonial period, as both vied to expand their colonies and the economic benefits that this entailed. These tensions reached fever pitch in the mid-eighteenth century which resulted in a number of battles between the British, French, and other colonial powers over colonies around the world, referred to as the Seven Years' War. Eventually the British gained control over New France and established the Province of Quebec in 1763. As Quebec was now under British authority, attempts were made to change the social hierarchy so that Quebec reflected a more British character. This was done by encouraging British migration, French Protestant migration, as well as preventing Catholics from holding public office and barring French Canadians from holding government posts and sitting in assemblies. However, attempts to change the social structure of Quebec were ineffectual, as there was insufficient British migration to Quebec, which was still overwhelmingly French Catholic. Consequently, the Quebec Act was passed in 1774 which restored French civil law, guaranteed religious freedom, allowed for greater political participation of francophones, and preserved the Catholic Church's social influence in Quebec society.

Catholicism continued to be influential in Quebec until the 1960s. According to Rymarz (2012), Catholic Mass attendance just prior to the 1960s exceeded 80% in major parts of the province on any given Sunday. This slowly began to change in the 1960s as religion was perceived as impeding social progress. In the place of religion, "there evolved a robust secular mentality characterized by, among other things, a marginalization of religion to the periphery of personal and public life" (Rymarz, 2012, p. 297). The erosion of the Church's influence is usually referred to as the Quiet Revolution. Although it took place in the 1960s, its roots can be traced to the *Grande noirceur* or the 'great darkness' a few years earlier, when there was a rise in conservative ideology and clerical power. It was a period when Quebec Premier Maurice Duplessis presented French Canadians as "a docile Catholic population that was reliable as an unaggressive labour force and…respectful of hierarchy" (Dickinson & Young, 2008, p. 271). Accordingly, francophones in Quebec were economically marginalized and relegated to working-class positions. This was a challenging time in Quebec society as it was being confronted with numerous changes. After World War Two there was a considerable inflow of immigrants to Canada, including Quebec. Linguistic and ethnic tensions were beginning to fester as a rising awareness of class and ethnic identity emerged. These changes helped bring about a revival of Quebec nationalism that formed the basis for the Quiet Revolution.

During the Quiet Revolution between 1960 and 1966, Quebec Liberal Premier Jean Lesage introduced a number of political reforms, transferring several key responsibilities from the Catholic Church to the government. These reforms were celebrated by Quebec society as a release from the Church and economic oppression. The Lesage reforms brought about a re-invigoration of Quebecois identity that was exclusively connected with the culture and language of the majority. This neo-nationalist ideology asserted that immigrant populations should be assimilated, adopting the language and culture of the francophone majority. Upon being elected Premier, Lesage rallied the French Quebecois population under the mantra of *Maîtres chez nous* (masters of our own house), seeking greater political autonomy for Quebec's distinct culture and identity from the rest of Canada. During this period, francophone identity was redefined and centred on the preservation of French language and nationalism. These transformations were especially directed towards the traditional education system in Quebec, which was under the administration of the Catholic Church. This was a classical college system which focused primarily on theology. Higher education was limited amongst French Canadians as their formal education was low and few could afford the luxury, which was primarily offered in English. Therefore, French Canadians were less educated and economically disadvantaged. Inspired by notions of economic progress, the Quiet Revolutionaries brought about a series of educational reforms that displaced Roman Catholicism from a near-monopoly of clerical influence. Hence, secularism and the French language began to define Quebec identity, which inevitably resulted in a growing desire to seek greater political autonomy.

Sentiments over Quebec nationalism have often resulted in tensions between Quebec and the rest of Canada, which have included two referenda geared towards Quebec sovereignty in 1980 and 1995. Through employing identity politics, which asserted the distinctiveness of Quebec society, as a means of political protection from being marginalized within Canada, Quebecers and nationalist political parties engaged in 'Us-talk'. 'Us-talk' is a racially coded way of speaking aimed at preserving power and privilege. In the Quebec context it has manifested through emphasizing the distinctiveness of Quebecois culture and identity in contrast to the 'Other'. This exclusionary 'Us-talk' lost some of its political currency after Jacques Parizeau, the former Quebec Premier, made his infamous speech on the eve of the sovereigntist defeat in the 1995 referendum. In this speech, Parizeau openly blamed the referendum results on ethnic minorities voting against separation. However, recent events in Quebec have seen a rehabilitation of the exclusionary 'Us-talk' reminiscent of Quebec's past. The reasonable accommodation debates, as well as discussions over the proposed Quebec Charter of Values, were clear examples of how divisiveness and alienation of ethnic and religious minorities from Quebec society have come to occupy political discourses. These discourses, which are discussed below, were emblematic of the sensitivities surrounding the preservation of Quebecois culture through French secularism in the aftermath of the Quiet Revolution.

UNDERSTANDING FRENCH SECULARISM IN QUEBEC

Laicité, or French secularism as I will be using the term, can be understood as a normative political culture in which there is a strict separation between church and state on matters of public policy. It differs from the term 'secularism', which some have described as the co-existence of multiple religious and non-religious perspectives in a given social context (Taylor, 2007). *Laicité* has traditionally been rooted in separating Catholicism from the state. In more contemporary times it has been geared towards dichotomizing Muslims as 'Other' in French society. As Selby (2011) notes, "[i]f during the first half of the twentieth century the separation of church and state was intended to displace Catholicism, in recent decades Islam has been increasingly depicted as the new challenge for French secularism" (p. 442). Within France this dates back to the post-war era when there was a large increase of Muslim immigrants arriving from North Africa as unskilled labourers in the 1940–1960s. The consistent growth of Muslim migrants over the decades brought about tensions, as state discourses framed Muslims as threats to French culture and society. This was apparent in the Stasi Commission Report published by the French government in 2003, which examined the application of secularist principles in France. The report emphasized *laicité* as a fundamental pillar of French society and essential for national unity and cohesion. However, the Stasi Commission Report positioned "Islam as overly 'political' and 'patriarchal' and describe[d] Muslim women as 'oppressed' by their religious tradition" (Selby, 2011, p. 445). Additionally, the report associated Islam with polygamy, genital mutilation, and forced marriages. This report led to the French government passing a law banning conspicuous religious symbols in public schools in 2004. The majority of cases in which the law was applied involved Muslim women wearing the head scarf (Al-Saji, 2010). Hence, Muslims have become the direct targets of French secularism in contemporary times through discourses of 'liberating' Muslim women from their oppressive religious beliefs and practices. Drawing from the work of Fanon, Alia Al-Saji (2010) argues that perceptions of Islamic symbols like the head scarf being threatening to French society dates back to the colonial era.

In his critical essay 'Algeria Unveiled', Fanon (1965) discusses the French colonizers' project of removing the Muslim head scarf from Algeria in the 1930s. According to him, the colonizers perceived the headscarf as a cultural identifier, believing that by eliminating the head scarf they would be taking steps towards destroying Algerian culture in the colony. Dismantling Algerian culture was essential, as the colonizers viewed themselves in stark contrast to the colonized. According to Al-Saji (2010), "[t]he representational apparatus of colonialism not only constitutes the image of the 'native' but posits this image in opposition to a certain self-perception of colonial society and against an implicit normalization of gender within that society" (p. 883). It is through this dichotomizing gaze that a civilized-self emerged in contrast to a barbaric 'Other'. This perception of the 'Other' constructed the Muslim head veil as a deviation from French society and was therefore deemed unacceptable. Similar instances of perceiving the *hijab* as 'Other' have occurred in Quebec and have resulted in exclusionary discourses, as noted by Al-Saji. She notes that, "in diverse contexts from France to Quebec, images of the veil have as their counterpart policies that enact the exclusion of veiled women" (p. 877). Hence, the Muslim head veil has come to symbolize opposition to French culture and society. Notions of French secularism have combined with discourses surrounding gender equality to frame Muslims as a threatening 'Other' in Quebec. French secularism has greatly impacted Quebec's integration model of interculturalism, which bears some similarities to Canada's model of multiculturalism.

MULTICULTURALISM, INTERCULTURALISM, AND MANAGING DIVERSITY

To put interculturalism in context we should recall that multiculturalism was instituted in Canada by Prime Minister Pierre Trudeau through the *Multiculturalism Policy* in 1971. This policy ensured that

all citizens can keep their identities, can take pride in their ancestry and have a sense of belonging. Acceptance gives Canadians a feeling of security and self-confidence, making them more open to, and accepting of, diverse cultures. The Canadian experience has shown that multiculturalism encourages racial and ethnic harmony and cross-cultural understanding. (Government of Canada, 1971)

According to Eve Haque (2012), the *Multiculturalism Policy* as well as the *Official Languages Act* were enacted to engender a sense of belonging and to counter tensions building in Canada resulting from changes in immigration policy, Indigenous Peoples' critical responses to the Federal government's attempts to abolish the *Indian Act*, and the growth of French language nationalism and sovereignty movements in Quebec in the 1960s and 1970s. The changes in Canada's immigration policies dramatically increased immigration. Hence the *Multiculturalism Policy* was a means to manage the changing make-up of Canadian society.

There have been a number of critiques of multiculturalism, which contend that it gives rise to the false notion that Western nations are living in a 'post-race' era. This implies that notable racial progress has been made and that we have now entered a phase in our societal development in which racism is a concern of the past. Consequently, the notion of multiculturalism ultimately masks the racist past of these nations while simultaneously cloaking the existing inequities, alienation, and prejudices that continue to impact racialized members of society. Embedded within multiculturalism are the notions of tolerance and benevolence, both of which are problematic. The notion of tolerance suggests that some are in a position to tolerate, while others are tolerated—that there is a power relation between some who get to judge who should be 'accepted' into Canada, on what terms, and others who do not. The notion of benevolence in multiculturalism fails to acknowledge immigrant contributions to society. As Sourayan Mookerjea (2009) explains, multiculturalism was instituted to:

> obscure our significant and now growing dependence on the import of migrant labor without access to citizenship rights and to impede the formation of public class solidarities between social groups. But the neoliberal reforms of the last two decades have made it difficult to contain the contradictions. (Mookerjea, 2009, p. 188)

In other words, Mookerjea argues that multiculturalism is not an expression of beneficence, but rather it is a way of masking Canada's dependence on its immigrant populations for economic growth and prosperity. Ghassan Hage (2000) has examined the notions of multiculturalism and tolerance in Australia, another former British colony with which some Canadian scholars have drawn parallels. Hage argues that multiculturalism, as celebrated by Western nations, is a form of 'nationalist inclusion'. This involves nationalist subjects envisioning themselves as possessing power in society and being in a position of tolerating its racialized 'Others'. According to Hage, "the difference between those who practice nationalist exclusion and those who practice nationalist inclusion is not one of people committed to exclusion versus people committed to inclusion, but rather one of people with different thresholds of tolerance" (p. 92). In other words, tolerance towards the 'Other' is only acceptable to a point. This was apparent in the *sharia* tribunal debates from 2003–2005, when there was public discontent against members of the Muslim community opting for faith-based mediation, which has been permitted in Ontario since 1991 (Service Ontario, 2009). The faith-based tribunals were a means through which faith communities were permitted to resolve civil disputes over divorce, child custody, and inheritance. Other faith groups in Ontario, including Jews, Indigenous Peoples, and Christians were able to opt for these tribunals to resolve conflicts within their communities. However, when there was talk of Muslims using these tribunals there were concerns over lapidation, flogging, chopping off limbs, and other tropes conjured up from the buzz word '*sharia*'. Ultimately, faith-based arbitration was discontinued in Ontario in 2005 because of the uproar it caused when Muslim communities opted for it. The public outcry of Muslims exercising their rights in this instance demonstrated how seeking religious arbitration exceeded the nationalist subjects' threshold of tolerance of Muslims and therefore was denied. Hence, multiculturalist practices, such as tolerance, fall short in giving the racialized 'Other' a true sense of equality because there is no redistribution of power, but rather a reliance on the nationalist subject to use their power to show benevolence to the 'Other'.

Interculturalism is Quebec's integration model for managing racial diversity. It came about in response to Canada's implementation of its multiculturalism policies and has been promoted and in operation officially in Quebec since the 1970s. According to Leroux (2010), the 1990 policy document *Au Québec pour bâtir ensemble: Énoncé de politique en matière d'immigration et d'integration* best articulates the policy implications of interculturalism which has three main principles: "French as the language of public life; a democratic society, where everyone is expected and encouraged to participate and contribute; and an open, pluralist society that respects democratic values and intercommunitarian exchange" (Gouvernement du Québec, 1990, p. 16). One of the key differences between interculturalism and multiculturalism is the notion of a moral contract between newcomers and Quebec society, which suggests that Quebec's common public culture is at the forefront. The adoption of interculturalism as Quebec's official stance towards racial diversity instead of multiculturalism is rooted in the notion of self-preservation. As Waddington et al. (2011) state: "Québec's opposition to multiculturalism is grounded in the belief that the Canadian government's policy of multiculturalism is a betrayal of Québec's historical status within the Canadian federation and undermines Québec's grounds for seeking greater political autonomy" (p. 314). As there have been ongoing tensions over safeguarding language and identity in Quebec, this approach ensured its preservation as a unique minority in Canada while it also offered "a means of partial or limited integration within Canada, releasing the Québécois from the fear of loss of their linguistic culture…providing a sustainable means of remaining within Canada" (DesRoches, 2013, p. 7). Thus, interculturalism takes a more assimilationist approach to integration of racial minorities in order to safeguard traditional Quebecois culture.

Some believe that interculturalism is conducive to social harmony. For example, Gagnon and Iacovino (2005) argue that interculturalism incorporates "immigrant or minority cultures into the larger political community [as] a reciprocal endeavour—a 'moral contract' between the host society and the particular cultural group, in the aim of establishing a forum for the empowerment of all citizens" (p. 30). Others have argued that the differences between multiculturalism and interculturalism are political in nature and that ultimately whether one is dealing with multiculturalism or interculturalism, both are political tools for building national subjects. Seen through this lens, Quebec, like Canada as a whole, engages in exaltation (Thobani, 2007), the process of attributing inherent qualities which characterize belongingness to the national imaginary, while excluding those who are deemed not to possess these qualities. This is evident as interculturalism promotes the notion of a "common culture", the French white Quebecois culture being accepted as the norm and given prominence. It is a culture which does not evolve or change. It remains constant and stagnant, fixed in a particular construct of French culture and identity, rejecting those who do not fit its mould. It is a culture that does not accept deviations and is exclusionary in nature. Therefore, interculturalism has been central to discourses of preservation in Quebec. As will be seen in the following section, the reasonable accommodation debates were a clear example of a resurgence of Quebec nationalist identity politics in contemporary Quebec society.

REASONABLE ACCOMMODATION DEBATES AND THEIR REVERBERATIONS

Some Western nations in recent years have displayed anxieties over the 'Other' and the extent to which immigrant populations should be integrated in society and their cultural/religious practices be accommodated. Quebec society is no different, and these concerns began to boil over in light of a series of highly publicized, and at times unsubstantiated, claims about incidents regarding accommodating religious minority groups between 2006 and 2007. Reasonable accommodation (RA) in Canada is a concept derived from section 15 of the Canadian Charter of Rights and Freedoms, which outlines equality rights. The term is most frequently employed in Canada and the US when discussing issues relating to labour law, where employers are required to accommodate employees for religious practices, physical disabilities, or other reasons to the point of undue hardship. In Quebec, the RA debates involved discussions around the extent to which religious minority practices should be accommodated in light of the values and culture of the Quebecois majority. According to Gada Mahrouse (2010), these debates were preceded by a string of highly publicized cases including a Sikh boy wanting to wear a *kirpan* to school, an 11-year-old Muslim girl being disallowed by a referee from participating in a soccer match because of her *hijab*, as well as a synagogue requesting an adjacent YMCA to frost their windows so that women wearing tight fitting clothes would not be visible to members of the congregation. A few other incidents exacerbated tensions such as the Quebec Human Rights Commission ruling against a local French university, ETS, forcing them to accommodate Muslim students attending the school with prayer space, as well as cases of disputes of pregnant Muslim women requesting women doctors in Quebec hospitals. These incidents received widespread media coverage, despite representing a fraction of the RA cases in Quebec. The vast majority of religious accommodation requests in the years leading up to the RA debates, which were few in number to begin with, came from Protestants and Jehovah's Witnesses (McAndrew, 2010). In relation to this point, Potvin (2010) observes, "not only was media coverage disproportionate to the actual number of cases of accommodation, but many newspapers…increased the number of incidents 'revealed', thereby setting the stage for one-upmanship and media hype" (p. 79). Media representations of these overly publicized incidents created anxieties and fueled fears over Quebec identity being threatened by the Muslim 'Other'. Consequently, in January 2007, a small Quebec town, Hérouxville, adopted a 'declaration of norms for immigrants' geared towards its (non-existent) immigrant population. The declaration entailed the following:

1. At Christmas, children sing Christmas songs.
2. No stoning women.
3. No burning women with acid.
4. No ceremonial daggers in school even if you're a Sikh.
5. Boys and girls can swim in the same pool whether Muslims like it or not.
6. Men can drink alcohol whether Muslims like it or not.
7. No walking around with your face hidden except on Hallowe'en.
8. Female police can arrest male suspects even if it troubles their egos.
9. Women are allowed to dance.
10. Women are allowed to drive.
11. Women are even allowed to make decisions on their own.

A number of these declarations appear to be banning practices commonly associated with perceptions of Muslim backwardness and barbarism. The declaration, not so subtly, made certain assumptions about the incivility of Muslim immigrant communities, while ironically white-washing gender inequality which existed, and continues to exist, in Quebec society. Despite the distasteful nature of the declaration, which presumed immigrant populations—particularly Muslim immigrants—were barbaric and in opposition to 'true Quebecois' values, a number of other municipalities across Quebec adopted similar declarations. Much of the anti-immigrant fervour from the RA debates focused particularly on Muslim women as Mahrouse (2010) observes:

> [a]lthough the debate was officially framed as being about secular versus religious values, the major preoccupation of the media reports on the Commission reveal that the overwhelming concern was not secularism per se but Muslim religious practice in Québec, in particular the wearing of the veil, which suggests that the oppression of Muslim women has come to be perceived as the greatest threat to Québec identity. (p. 92)

Mahrouse (2010) further elaborates that the focus around Muslim women in the RA debates was framed around a discourse of secularism versus religions in a general sense. However, in the post-9/11 climate, these debates of secularism versus religion in Western nations have allowed for the policing of some forms of religious expression and not others. In other words, secularism is increasingly being used as a pretext to attack particular religions, the brunt of which is borne by Muslims.

As fears of the impending erosion of white francophone Quebecois culture and identity grew, political parties were able to gain ascendency by politicizing the debate over the accommodation of minorities in the March 2007 provincial elections. The Action Démocratique du Québec (ADQ), which prior to these elections was merely a fringe third party overshadowed by the Quebec Liberals and the Parti Quebecois, bolstered its reputation by being the first party to take a strong and vocal position on RA, framing it as an issue of *un*reasonable accommodation for the white Quebecois majority. The leader of the ADQ, Mario Dumont, clearly articulated his party's views regarding accommodation of minorities in his *Open letter to the Quebecois*, published by all francophone dailies on January 16, 2007. They disseminated a discourse hinging on the notion that the Quebecois nation's racial origins, being from "European stock", were at odds with those needing accommodation (i.e. immigrant communities). Thus, accommodating immigrants and ethnic minorities was *un*reasonable from their perspective. Many of the principal points in this letter would later form important tenets of the party's platform, which according to Bilge (2013) was "among the most anti-immigrant and pro-assimilationist party platform[s] witnessed in post-1960 Canadian politics for a long time" (p. 168). Ultimately, what were initially a few isolated incidents of religious minorities seeking accommodations in order to practice their faith became an occasion for the media and politicians to acquire gains. As Wong (2011) states, "the media and the politicians saw an opportunity to draw in more readers and votes, respectively, and, as a consequence, collectively fanned the flames of racism in the public sphere" (p. 147). This was particularly troubling given that no one spoke out against the number of white Christian requests for accommodation, which far outnumbered the ones that were being sensationalized involving Muslims, of which, some were not proven to have actually happened (Leroux, 2013).

The RA debates illustrated an important point; which citizens were considered reasonable and unreasonable in Quebec society. These debates were used by politicians and the media to delineate reason from irrationality. The white francophone majority were deemed to be the possessors of reason, whereas the immigrant 'Others' who lacked conformity to the majoritarian culture and made *un*reasonable demands were deemed to be irrational. In order for the 'Other' to be considered reasonable and attain the status of a 'preferred' immigrant they were required to accept the norms of 'reason' as defined by the French white majority. As Jiwani (2006) observes,

> [t]he preferred immigrant fits the mould of the reasonable person. But, unlike the reasonable person, who is most likely to be born in the country and who is **White, the preferred immigrant tends to be a person of colour. This person does** not bring conflicts over from her/his ancestral lands of origin…At the same time, the preferred immigrant also believes in the system, adhering to the same liberal beliefs as those of the reasonable person. (p. xiv)

Through this "discourse of domination" (Jiwani, 2006), the white Quebecois majority defined what was rational and what was not. Thus, what did not conform to notions of rationality should have been restricted, which led to the heated debates over RA.

In response to this perceived crisis over RA, the Quebec provincial government established a consultative commission in February 2007 headed by sociologist Gérard Bouchard and philosopher Charles Taylor. The commission's mandate was to:

(a) take stock of accommodation practices in Québec; (b) analyse the attendant issues bearing in mind the experience of other societies; (c) conduct an extensive consultation on this topic; and (d) formulate recommendations to the government to ensure that accommodation practices conform to Québec's values as a pluralistic, democratic, egalitarian society. (Bouchard & Taylor, 2008, p. 17)

The commission's final report was published in April 2008. The synthesis and analysis of the 300-page report concluded that the perception of Quebec identity being under threat was erroneous and that the collective wellbeing of Quebec society was not in danger (Bouchard & Taylor, 2008). On the one hand, some stated that the report produced a well-documented and thorough analysis of a number of the pressing issues relating to reasonable accommodation, as a number of Arab and Muslim groups welcomed the recommendations of the report (CAIR-CAN, 2008). However, in subtle ways, the Commission reinforced the racialized hierarchies that it was attempting to overcome. This was most obvious in the consultation process. White French Quebecois would regularly vent their concerns over the loss of Quebec identity, nostalgically recalling the days when Quebec culture was uncontaminated by the 'Other'. Meanwhile, immigrant groups would try to alleviate the fears of the white Quebecois majority reassuring everyone that they were not threatening and were committed to Quebec values and culture. Minority and immigrant groups "were always on the defensive, having to justify their presence, and commitment to Quebec values, while French-Canadian Quebecois were in a position of granting validation and approval, in effect, acting as judges of what was tolerable and what was not" (Mahrouse, 2010, p. 89). Thus, instead of alleviating misguided fears and paranoia of the threatening 'Other', the consultation process served as a platform to reify positions of privilege and dominance by bringing to the surface the fact that certain members of Quebec society were able to define who did and did not belong.

Another way in which the Commission reinforced racial hierarchies was by shifting the debate over RA away from strictly legal issues to being symptomatic of problems related to Quebec's sociocultural integration model of interculturalism. The overall consequence of employing this approach led the Commission to give "greater prominence to a general request for majority generosity and tolerance, rather than a demand that certain minority rights be upheld" (Mahrouse, 2010, p. 90). The white French Quebecois majority were positioned to show benevolence by tolerating practices of the 'Other' despite the fact that freedom of religious expression is a right guaranteed in Quebec and Canada. As the statement on the report's cover—"dialogue making a difference"—suggested, the assumptions embedded in this report were that the RA debates stemmed from ignorance and miscommunication, and that by engaging in dialogue, these differences and problems could be resolved. What was absent from the report was an analysis of the power dynamics which framed the debates.

Another troubling issue which manifested in these debates was the failure to acknowledge that immigrants were contributing members to society on whom Quebec was heavily dependent for its economic growth and sustainability. Quebec's demographic weight within Canada has been steadily decreasing. According to a report by Service Canada in 2012, the weak demographic growth in Quebec may possibly bring about a negative natural increase rate (births minus deaths) within two decades, in which case only a positive net migration would yield population growth in Quebec. Simply put, in the next twenty years, Quebec may be utterly dependent on immigration for its survival. Therefore, empowering immigrant populations in ways that their religious and cultural practices are *accepted* and not accommodated is essential because it may facilitate their integration and engender a sense of belonging to Quebec society. Arguably, then, Quebec not only has an obligation to accept its immigrant populations but has a vested interest in doing so.

The fallout of the RA debates profoundly affected Quebec's political landscape. The ADQ's platform in the 2007 election brought to the forefront a number of issues which have, and in all likelihood will continue to, structure nationalist debates in the foreseeable future. The Quebecois identity politics used by the ADQ, framing accommodations for the 'Other' as threatening white francophone culture, brought about major political gains for the party in the 2007 election. However, this amounted to nothing beyond a short-lived official opposition party status. Though Dumont is no longer directly involved in Quebec politics, some argue that his platform greatly influenced the Parti Quebecois (PQ) and its platform while holding a minority government under the leadership of Pauline Marois from September 2012 to April 2014. The most blatant example of this could be seen in the proposed Bill 60, more commonly referred to as the Quebec Charter of Values tabled by the PQ government in 2013. The guidelines of this charter of secularism and religious neutrality proposed that no state employee or employee of a state-funded institution be permitted to wear conspicuous religious symbols. This would prevent teachers, daycare workers, hospital staff, and government employees from wearing a *hijab*, Sikh turban, Jewish skull cap, or a large cross. Ironically, the large cross which hangs from the National Assembly would have been excluded from this ban, as the PQ claimed that some religious symbols have become purely secular in nature and reflect Quebec's culture and not a religion (Brean, 2013).

Public hearings on Bill 60 took place in January 2014 in Quebec City and were heard by PQ representative Bernard Drainville. As with the Bouchard-Taylor Commission consultations, at the hearings on the proposed charter, a number of white Quebecois voiced their anxieties and fears of the 'Other'. Perhaps the most virulent of these came from Claude Pineault and Genevieve Caron, a couple from a small town northeast of Quebec City. During the hearings, the couple described how they were traumatized on their vacation to Morocco when they were asked to take off their shoes when entering a mosque and when they saw Muslims praying. Pineault went as far as implying Muslim dress could be a se as he claimed veiled Muslims tried to steal his wallet while he was on v lamented the idea of wearing such "disguises" in Quebec society. Altl testimonies were not representative of all of the pro-charter voices, they with Dumont's and the PQ's 'Us-talk' where the 'Other' was perceived as irrational and aberrant and therefore not worthy of accommodation. Pineault's belief that people wearing veils was 'unthinkable' in Quebec society demonstrated his sense of power to define what was socially acceptable in Quebec. Perhaps Genevieve Caron's experience was so 'traumatic' because she felt that bowing on all fours (in prayer) was a complete disjuncture from her notion of Quebecois culture, while not even giving a thought to the thousands of Quebecois Muslims who perform the same rituals. Do their practices not form a part of Quebec culture as thousands of Muslims in Quebec identify themselves as Quebecois? Could their practices ever be accepted as a part of Quebec culture? The RA debates, immigration codes of conduct, and the proposed Bill 60, were all examples of the 'civilizing European' trope, discussed in Chapter Two. These instances demonstrated how there was an assumed backwardness inherent within immigrant, particularly Muslim communities, which required policing and civilizing in order to be accepted members of Quebec society. The policing of Quebec's racialized 'Others' has also manifested through secular and liberal feminist discourses.

RACISM DISGUISED AS SECULAR AND LIBERAL FEMINIST DISCOURSES

A number of Western nations and states have increasingly imagined themselves as champions of gender equality and sexual emancipation. This view was evident when the Quebec National Assembly adopted a Bill in the aftermath of the RA controversies which gave gender equality precedence over religious freedom through the addition of the sex equality provision in the Quebec Charter of Human Rights, even though sex discrimination was already protected against in this charter. Hence, gender equality has been given such prominence that it was the only one of Quebec's 'core values' that was in need of additional constitutional protection. This situation, as described by Bilge (2012), is a manifestation of sexularism. Sexularism can be understood as:

> a contemporary discourse offering a teleological narrative of the secularisation process, believed to lead inevitably to gender and sexual equality. From the sexularist stand, religion is deemed unambiguously oppressive to women and non-heteronormative sexualities—an assumption that heavily relies on hierarchical binaries... and produces the West as the site of gender equality and sexual emancipation thanks to secularism. (p. 307)

Through a sexularist discourse, Muslims are seen negatively not only because of the association with the religion of Islam, but also because a number of Muslim women wear *hijab*, which in Western societies has become synonymous with misogyny and oppression.

Underlying sexularist discourse is the notion that women have entered into a phase of modernity thanks to secularism. These gains need to be protected at all costs, hence religion, particularly Islam, is seen as an open threat to Quebec society because of perceived symbols of oppression like the *hijab*. This became apparent in the Bouchard-Taylor Commission proceedings in which significant negative images of Muslim women wearing the *hijab* were circulated. Hence, these proceedings became a platform where "the figure of the veiled woman conveniently served, once again, to position non-Muslim Quebecers as the epitome of progress and tolerance" (Mahrouse, 2010, p. 92). What was strikingly absent from these discussions over the oppressive nature of the *hijab* were the voices of the women whom were supposedly oppressed. The irony of these discourses was that they claimed to centre on freedom and the liberation of women, while marginalizing and silencing the same women who they sought to 'liberate'. This framing of the *hijab* as oppressive, according to Bilge (2010) is typical of liberal/universalist feminist discourses. Bilge (2010) notes that there are other feminist discourses, namely, postcolonial feminist accounts, which frame the *hijab* in a resistance discourse. In other words, the *hijab* symbolizes "resistance against Western hegemony, commodification of women's bodies and post-9/11 Islamophobia" (p. 14). However, like the liberal/universalist discourses concerning the *hijab*, this frame also fails to address the reasons given by veiled women themselves as to why they cover—reasons involving morality, modesty, virtue, and divinity (Mahmood, 2005).

In addition to framing Muslim women as passive and oppressed, reinforcing the 'imperilled Muslim woman' archetype, liberal feminist discourses also framed Muslim men as dangerous and threatening. This frame was visible in Quebec society over discussions relating to 'honour-based violence' during the Shafia murder trial. In January 2012 the Shafia murders received widespread media attention, when Mohammad Shafia, his wife Tooba Yahya, and their son Hamed were convicted of killing Shafia's three teenage daughters and his first wife over their alleged immoral behaviour. According to Dana Olwan (2013), the violence surrounding these tragedies were framed as belonging outside the national imaginary, as media reports "established honour-based violence as a foreign and imported phenomenon, driven by cultural and ethnic manifestations of murderous patriarchal honour" (p. 539). The three members of the Shafia family who were convicted of the murder were reproduced in the media as alien to Canadian norms and standards. The three teenage victims were portrayed as trying to fit into Canadian society, fleeing from their oppressive backwards culture. Media reports mentioned how the teenage daughters' rebellious behaviour, which included wanting to have boyfriends, clashed with their father's more traditional Afghan cultural practices and eventually reached an impasse resulting in their deaths. As opposed to framing this case as an instance of domestic violence, the media, the Crown prosecutors, and even the presiding Judge insisted on this particular case being an honour-based murder. In the aftermath, the Quebec government mandated the Quebec Council for the Status of Women to examine the phenomenon of honour-based crimes. After studying a grand total of seventeen cases of honour-based violence in Canada since 1991, the Council provided the provincial government with seven recommendations to help stop honour-based crimes. These include:

1. Develop a policy to fight against honour-based violence, in consultation with women's groups and community organizations.
2. Develop an action plan that includes the following measures:
   o Train all workers (including youth protection officials, police, judiciaries, teachers and medical professionals) who deal with people at risk of honour-based violence, including forced marriage and genital mutilation.
   o Develop tools to help workers recognize the signs of honour-based violence and to help them evaluate potential risks.
   o Inform women and minorities affected by honour-based violence about their rights and the resources available to help them.
   o Increase funding for organizations that support women affected by honour-based violence, so that they can offer monitoring, extended accompaniment and adapted housing.
   o Develop a strategy aimed at helping youth, such as a guide on how to prevent honour crimes, or a guide on the rights of Canadians.
3. Review the strategy to fight against the practice of female genital mutilation.
4. Put mechanisms in place to protect immigrant women who have been sponsored by their spouses and inform them of their rights in cases of fraud or violence. Also monitor women sponsored by their spouses until they obtain their citizenship, in order to ensure their safety and their rights are respected.
5. Examine the laws in place to ensure that children and adults who are threatened by forced marriages are protected by our legal system and, if necessary, ask the federal government to modify its legislation to ensure those protections are in place.
6. Review the Youth Protection Act, the criteria for the evaluation and the intervention of the department of youth protection, keeping in mind the particular risks linked to honour-based violence.
7. Co-ordinate the implementation of an outreach strategy to challenge the patriarchal concept of honour at the core of some of the communities in question, and actively promote awareness about equality between men and women (CBC News, 2013).

What was troubling about the publishing of these recommendations along with a report was not that action was taken to help prevent honour-based violence against women, as violence against women is a serious social ill and problem that continues to plague society. Rather, what was problematic was that the impetus for these actions came from the Shafia murder trial. This case demonstrated how honour killings were believed to be "a foreign and imported phenomenon brought to Canada by immigrants who fail[ed] to assimilate to national and 'western' ideals of gender equality, the crime [was] also viewed as an extreme form of violence that must be managed and ultimately expelled" (Olwan, 2013, p. 533). As the terms 'honour killings' or 'honour-based violence' are frequently used when Muslims or people who come from predominantly Muslim cultures commit acts of violence against women from their communities, it comes as no surprise that these murders were labeled in this way.

Publishing a report specifically for 'honour-based violence' may have the unintended consequence of lessening the impact of violence against women that has not been categorized in this manner. It was apparent from the Shafia murders that domestic violence when categorized as an 'honour killing' received widespread media attention and government involvement. However, do similar forms of gendered-based violence enacted by other communities, including the white majority, receive as much attention by the media or the government? In August 2012, Nikolas Stefanatos, a man residing in Brossard, Quebec, assaulted his girlfriend Tanya St-Arnauld in a jealous rage. In addition to throwing several objects at St-Arnauld, Stefanatos threw a highly corrosive acid seriously burning 20% of her body. Media reports described Stefanatos' actions as an acid attack, an instance of domestic abuse, and a bout of jealous anger, but not as an act of honour-based violence, even though it bore the traits of such a crime. Stefanatos' actions did not usher in concerns over honour-based violence being endemic in other parts of Quebec society, which needed to be investigated by governmental bodies. Rather his actions were viewed as an isolated incident of domestic violence independent of any cultural or religious affiliations.

In the aftermath of the Shafia murders, it is striking that the Quebec government would go to the trouble of mandating an organization to study, collect information, and publish a report over 'honour-based violence'. There have only been seventeen cases of 'honour-based violence' in Canada over a span of twenty years, an average of less than one case per year, while in 2009 alone there were over 18,000 cases of domestic violence in Quebec, 82% of which involved female victims (Sécurité Publique Quebec, 2009). The result of these fixations with 'honour-based violence' is that it masks the existence of this violence when committed by men from non-Muslim communities, as well as the violence suffered by women belonging to non-Muslim communities. This is highlighted by Olwan (2013), as she notes the contradictions littering policies about honour killings in Canada, where the state has committed "over $2.8 million dollars to community projects targeting honour related violence while simultaneously stripping Native women's associations from funding crucial for their work" (p. 549). This was in reference to the federal government's decision in 2010 to defund Sisters of Spirit, an association which worked towards exposing and ending violence against Indigenous women.

Labeling forms of domestic violence specifically as 'honour-based violence' reinforces the 'dangerous Muslim men' archetype. The Council, when providing these recommendations, explicitly mentioned that honour-based violence was not exclusive to any particular culture or religion, but their recommendations repeatedly refer to female genital mutilation and forced marriages—tropes often associated with Muslim cultures. They also emphasized the protection of rights of women from immigrant communities. What was clear from these recommendations was that non-immigrant communities were not particularly at risk of honour-based violence, even though honour-based violence and other forms of violence against women have the same basis, namely; power, control, the subjugation of women, male patriarchy, and a perceived sense of superiority resulting from gender discrimination.

Anti-Muslim liberal feminist discourses in Quebec also surfaced over the PQ government's proposed Charter of Values. Those championing the charter saw Bill 60 as an advancement towards eliminating perceived symbols of oppression like the *hijab* from Quebec society. However, critics contended that this charter would have the *de facto* result of further marginalizing women who already faced barriers to employment (Jabir, 2013). Furthermore, after the Charter of Values was unveiled, there was a documented rise in hate crimes against Muslim women (Garber, 2014). Ironically, this proposed legislation did nothing to liberate Muslim women who wore the *hijab*, but served as a means of oppressing them, as many Muslim women stated that they no longer felt safe to leave their homes by themselves as a result of harassment they faced in the aftermath of the proposed charter (CTV News, 2014).

The Quebec Liberals also proposed a charter of values during their 2014 provincial election campaign. This version would have allowed for religious symbols such as the *hijab*, Sikh turban, and Jewish skull cap to be worn by government employees or employees of government funded institutions. The only exceptions would be women who wore the 'chador' and/or face coverings because according to the Quebec Liberal Party such clothing was symbolic of "'submission and oppression' of Muslim women to men" (Dougherty, 2014). The chador is a long flowing garment that covers a woman's body except for her face, and is a cultural dress typically found in Iran. Whether there were women in Quebec who even wore this garment at the time was unclear. However, what became clear from this Liberal discourse was that attempts to champion human rights for Muslim women continued to perpetuate notions of Muslim women's dress being a signifier of their perceived oppressed status, despite the fact that studies have shown that most women in Canada who wore face covers did so by choice (O'Brien, 2014). Given the presence of anti-Muslim biases in the RA debates, through the notion of interculturalism, and secular/liberal feminist discourses, all of which are perpetuated by state power within Quebec, the question arises whether and how educational institutions are addressing these issues. More importantly, as schools are state-run institutions, would it be fair to assume that they facilitate anti-Muslim racism as other parts of the state have done, as seen from the analysis above?

EDUCATIONAL INSTITUTIONS IN QUEBEC

The educational landscape of Quebec secondary schools has changed dramatically over the past 30 years due to an increased and diverse influx of immigrants. Teacher training institutions appeared to have made significant changes to their programs in order to better equip future educators to manage ethnocultural, religious, and linguistic diversity in the classroom and to help foster citizenship in a pluralistic society. The *Centre d'études ethnique des universités montréalaises* recently conducted a study to examine how well Quebec universities were addressing these issues in their teacher training programs. According to the report, there was significant progress in the 10 years after the educational reforms in Quebec in 2000, with 40 courses across universities in Quebec that "deal effectively with ways of taking diversity into account in an educational milieu" (Larochelle-Audet, Borri-Anadon, & McAndrew, 2013). These courses exposed future teachers to concepts such as integration, prejudice, and discrimination. The courses also provided information relating to ethnic relations, immigration to Quebec, and how to adapt educational practices for diversity. Additionally, the report mentioned that a growing number of tenured professors were devoting much of their teaching and research to issues relating to ethnocultural, religious, and linguistic diversity in educational milieus.

Despite these improvements, the report also identified a number of shortcomings that these educational institutions needed to address, namely that this type of teacher training has developed in an unorganized manner with a lack of collaborative efforts between professors and institutions. The report suggested that a possible cause for this problem was the lack of definitive guidelines from the government. The report states: "This somewhat makeshift development is also related to the often ambiguous institutional anchorage of teaching diversity, due to the absence of clear Ministerial requirements and guidelines covering its legitimacy and the objectives it ought to target" (Larochelle-Audet, Borri-Anadon, & McAndrew, 2013). Although this report provides useful information to address important and pressing issues relating to teacher education, one area which should have been examined to truly understand the efficacy of these programs would have been to talk to racialized youth who attended Quebec schools. Engaging in such a dialogue could explore if racialized students felt the programs with which their teachers engaged the class effectively addressed issues and problems relating to ethnocultural diversity in Quebec schools. The assumptions embedded in the report presume that if teacher training programs offer the right mixture of courses and impart the right concepts, there should be fewer problems in Quebec schools concerning racial tensions, prejudices, and interethnic conflicts. However, to better gauge their experiences, students themselves, particularly racialized youth should have been consulted.

Another study has looked specifically at issues relating to racism towards Muslims in Quebec school textbooks (McAndrew, Oueslati, & Helly, 2007). Previously, it was found that there has been significant misinformation about Muslims and Islam in Quebec textbooks throughout the 1980s which contained factual errors, perpetuated stereotypes, and which viewed Muslims and Islam from an ethnocentric perspective (Dunand, 1989; Schultze, 1994). McAndrew, Oueslati, and Helly looked at textbooks used in French secondary schools across Quebec throughout the 2003–2004 school year to examine how these texts represented Islam and Muslims. They examined 21 French textbooks to see how they presented Islam and Muslim cultures, the Muslim world at an international level (i.e. historical events, events between civilizations, and political situations), as well as Muslims in Quebec and Canada. The findings of this study were similar to those in other parts of Canada and the US which found that textbook representations of Muslims reinforced notions of 'Otherness' (Ali, 2013; Sensoy, 2009). In the 117 excerpts that were identified, they noted that there have been some improvements in the ways Muslims and Islam have been represented in textbooks since the 1980s. However, their study revealed that "ethnocentric and stereotypical presentations, as well as factual errors, still abound" (McAndrew, Oueslati, & Helly, 2007, p. 173). In particular, it was found that there were problems in the covering of "historical events that largely legitimizes Western actions, a strong tendency towards homogenizing and essentializing Muslim cultures, as well as a near total absence of Muslims as Quebec and Canadian citizens" (p. 173). McAndrew, Oueslati, and Helly suggested that these problems existed because of a lack of expertise on the part of those writing these texts, fueled possibly by media biases against Muslims and Islam, as well as the tendency for high school textbooks to deal with complex issues through simplistic explanations. This study was quite insightful, as it shed light on subtle forms of racism that existed within educational institutions in Quebec. However it did not describe the lived realities of Muslim students who attended educational institutions and who were the expert practitioners of their lives. Though this study uncovered misinformation in the materials used by educational institutions in Quebec, it fell short in describing the impact that this could have on students, particularly Muslim students.

CONCLUSION

Quebec society has had a tumultuous and troubled relationship with the Muslim 'Other' in the post-9/11 context through the notions of French secularism and interculturalism, the reasonable accommodation debates, and liberal feminist discourses. Sexularist discourses in Quebec have constructed visual signifiers worn by Muslim women, like the *hijab,* as oppressive and misogynistic, under the guise of gender equality. These discourses, which have framed Muslim women as 'imperilled' have also manufactured the perception of the 'dangerous Muslim man'. This occurred in media and political discourses surrounding the perceived crisis of honour-based violence and honour killings in Canada. Additionally, the RA debates, the Hérouxville immigration code of conduct, as well as the proposed Bill 60 have reinforced the notion of the 'civilizing European'. These archetypes have been mediated by Quebec identity politics, state policies of interculturalism, as well as liberal feminist discourses in Quebec.

Research on teacher training programs in Quebec, as well as studies that have examined Muslim representations in French textbooks used in Quebec secondary schools have failed to describe the lived realities of Muslim students. This book differs from those previous studies as it aims to investigate the lived experiences of Muslim students in secondary schools in the post-9/11 context. The following chapter will further contextualize Islamophobia by examining how it exists in the realm of popular cultural knowledge production.

NOTE

[1] There are a total of 10 provinces in Canada and 3 territories. When looking at provinces and territories combined, Quebec is second largest, preceded by the Territory of Nunavut.

CHAPTER 4

POPULAR CULTURAL ISLAMOPHOBIA

Muslim representations in Films, News Media,
and Television Programs

INTRODUCTION

Thus far in the book, we have examined Islamophobia from a theoretical perspective, as well as how it manifests in political discourse, and policies and legislation in the context of the War on Terror. Negatively evaluated beliefs and perceptions of Muslims in the post-9/11 context have also been strongly influenced and informed by representations in popular cultural mediums such as film, news media, and television programs. The impact of media in the construction of race has been discussed in great detail by Stuart Hall (1996), as he states, "the media construct for us a definition of what *race* is, what meaning the imagery of race carries, and what the 'problem of race' is understood to be" (p. 161). Indeed, after 9/11 depictions of Muslim terrorists flooded TV and cinema screens reinforcing narratives in the news media about 'dangerous Muslim men' and 'imperilled Muslim women'. This chapter examines Muslim representations in popular cultural mediums after 9/11. The reason I have devoted an entire chapter on analyzing Muslim representations in popular cultural mediums is because a number of people I interviewed for this book directly and unambiguously discussed how they felt the 'media' negatively portrayed Muslims and that these depictions have facilitated the growth of stereotypes of Muslims in Canadian society and secondary schools. This chapter examines the types of media that participants discussed in the interview process to demonstrate how these media have circulated the tropes of 'dangerous Muslim men', 'imperilled Muslim women', and Muslim cultures as being monolithic. All the media that was examined in this chapter was from the post-9/11 context as all the participants in this study attended secondary school during this time frame.

The films examined in this chapter are: *The Kingdom* (2007), *Iron Man* (2008), and *Body of Lies* (2008). There have been a number of more contemporary films that have disseminated anti-Muslim racism such as *The Dictator* (2012), *Argo* (2012), and *Zero Dark Thirty* (2012), that also resonated with participants' comments. However, the reason for analyzing these older films was because participants that mentioned how there were media biases against Muslims in Hollywood films were primarily the Muslim male particpants, who all attended secondary school the years that these films were produced and in theatres. Some of these films, like *Iron Man* and *The Kingdom* were specifically mentioned or commented on by participants.

I have included the film *Body of Lies* in this analysis because it was a fairly popular film during the same time frame of the aforementioned films and included a number of messages similar to those discussed by participants. These films often portrayed Muslim men as dangerous and threatening characters whose story lines revolved around terrorism. The news media that was analyzed in this chapter similarly included stories relating to 'dangerous Muslim men' but also examined stories that employed the 'imperilled Muslim woman' archetype.

In analyzing news media, this chapter examined events involving Muslims from the post-9/11 context that received major news coverage from Canadian and American news outlets. The events that were examined in this chapter included news coverage of the 9/11 terror attacks and the ensuing War on Terror, as well as North American terror plots. The reason for examining the news coverage of 9/11 and the War on Terror was because three of the five Muslim women participants were attending secondary school during the time of this event, which had a major impact on their secondary school experiences. Additionally, other participants alluded to how the invasions of Afghanistan and Iraq impacted their experiences in secondary schools. I have also included an analysis of news coverage relating North American terror plots because these stories directly related to participants' comments relating to how Muslims were automatically labeled as terrorists in news media, whereas the same designation was not given to non-Muslims who commit similar acts.

The analysis of television shows in this chapter consisted of examining FOX Television's drama *24* (2001–2010, & 2014). I decided to analyze the show *24* as opposed to a more contemporary program such as *Homeland* (2011–) because *24* was mentioned specifically by multiple participants as being a popular television drama which disseminated anti-Muslim stereotypes and racism. Of all television shows from the post-9/11 context that had Muslim characters, *24* has been the longest running and most successful to date. Additionally, this television program aired during a time frame that most of the student participants attended secondary school and is therefore a logical choice to include in my analysis of television programs for this study.

ANALYSIS OF HOLLYWOOD FILMS

The Kingdom. The Kingdom, directed by Peter Berg and starring Jamie Foxx, takes place in the Kingdom of Saudi Arabia, where an American oil company's housing compound is brutally attacked by a terrorist group. The terrorist attacks were devastating, causing the death and injury of hundreds of Westerners, including FBI agents who arrived at the scene of the attacks when secondary explosives were detonated. A team of elite FBI agents manages to get special access into Saudi Arabia to investigate the incident with the intent of bringing the terrorists to justice. This film frequently employs the trope of 'dangerous Muslim men' from beginning to end. The attacks described in this film were loosely based on terrorist attacks on a Western compound in Riyadh, Saudi Arabia in 2003, where 30 people were killed; however, as Shaheen (2008) mentions, "Berg mutates these real tragic events, cleverly manipulating viewers into thinking his movie's false scenes are what really happened" (p. 129). In Other words, the film falsely portrays itself to be depicting actual events.

In the opening scene of the film, viewers were exposed to incompetent Saudi police officers easily being fooled into giving terrorists access into the compound, which was then followed by scenes of Muslim terrorists indiscriminately killing civilians, most of whom were women and children. The faith of Islam was explicitly linked to the motives of the terrorists, as one scene clearly showed a terrorist reciting the *shahadah*, Muslim declaration of faith, before blowing himself up along with scores of innocent civilians. While the bloodbath takes place on the compound, the head terrorist and his associates watch contently from a safe distance at the death and destruction being waged on Westerners. Amongst those most vigilant was the ring leader's teenage son who was clearly desensitized to the killing of Western children his own age. Hence, Muslims of varying ages were depicted as engaging in, or being supportive of terrorist activities—a sentiment reminiscent of the experiences of a number of the Muslim participants discussed in Chapters Five and Six.

In the final scene, the grandson of the slain lead terrorist, who initially was repulsed by the imagery of indiscriminate killing of innocents taking place at the outset of the film, takes solace in his grandfather's parting words to him, "we're going to kill them all." The film then concludes focusing on the beady, menacing eyes of the young child who is to represent the next generation of terrorists, fully charged with rage, hate, and spite for the West. The only exceptions to the Muslims-as-terrorists depictions in this film were incompetent Saudi Arabian police officers who were portrayed as completely clueless and inept. Even the Saudi civilian population in this film was framed as hostile and ready to wage war against Americans.

From the moment the elite FBI team set foot on Saudi Arabian soil there was a constant concern for their security, giving the impression that Saudi Arabia, likened to "Mars" by one of the FBI agents, was a lawless land filled with manacing anti-Westerners just itching to exterminate any American within sight. The agents were constantly asked if they were wearing their bulletproof vests, implying they were constant targets under threat. All these fears for the Westerners' safety were deemed warranted by the film's end as the FBI agents wandered into the Saudi Arabian neighbourhood housing the lead terrorist. Within minutes of setting foot onto the terrorist's turf, Saudi Arabian civilians were firing grenade launchers, automatic weapons and explosives at the FBI agents and the sole competent Saudi Arabian officer in the film. This elite FBI team of three was able to emerge unscathed and defeat the entire terrorist neighbourhood resulting in a massive body count of dead Muslims strewn all over the neighbourhood. The only casualty on the side of the 'goodguys' was Al-Ghazi, the competent Saudi Arabian police officer helping the FBI. Consequently, whatever fleeting positive images about Saudis that were presented in this film were erased from the collective memory of the viewers as Al-Ghazi ends up on the side where all the 'badguys' ended up, amidst the body count of dead Muslims at the conclusion of this film. His death demonstrated the inability of contradictions to exist in the contrived 'Muslim world' depicted in this film. Al-Ghazi's 'Otherness' associated with being Muslim was incompatable with 'Westerness', hence being on the side of Westerners was an irreconcilable union bound to result in his demise. The 'dangerous Muslim man' archetype, has been further developed in other films by depicting an inherent backwardness in Muslim men.

Iron Man. *Iron Man,* directed by Jon Favreau, was a film adaptation of the Marvel comic book character Iron Man. In this film, millionaire genius inventor, Tony Stark, played by Robert Downey Jr., was the head of a military contracting company, Stark Industries, which provided arms to the U.S. military throughout its mission in Afghanistan. While Stark was visiting Afghanistan to promote his new advanced technology missile, the Jericho, he gets captured by a group of Afghan terrorists. The terrorists demanded that Stark manufacture a Jericho missile for them in exchange for his freedom. Initially Stark refused the offer, but was then coerced through torture. Ironically, the intimidation techniques employed on Stark by the Afghan terrorists bore a striking resemblance to methods employed by U.S. military personal on Afghan detainees in prisons in Bagram and Guantanamo Bay (Begg, 2006), thus flipping reality completely on its head. Eventually Stark agreed to build the weapon; however, in secret devised a plot to instead create a bullet proof body armor suit. The suit was fully equipped with weapons, flame throwers, and rockets which enabled him to escape his captors and eventually become the superhero Iron Man.

This film negatively depicts Muslims throughout the scenes in which Stark was a captive in Afghanistan. For the most part, Muslims in this film were portrayed as inept, stupid, and incompetent terrorists who were easily duped by the protagonist. This was most evident in the scenes where Stark was busy building his armor suit, which bore no semblance to the Jericho missile he was supposed to make, under the direct supervision of his captors. From time to time, the terrorists commented how the suit did not look like the missile; however, they were not intelligent enough to figure out what Stark was up to. Another scene in which the terrorists were portrayed as incompetent was when Stark's business partner Obadiah Stane, who was secretly plotting to get rid of Stark, came to Afghanistan to meet Stark's former captors. In this scene, the terrorists managed to salvage a prototype of the suit that Stark created while he was captured. The terrorists attempted to make a business deal with Stane; however, once again they were duped by the whimsical technological devices of the far more intelligent and advanced Westerner. Within minutes, Stane had them all eliminated and removed the technology which they were too incompetent and primitive to be the custodians of. The white characters in these scenes, which were embodiments of the 'West', were portrayed as technologically advanced and intellectually superior. In stark contrast, the darker skinned villains, emblematic of the 'Muslim Other' were unable to possess and handle Western technologies.

In addition to being portrayed as backwards and inept, Muslims were also portrayed as being violent. The terrorist group in this film not only inflicted violence on Western military targets, but also focused much of their killing and bloodshed towards their own people: Afghan civilians. Hence, Afghani people were portrayed in this film as either being violent terrorists or helpless civilians who were unable to fend for themselves. In one scene when the same terrorist group that captured Stark was raiding a village, the powerless Afghan civilians were desperate for a savior. Seeing as how their own people were too incompetent and backwards to do anything about their plight, who could they turn to? Cue the benevolent, ingenious, Western superhero; Iron Man, with his fancy weaponry to save the primitive Afghanis from their own wicked, backwards people. In a not-so-subtle fashion, this scene reproduced the archetypal figure in the War on Terror of the 'civilizing European' whose imperial actions of intervention were justified as acts of benevolence, saving the savages from themselves and their backwards culture.

The only Afghani character in the film who was not portrayed as being a terrorist or a weak dependent civilian was Dr. Yinsen, a co-captor of Stark in Afghanistan who, like Al-Ghazi sacrifices himself, for the ultimate good; protecting and saving the Westerner. This 'good Muslim' was uniquely Westernized and in no way resembles other Afghani people in the way he dressed, spoke and presented himself. Hence the overall impression viewers were left with after watching this film was that Muslims were either backwards ruthless terrorists or primitive feeble non-combatants in need of Western support for their deliverance from their own people. The only way to avoid this degrading dichotomy was by adopting a Westernized *modus operandi*. This theme also manifested in the film *Body of Lies*.

Body of Lies. Body of Lies, directed by Ridley Scott, was an action thriller starring Leonardo DiCaprio and Russell Crowe. This film portrays clear contrasts between success, modernization, and progress (the West) and primitiveness, poverty and regression (the East). In this film, CIA agent Roger Ferris is operating out of Jordan in America's War on Terror, under the supervision of his deceitful boss, Ed Hoffman stationed at CIA headquarters in Washington. The opening scene of the film featured a radicalized Muslim cleric preaching hate and violence towards the Western world, giving credence to his radicalized views throughout the film by quoting verses of the Quran completely devoid of their context. Muslim terrorists in this film manage to wreak havoc causing mass destruction in various countries across Europe including the U.K. and Netherlands, giving the impression that Muslim terrorist cells are covertly operating all over the Western world completely undetected. As was the case in *Iron Man,* Muslim men are depicted as primitive and belonging to an era of centuries gone by. The terrorists avoid using technology to evade detection because, as Hoffman mentions "our enemy has realized that they are fighting guys from the future". As such, these terrorists have "turn[ed] their backs on technology". This primitiveness and archaism from the Muslim world is contrasted with the sophisticated and advanced technological tools used by the CIA, which symbolized Western triumphalism and superiority over the East.

In addition to notions of primitiveness, Muslim religiosity is often equated with extremism in this film. For example, in one scene, the suave, debonair, and

Westernized Hani Salaam, who is the head of the Jordanian intelligence meets a former friend, Mustapha Karami, who has turned towards terrorism. During their discussion Salaam notes how Karami has become a "jihadist" and that his transformation was related to his newly found religiosity. At the end of this scene Salaam manages to buy off Karami by giving his mother, a Palestinian refugee, a comfortable life away from the refugee camps. When asked by Karami what he must do in return for helping his family, Salaam responds saying, "be a good Muslim. Continue your life with your brothers from Al-Qaeda. We will devise a way to talk." Thus, with a few trinkets from the wealthy Westernized Hani Salaam, wearing a Western suit, the poor Muslim terrorist wearing his shabby 'Islamic' style clothing sells his principles and becomes an informant for the Jordanian intelligence services. The contrasts in this scene clearly depict 'good Muslims' and 'bad Muslims'. Salaam, the 'good Muslim' dressed in his Western suit is leading the charge on the War on Terror in his country. Karami, the 'bad Muslim' with his newly found religious devotion and 'Islamic' style clothing was depicted as a-would-be terrorist if it were not for the 'good Muslim' policing his behavior.

The Islamic faith was not completely denigrated in this film, as one of the final scenes explained how the Quran did not advocate indiscriminate killing. In this scene Farris was being held captive by terrorists who were about to kill him. In a plea to spare his life, Farris states that "there is no place in the Quran for killing innocent civilians". Unfortunately, this interpretation of the Quran came from someone who was not a Muslim himself. Hence, in this film fringe elements and radicals who in no way represent the Islamic faith as a whole, continuously misinterpret and misquote the teachings of the Quran to justify their sordid and twisted ideas and the only mainstream understanding of the Quran to counter these inaccuracies came from someone who has been at war with Muslims throughout the film. Thus, viewers were left with a paradoxical impression that the Islamic faith, when interpreted by its own adherents, is violent and against the West; however, is not so ghastly and aggressive when it was interpreted by non-Muslims. Because Arabs/Muslims were predisposed to violence they were only able to interpret their scriptures through violence. The civilized Westerner who was benevolent and diametrically opposed to the Arab mindset was able to sanitize the Islamic faith through his interpretations of Islamic Holy Scriptures. The film ends shortly after Farris is rescued from the terrorists and meets with Hoffman who offers him a safer and more stable position in Washington. Farris declines saying that maybe he will stay in Jordon. Hoffman, shocked at the idea exclaims, "Nobody likes the Middle East, there's nothing here to like" solidifying the 'Otherness' of the Muslim world presented in this film.

All the films discussed in this section consistently portray Muslims through archetypes that have emerged in the War on Terror. As Morey and Yaqin (2011) note, Muslim characters in films such as these have "their 'Muslimness' marked out in some way. Their existence as subjects with any other affiliations or interests are effectively voided" (p. 119). In other words, Muslims are portrayed monolithically through tropes ascribing violence and terror as inherent qualities. News media coverage of events involving Muslims have had similar representations.

ISLAMOPHOBIC ARCHETYPES IN NEWS MEDIA

Terrorist attacks of September 11 and the War on Terror. The terrorist attacks of September 11, 2001 were a series of attacks which targeted major important and symbolic structures in the United States. The most devastating of these attacks was on the twin towers of the World Trade Center in New York City, which were strategically hit by two airplanes within minutes of each other resulting in the collapse of both buildings. A third plane hit the Pentagon destroying sections of the edifice and a fourth plane was on route to Washington D.C. when crew members and passengers attempted to regain control of the pane, resulting in the plane crashing in Shanksville Pennsylvania. The alleged hijackers of the planes were all Arab-Muslim men who were members of the terrorist organization al-Qaeda.

The terrorist attacks on September 11 marked a major turning point in the US, as these attacks were the greatest threat to American national security in recent history. As such, there was a seemingly endless amount of news coverage of these attacks in the US as well as in Canadian media. The world was in shock at these attacks. Amidst the bewilderment, media and political discourses were rife with irrationality, prejudice and loaded terminology. In this analysis, political and media discourses were examined simultaneously, as political and media discourses in relation to the War on Terror have become inextricably linked (Alsultany, 2012). Describing how governmental and media discourses were interrelated throughout the War on Terror, Alsultany (2012) mentions, "the Bush administration needed to frame the ways that people across the country thought about and talked about the events of 9/11, and the ways that we should respond to such events" (p. 7). Thus, governmental discourses of "they hate us for our freedoms" were disseminated through the media to garner support for the War on Terror.

Whether it was CNN, ABC, NBC, CBS, MSNBC or FOX a similar type of narrative was regularly reproduced in the media coverage of the 9/11 terror attacks (Mogensen, 2007). Reductionist views were disseminated by "experts" like Jeane Kirkpatrick who argued that America was at war with Islam. Charged language was featured in news casts boasting headings like "War on America", "America Under Attack", and "America's New War". Media outlets presented images of Palestinians celebrating the terrorist attacks—a sentiment which was shared by an extreme minority of Muslims worldwide. Ann Coulter, one of the most outspoken right-wing columnists in America stated: "not all Muslims are terrorists but all terrorists are Muslims—at least all terrorists capable of assembling a murderous plot against America…We should invade their countries, kill their leaders and covert them to Christianity" (cited in Abukhattala, 2004, p. 157). It would appear that the precarious atmosphere of 9/11 emboldened Coulter to vent these incoherent and inaccurate views despite the fact that the U.S. State Department's figures suggested that terrorism prior to 9/11 originating from Middle Eastern Muslim countries ranked sixth in occurrence and frequency (Said, 1997). Caricatures of the hijackers regularly appeared in editorial cartoons, which recycled images often associated with Islam and Muslims; a scraggly beard, turban, and Eastern style clothing (Gottschalk & Greenberg, 2008). However, a cursory analysis of the hijackers reveals that they were, for the most part, clean-shaven and donning Western clothes. Hence, the public was presented with erroneous images of the Muslim 'Others' responsible for these acts.

The biased news coverage of these events has been discussed at length by Kirsten Mogensen in her study of T.V. journalists covering the 9/11 attacks. In this study Mogensen (2007) concluded that journalists from major media outlets including CNN, ABC, NBC, CBS, MSNBC, and FOX "consciously [chose] not [to] be objective, neutral, or impartial, and they often explained their actions by referring to the feelings of the viewers" (p. 314). In other words, at a time when Americans felt uncertainty, fear, anger, and rage, journalists felt justified in abandoning impartiality on their commentaries of these events. Additionally, media coverage of these attacks in the US facilitated anti-Muslim sentiments as right-wing and mainstream media outlets frequently featured figures like Steven Emerson and Danial Pipes as "terrorism experts". These "experts" would regularly disseminate misinformation about American Muslims, making baseless claims such as the vast majority of mosques in the US were being controlled by Muslim radicals (Kumar, 2012).

Ross Perigoe (2007) also found biases in the media coverage of 9/11 from Canadian media outlets, as he mentions, "In Canada, coverage of the attacks produced, for White Canadians, feelings of insecurity, vulnerability and suspicion of the Muslim community" (p. 332). Perigoe's analysis of *The Gazette*, the largest English language newspaper in Quebec and the eighth largest newspaper in Canada, found that journalists disseminated ideas and frameworks which casted the Muslim community in a negative light. *The Gazette* perpetuated ideas of Muslims from Muslim majority countries as being backwards, oppressive and misogynistic, whereas their coverage of Muslims from the West was centered on the unavoidability of a backlash. According to Perigoe (2007), framing Muslims from Western countries in this manner created the expectation that attacks against them "were not only inevitable, they were also justified—since even the Muslims themselves expected them" (p. 329). Ironically, *The Gazette* did not document any acts of violence perpetrated against Muslims from September 18 to September 30 despite the fact there was evidence suggesting that such attacks were taking place (Perigoe, 2007). According to Perigoe, *The Gazette*'s coverage of 9/11, like the coverage found in the major American media outlets, constructed an image of these events which justified a reaction of retribution and war. Hence, Media discourses in the US and Canada perpetuated identical perceptions of Muslims.

The war that ensued from the 9/11 attacks, referred to by the Bush administration as the War on Terror, toed a common line in the media, providing unconditional support for retaliation against this catastrophic event. Any type of decent from media personalities was severely reprimanded, as Anthony DiMaggio (2008) states,

> Prominent figures in the media have been subject to a number of punishments intended to skirt foundational anti-war opposition to the Bush Administration. These punishments include intimidation, firings, and the use of censorship in order to limit messages questioning pro-war propaganda. (p. 146)

News personalities from major news networks, including CNN's Christiane Amanpour, claimed that they felt intimidated by the pressure tactics of the Bush administration if they did not fully give support to the War on Terror (DiMaggio, 2008). Similarly, political analyst Bill Maher, despite being a rabid Islamophobe, was fired from his job with ABC when he began criticizing the cowardly tactics of aerial bombings employed in the war. Phil Donahue, who had a consistent record of anti-war criticism, was taken off the air even though his show was the highest rated program on MSNBC at the time. The reason given by MSNBC for Donahue's sudden dismissal was that he represented a "difficult public face for NBC in a time of war" (DiMaggio, 2008, p. 147). Hence, not only was critical dialogue nonexistent in the media coverage of the terrorist attacks of 9/11, but it was also absent in the coverage of the War on Terror. As Simon Cottle (2006) observes, "journalism post-9/11 and the reporting of the global War on Terror…clearly reproduce agendas and representations that support state interests and policies" (p. 191). In other words, media discourses confirmed and perpetuated political discourses regarding these conflicts. A number of these political discourses surrounded the plight of the 'imperilled Muslim woman'.

As discussed in previous chapters, saving oppressed Muslim women from dangerous Muslim men was a rallying call used to garner support for the War on Terror. Conservatives and liberals both voiced their support for the invasion of Afghanistan on the premise that it would liberate Afghan women. The framing of the War on Terror as being an act of benevolence couched in liberal feminist discourses was necessary as the "they hate us for our freedom" explanations for the 9/11 attacks relied "on the presentation of the oppressed Muslim woman as evidence of this hatred of freedom and also as a key to understanding and winning the War on Terror" (Alsultany, 2012, p. 73). Prominent political figures like Laura Bush and Hillary Clinton openly spoke in support of this invasion to liberate Muslim women, whose opinions were widely circulated in the media. What was often neglected in political and media discourses were discussions of how this conflict inflicted violence on Muslim women, which inevitably resulted from the militarized nature of this conflict. The motives of liberating Muslim women in Afghanistan through the War on Terror needs to be seriously questioned, as women had been suffering in Afghanistan prior to 9/11, however their plight only became worthy of intervention when it served a strategic political end.

North American terror plots: The classifications of 'terrorist' and 'terrorism' in media. Words like 'terrorism' and 'terrorist' in the aftermath of 9/11 have

71

increasingly become subjective terms highlighting Arab and Muslim violence disproportionately to acts of violence committed by other religious and ethnic groups. In addition to examples previously discussed, the Hutaree Militia bomb plot further illustrates this point. The Hutaree militia were a group of 9 Christian militants based in Michigan who allegedly hatched a plot to kill a police officer with the intent to carry out bomb attacks at the funeral, using landmines and roadside bombs in May 2010. The motivations of the accused in planning these attacks were religious in nature, as they described themselves as "Christian warriors" on their website. This fact was downplayed by the media, which has not been the case when Muslims hatched similar plots. As Sheehi (2011) observes, media coverage of this plot was in stark contrast to how Islam and religious affiliation are highlighted when Muslims have engaged in similar attempted plots. Another example of news media's reluctance to use the term terrorism to define clear acts of violence and terror committed by non-Muslims was the attempted mosque bombing in Jacksonville, Florida on May 10, 2010. A pipe bomb was detonated at a local mosque in Jacksonville at a time when Muslims were in the facility for evening prayers. According to FBI investigators, the blast was powerful enough to send debris over 100 feet away. Though no one was hurt in this explosion, had the bomb been placed closer to the prayer hall it could have very easily resulted in numerous injuries and possibly deaths. However, media outlets did not deem this event to be an act of terrorism.

In contrast to the media coverage of the Hutaree militia and the Jacksonville mosque bombing, Muslim fanatics who hatched similar failed terror attacks such as Umar Farouk Abdulmutallab (a.k.a. the Underwear Bomber), Faisal Shahzad (a.k.a. the Times Square Bomber) and Mohamed Osman Mohamud (a.k.a. the Christmas Tree Bomber) were all featured prominently in news media and were unflinchingly labelled as terrorists. When Major Nidal Hasan, a former Army psychiatrist at the Fort Hood military base in Texas went on a shooting spree killing 13 people and injuring 30 others in November 2009, media outlets immediately labeled his actions as religiously inspired terrorism (DiMaggio, 2009). However similar acts of violence involving the killing of innocent civilians such as the Virginia Tech massacre in 2007, the Aurora shooting in 2012, or the Washington Navy Yard shooting in 2013 were not labeled as acts of terrorism in the media. Media discourses surrounding these events did not mention religious affiliations or beliefs as being motivating factors for these massacres. Rather, in all these instances, media discourses attempted to make sense of these violent acts by questioning the perpetrators' sanity and mental state. In other words, these actions, when committed by non-Muslims, can only be explained as resulting from some type of mental deficiency. One can draw parallels of the media coverage in the Canadian context in the alleged "Project Samosa" terror plot in August 2010.

The "Project Samosa" terror plot involved the arrest of three Canadian men in the Ottawa region; Hiva Alizadeh, Misbahuddin Ahmed, and Dr. Khurram

Sher, who were involved in an alleged plot, the parameters of which were never defined or articulated (Cobb, 2014). Canadian media outlets were unhesitant in pronouncing the accused, all of whom were Muslims, to be terrorists before they had been found guilty of any crimes. In an article printed by the *Montreal Gazette* on August 28, 2010, assertions were made that the accused in this case had plans to bomb Montreal's metro system (Curran, 2010). Yet in the same issue of the *Gazette,* another article debunked these claims quoting a spokeswoman from the Société de Transport de Montréal who had stated "we checked with the police and authorities and…it's not true" (MacLeod, Nease, & Seymour, 2010). This pattern of throwing out unfounded accusations also occurred in the *National Post*'s coverage of the alleged terror plot. In an article printed on August 27, 2010, the *National Post* described how one of the accused, Misbahuddin Ahmed, an X-ray technician at an Ottawa area hospital, "worked near to where radioactive isotopes are stored, but had no official access to them. Isotopes, used to diagnose and treat illness such as heart disease and cancer, can also be used to build so-called dirty bombs" (Nease, 2010). Why did the *National Post* feel it necessary to mention this piece of information unless to imply the accused was making "dirty bombs"—a claim which had no grounding. Terms such as "radicalized," "terrorist cell" and "al-Qaeda inspired" were regularly featured in newspaper articles across Canada, including the *National Post, Ottawa Citizen,* and *Montreal Gazette,* all alluding to the presumption of guilt before the accused had an opportunity to defend themselves in court. Would this have been so had the accused been white Christians, as was the case in the Hutaree militia? If so, would such an operation be insensitively named "Project Macaroni and Cheese" or some other type of food which is stereotypically associated with people who are white, or possibly "Project Fried Chicken" had the accused been African Americans?

This knee-jerk reaction of equating Islam and terrorism creates a paradoxical situation—when terrorist acts are committed by Muslims, political and media discourses surrounding Muslims are validated. When Muslims denounce these attacks it gives the impression that they are denouncing Islam, thus producing 'good Muslim' 'bad Muslim' discourses. This process of singularly identifying Muslims as terrorists in the media creates a climate in which statements such as those voiced by FOX News host Brian Kilmeade, who claimed "not all Muslims are terrorists but all terrorists are Muslims" (cited in Media Matters, 2010), can be expressed in public forms. The pervasiveness of these types of discourses becomes problematic as it legitimizes "their public expression and increases the threshold of the public acceptability of racism. Racism becomes 'acceptable'—and thus, not too long after, 'true'" (Hall, 1996, p. 162). Such a simplistic and un-nuanced approach at examining present day acts of terrorism can easily be manipulated to draw erroneous conclusions. Television dramas in the post-9/11 context have attempted to present more complex portrayals of Muslims, however they still present archetypal images associated with the Islamic faith.

THE MUSLIM THREAT IN THE WORLD OF *24*

24 was a widely popular and successful television program that aired on FOX Television from 2001–2010 and again in 2014. The show received numerous awards and nominations including winning Best Drama Series in the 2003 Golden Globe awards and Outstanding Drama Series in the 2006 Primetime Emmy Awards. Kiefer Sutherland also won an Emmy Award for Best Lead Actor for his portrayal of Jack Bauer on the show the same year. The popularity of the show reached far beyond its North American audiences as the show has aired in Africa, Australia, Europe, and the Middle East. The premise of the show was unique, as it took place in real time. Each season consisted of twenty-four episodes and therefore the season portrayed one full twenty-four-hour day in the life of Jack Bauer, a special agent working for a fictional government agency called the Counter Terrorism Unit (CTU) based out of Los Angeles.

As one can imagine, this show whose plot centred on fighting terrorism and aired a couple of months after the 9/11 attacks, regularly portrayed Muslim characters as the main antagonists. Five of the nine seasons featured Muslim characters as the main terrorist plotters on the show. In each of the five seasons featuring Muslims, the terrorists' plots involved detonating weapons of mass destruction on Western soil. A hallmark of the show was the ticking time bomb scenario, as viewers would see the timer appear at various times throughout the show, usually prior to and after commercial breaks. This technique reinforced an atmosphere of urgent realism on the show. It gave the perception that disaster could strike at any moment and that there was an impending threat that needed to be resolved before time runs out. In such a charged environment, Bauer was constantly faced with having to make decisions for the greater good. A regular theme on the show was that of the ends justifying the means. To this end, Bauer regularly engaged in torture in his interrogation of suspected terrorists. The show demonstrated how torture was an extreme measure in urgent situations, as there would usually be a bomb that was set to go off within the twenty-four-hour time frame that would result in the deaths of thousands of American civilians. Bauer was portrayed as a tortured soul for the violence he had inflicted in efforts to serve the greater good. He was often reprimanded by other periphery characters on the show for his techniques to acquire the information that was needed. However, in the world of *24*, Bauer's decisions were always a necessary evil and were sanitized by saving thousands of American lives. This show, probably more than any other in the post-9/11 context has been instrumental in legitimizing the violent policing that came about from the War on Terror, as it regularly justified the logic of torture. In the first five seasons alone there were 67 scenes that involved torture, more than any other show on television during that time span (Bayoumi, 2015).

One of the unpleasant byproducts of the War on Terror was the torturing of Muslims for information regarding national security. The Bush administration set up the infamous Guantanamo Bay prison in Cuba in which prisoners were designated enemy combatants and thus, according the US government, were no longer within the parameters of the Geneva Convention. Numerous stories abounded of the torture of inmates including Canadian citizen Omar Khadr, who was fifteen years of age when he was sent to the prison. Similarly, stories of the inhumane treatment of inmates at the Abu Ghraib prison in Iraq surfaced when pictures of Army personnel sexually and physically abusing prisoners leaked out. These prisons and others like them in the aftermath of the War on Terror were deemed a necessary evil in the fight against terror. *24* brought the reality of a terrorist threat to television screens across North America and beyond, and in doing so showed audiences how fighting terror came at a price. In the end, torture in *24* was always deemed an inconvenient necessity to save the lives of countless innocents. This has brought about unfortunate consequences in the post-9/11 context. As Alsutany (2012) observes, "*24* has helped make the real torture of Arabs and Muslims seem like a necessary evil—regrettable, perhaps, but essential for the safety of our nation" (p. 40).

24, like other post-9/11 dramas, did make attempts to show Muslim characters with some levels of complexity, as opposed to the pre-9/11 characterizations which relied more on one dimensional depictions. Alsultany (2012) refers to these attempts as "simplified complex representations". Alsultany argues that simplified complex representations are the "representational mode of the so-called post-race era, signifying a new era of racial representation. These representations appear to challenge or complicate former stereotypes and contribute to a multicultural or post-race illusion" (p. 21). Ultimately, these simplified complex representations are ineffectual because they are couched in discourses legitimizing the War on Terror, thereby associating Muslims with terrorism and reinforcing the 'dangerous Muslim man' archetype. In other words, tying Muslims and Arabs to storylines revolving around terrorism does nothing to challenge stereotypes of Muslim/Arab terrorists. Season two of this series was the first season that employed Muslim terrorists as the main antagonists.

The opening scene of season two shows a man being tortured in a South Korean dungeon to provide information about a terrorist plot about to take place somewhere in the US. Upon extracting the information from the detainee, US authorities were informed of a nuclear bomb set to go off in Los Angeles within the next twenty-four hours. Muslim terrorists, from an undisclosed Muslim country, were behind this plot. Throughout the season viewers were introduced to different characters who may or may not have been working with the terrorists. One character, Reza Naiyeer, a young Arab man working for a wealthy businessman named Bob Warner, was suspected of being involved in the plot. Reza was of Arab decent but was raised and educated in London, England. He was preparing for his marriage to Marie Warner, his employer's daughter, when he was approached by CTU for questioning related to the terrorist threat. Reza denied knowledge of the threat, however after searching through his personal effects, a connection was found between him and Syed Ali, the terrorist planning the attack. Viewers were led to believe that Reza was somehow involved with the plot, however as the season progressed it turned out Reza's connections to the terrorists were forged by his fiancée Marie, who was working with Syed Ali all along. The character of Reza was emblematic of the 'good Muslim'. Reza dressed in Western clothes, had a Western accent, was raised and educated in the West, and was marrying a blond hair blue eyed woman. He himself was disillusioned when he was being questioned by CTU for being connected to the plot as he stated: "I grew up in London. I'm marrying an American girl, a Protestant. So, if you're going to racially profile me you should at least get it right". Eventually, viewers came to learn that the most unsuspecting of characters, Marie Warner, was a key figure in the terror plot and questions surrounding how Marie became a Muslim radical emerged.

Once Marie's involvement in the plot came to light, her disillusioned sister Kate explains how Marie was once a political activist in her youth. Upon her mother's death, Marie went missing in London for several weeks and returned home more subdued and passive. This, according to Jack Bauer, was indicative of her descent into radicalism, as he stated "that's precisely what happens when you're radicalized. Handlers train you to stop talking about anything…You're better able to blend into the background." As the character of Marie and her complexities unfold, viewers begin to hear discourses reminiscent of state anti-terror policies.

According to Kundnani (2014), in the post 9/11 context authorities have identified behavioural, cultural, and ideological signals which can predict who will become a terrorist. Radicalized individuals will typically pass through four stages: *preradicalization, identification, indoctrination*, and *action*. Marie Warner as a youth was politically active, which was an indication of *preradicalization*. While in London, Marie became Muslim and radicalized, hence her periods of *identification* and *indoctrination* took place while missing in London. Finally, Marie's character moves onto the last stage of *action*, attempting to detonate a nuclear bomb on US soil. What is troubling with these discourses of predicting terrorism is that, with the exception of the last stage of 'action', they attempt to criminalize beliefs and behaviours which are not illegal, as the goal of identifying would-be-terrorists is to prevent a crime before it happens. This line of thinking implies that "terrorism can only be prevented by systematically monitoring Muslim religious and political life" (Kundnani, 2014, p. 12). Hence, Marie's character transformation is in line with state discourses of radicalization and terrorism. As a youth she was politically active, this eventually led her to identify with violent ideologies and easily become indoctrinated, so much so that she was willing to engage in terrorist activities. The logic therefore goes that, had they identified and 'fixed' Marie's radical beliefs earlier on, it may have prevented her decent into violent extremism and murder.

Marie's character was an example of how Islam was a corrupting force, needing to be protected against. Marie Warner was a white upper-class American girl. She had wealth, beauty, and a loving family. Her political leanings were indicative of her spoiled liberal upbringing, which sowed the seeds of her eventual radicalization. Once her family unit was shaken (i.e. the death of her mother) she fled the safety of her home to London and disappeared. While in London, the Islamic faith acted as a corrupting agent, as she transformed from an innocent white American girl to a hard-core Islamic terrorist ready to mercilessly Murder hundreds of thousands of innocent civilians. The moral values that she was brought up with, as embodied by her sister Kate who joins the fight against terror by working with Bauer, were completely undone within a span of a few weeks through the faith of Islam.

Alternative depictions of Muslims on television? Television representations of Muslims have not all been as negative as those on *24*. Popular prime-time dramas such as ABC's *Lost* (2004–2010) and NBC's *Community* (2009–2014) both had Muslim characters which were generally portrayed positively. However, despite these characters' positive representations, Muslims were ultimately perceived as 'Other' on these shows. The Character of Sayid Jarrah on *Lost* was an intelligent and logical character, whose technological knowhow was vital to the survivors of Oceanic flight 815, who were stranded on an island possessed of supernatural powers. This character always provided good advice and fought for the well-being of the characters on the show. However, Sayid's character screamed of 'Other', as prior to crashing on the Island with the rest of the survivors, he was a self-admitted Iraqi torturer. Though Sayid's character was troubled by his violent past, he nonetheless applied his skills of torturing on various characters on the show. The instances when Sayid tortured individuals on the island, as was the case in *24*, revolved around circumstances of necessity. Sayid's actions were necessary evils that the other protagonists on the show did not have the biological make up to inflict on other human beings. Hence, whenever the 'good guys' needed to do an 'evil' they were able to sanitize their actions through the character of Sayid, who was the only one capable of doing such horrible actions.

The character of Abed Nadir on *Community*, like Sayid, was generally portrayed in a positive light. He provided comic relief on the show through his constant referencing of American pop-culture. Abed was portrayed as an awkward individual, in part because of his difficult childhood having a Palestinian father who did not understand him, and a Polish Mother who was absent from his life from an early age. Abed was a key member of his study group on the show, however whenever family members of his 'Islamic' heritage made appearances they reproduced stereotypical representations of Muslims. Abed's father was a loud, irrational man, who had a heavy accent and would scream gibberish, which was supposed to be Arabic. Abed's cousin, Abra, also made an appearance on the show. She was clad in a *burqa*, similar to those worn by women in Afghanistan. Abra's character embodied the 'imperilled Muslim woman' archetype as she was only seen as happy once she was 'liberated' from her 'Islamic' culture, symbolized through her dress.

Other shows like TLC's *All-American Muslim* (2011–2012) have made attempts to show Muslim-Americans as regular people with similar challenges and aspirations in life as most middle-class Americans. This deviance from media and political discourses, showing Muslims as other than terrorists or oppressed, brought about a number of problems for the producers of the show. Right-wing zealots like Pamela Geller and Robert Spencer pressured advertisers to withdraw their sponsorship of the show. They argued it promoted ideas which normalized Muslims, masking the threat that they pose as a stealth fifth column to American society. Criticism of the show by the political right eventually resulted in 65 advertisers pulling their ads from TLC (Lean, 2012). Hence, in the post-9/11 context producing television programs which provide a counter discourse to political and media narratives of Muslims has been faced with opposition. In such a climate, the impact of a show like *24* is more far reaching.

CONCLUSION

Islamophobic images have been prevalent in a number of popular cultural mediums such as films, news media, and television programs. Muslim representations in *The Kingdom, Iron Man,* and *Body of Lies*, news media coverage of the 9/11 terror attacks, the War on Terror, as well as the television drama *24* have systemically reproduced notions of Muslim men being violent and threatening, Muslim women being oppressed, and Western nations as being inherently progressive and civilized in contrast to Muslim majority nations. This discussion of Muslim representations in popular cultural media help to contextualize the types of biases and racism that Muslim youth living in Western nations encounter in their interactions with society as well as in social institutions such as schools.

Having historicized, theorized, and contextualize the phenomon of Islamophobia in the first four chapters, my intent was to help the reader understand Islamophobia in the West. The second half of the book will discuss the lived experiences of Islamophobia. The following chapter will explore the phenomenon of Islamophobia in Canadian secondary schools since 9/11. The chapter will provide a portrait of the 'realities on the ground' by drawing from interviews from current and former Muslim female students who attend(ed) secondary schools in Quebec with the intent of uncovering the factors which may have facilitated anti-Muslim racism and Islamophobia in their schools.

PART 2

EXPERIENCING ISLAMOPHOBIA

Islamophobia in Practice

Before delving into my discussion of Muslim youth experiences in secondary schools, I believe it would be useful to briefly discuss some details about participants to better contextualize the discussions in the following chapters. All participants resided and attended schools in the Montreal and the Greater Montreal Region of Quebec, Canada. Four of these schools were located in Montreal, while the other eight schools were located in suburbs or neighborhoods outside the city. There were five female Muslim student participants. The pseudonyms of the Muslim female student participants were: Sarah, Maryam, Noor, Ayesha, and Amina. Sarah, Maryam, and Amina were of Pakistani origin, Ayesha was Syrian, and Noor was French Canadian. All five of the female student participants were born and raised in Quebec. The four non-French Canadian participants had parents that immigrated to Quebec before they were born. There was a total of seven Muslim male student participants. The pseudonyms I used for Muslim male student participants were as follows: Yusuf, Malik, Ismail, Ahmad, Adam, Zaid, and Ali. Yusuf, Malik, Ismail, and Zaid were of Pakistani origin; Adam and Ali were of Indian origin, and Ahmad was Algerian. All of the male participants were born and raised in Quebec and their parents immigrated to Canada before they were born.

Ideally I wanted to interview the same number of male and female Muslim student participants to have equal representation. I felt this was important because the experiences of Muslim women in educational contexts have been very distinct from Muslim males' experiences (Razai-Rashti, 2005; Zine, 2006). However, after a lengthy recruitment process the male to female ratio was slightly unbalanced as I had seven Muslim male and five Muslim female participants. Male participants were very forthcoming and not difficult to find. Female participants were not as enthusiastic about participating in this study. I cannot say for certain why I had such difficulty in attracting female participants. However, it may relate to sensitivities that often accompany narratives of Muslim women in educational institutions (Mossalli, 2009; Rezai-Rasti, 2005; Zine, 2006) and reluctance to want to share such sensitive information with a stranger.

I decided to limit the number of Muslim student participants to a maximum of twelve because I wanted the interviews to go into as much depth as possible and allow for follow-up interviews where necessary. Hence, this book provides rich detailed data to draw from, which may not have been attainable if I conducted shorter interviews with a larger number of participants. As I only interviewed a total of twelve student participants, this book does not claim to draw generalizing conclusions for all Muslim students in Canadian secondary schools. Rather, my focus is to provide a glimpse of the lived experiences of marginalized members of society, which nonetheless resonate with other narratives and studies of Muslim Canadian experiences with race and racism.

As I had interviewed former and current Muslim students, a concerted effort was made to find participants who attended or graduated from high school in different years since the 9/11 attacks. In other words, participants were not all the same age and I was able to acquire a range of insights from participants who were at high school at various intervals in the years after 9/11, as will be discussed in more detail in Chapters Five and Six. This was done to examine if attitudes towards Muslims remained consistent or if there have been variations in the post-9/11 era. It may not seem immediately obvious why former Muslim students were interviewed in this study, however, it is my contention that the lived experiences of Muslims who attended high schools in the post-9/11 context were fairly recent at the time of the interviews and therefore they could easily recall their encounters during this time. Some have criticized relying on memories when conducting ethnographic research, claiming this to be subject to one's present perspective, malleable, and susceptible to inaccuracy or loss (Davis & Starn, 1989). However, as Frank Pignatelli (1998) has observed, memory has the potential to enrich a critical ethnography and can bind "the rich potential of the narrative to fascinate, seduce, and draw us closer to the practical, activist intentions of a critical ethnography" (p. 407). In other words, relying on memory or the use of telling stories is in line with some of the foundational principles of critical ethnography, which is to give voice to socially marginalized members of society. Hence, these narratives are relevant even if they rely on memory. From this perspective, memory is not simply a "repository from which memories can be retrieved...Memory is active, always in the present, and a construction, transaction, and negotiation, as opposed to a reproduction" (Roberts & Roberts, 1996, pp. 17, 29). Despite the concerns raised by Davis and Starn, I believe that relying on the memories of participants helped provide reflective responses about their experiences. Through narrating their stories, I argue participants engaged in an introspective process, which may have brought to light understandings of issues that were elusive while living through these moments. These former students still possessed valuable insights about perceptions of Muslims in Canadian educational contexts in the aftermath of the 9/11 terrorist attacks. The fact that they were no longer secondary students should not have disqualified or devalued their contributions and insights into these issues.

In addition to interviewing former and current Muslim students, I also interviewed six teacher participants to inquire about their anecdotal experiences and observations regarding anti-Muslim bias and racism in their schools. This segment was interviewed to see if they had noted similar experiences to student participants. Furthermore, educators are often privy to experiences in their classrooms that can provide invaluable insights, especially in regards to racist attitudes towards Muslims. Teachers are located differently from students and their differing perspectives can provide a more holistic understanding of the context being studied. Efforts were made to include an equal number of male and female teacher participants. As such, there were a total of three male and three female teacher participants. Three of the teacher participants were Muslims and three were non-Muslims. Of the three Muslim participants there were two men and one woman, whose pseudonyms were Hamza, Ibrahim, and Alia respectively. Hamza was of Indian origin, but was born and raised in Quebec. Ibrahim was from Pakistan and immigrated to Quebec when he was a university student, and Alia was of Pakistani origin and was born and raised in Quebec. There were two women non-Muslim teacher participants and a third participant who was a male, their pseudonyms were Laura, Jessica, and Jeff respectively. Jeff was of Italian origin, Laura was of Greek origin, and Jessica was French Canadian. All of the non-Muslim teacher participants were born and raised in Quebec. Attempts were made to have a diverse range of teachers who taught core subject areas. Hence I was able to interview one Social Studies teacher, one Science teacher, one Fine Arts teacher, one Mathematics teacher, and two Ethics and Religious Culture teachers. Teachers made reference to their experiences in relation to their subject areas as well as from their perspectives as members of their school communities. More details relating to each category of participant will be discussed in Chapters Five and Six. Below is a table summarizing my participants by category, gender, location, and language.

Type of participants	Gender	Area	Language spoken
Teachers	• 3 male • 3 female	• 6 from Greater Montreal region	• 5 English • 1 French
Muslim students	• 7 male • 5 female	• 4 from Montreal region • 8 from Greater Montreal region	• 6 from French Schools • 6 from English Schools
Total	18	18	18

The overall goals of Chapters Five and Six are to paint a portrait of these Muslim students' lived experiences and to understand what factors may have facilitated Islamophobia in their schools. My analysis of Muslim female and male student experiences in the proceeding chapters was done thematically to see what issues emerged within each category of participant. Chapter Five discusses Muslim female student participants' experiences and Chapter Six examines the experiences of Muslim male students, as well as teacher participants' experiences. Upon completing my discussion of each of the groups' interviews, I will identify similarities and trends in participants' responses in the concluding chapter. I turn now to begin my analysis by examining the experiences of Muslim female students in Canadian secondary schools in the post-9/11 context.

UNVEILING THE LIVED REALITIES OF MUSLIM FEMALE STUDENTS IN CANADIAN SECONDARY SCHOOLS

THE PARTICIPANTS

All of the female student participants were interviewed individually and attended different high schools in Montreal and the Greater Montreal Region. Only one of the five Muslim women interviewed was still in high school at the time of interviewing. All five women were from middle-class socio-economic backgrounds. Two of the participants attended French public secondary schools and the other three attended English public secondary schools. As previously mentioned, the names used for the Muslim female participants in this study were Sarah, Maryam, Noor, Ayesha, and Amina. All women wore the *hijab* in high school and continue to do so. All identified as practicing Muslim women. Sarah was a high school student in grade eleven at the time of the interview. There were only a handful of Muslim girls at Sarah's school, who like her wore the *hijab*. Consequently, Sarah was one of the only visible Muslims in her school. Maryam was a university undergraduate student at the time of the interview. She was not in high school during 9/11. Therefore, Maryam, like Sarah, was a high school student in Quebec secondary schools in the aftermath of 9/11. Maryam was an activist who worked with grassroots organizations within her community to help organize Muslim events.

Noor, Ayesha, and Amina were older than the aforementioned participants and were all attending secondary school at the time of 9/11. Noor grew up in Montreal and was a convert to Islam who took the *shahada* (formal declaration of accepting the Islamic faith) when she was fourteen years old. She was in grade ten when 9/11 happened. Noor's husband was born in Pakistan and immigrated to Canada when he was 19 years old. Noor's husband and children were all Muslims. However, Noor's parents and extended family were all non-Muslims at the time of the interview. Ayesha had recently graduated from university at the time of the interview. She was in grade seven during 9/11. Her family was not always very religious, but after 9/11 there was a shift in her and her siblings' outlook which caused them to incline towards and identify more with Islam. Amina completed her university studies three years prior to the interview and had worked for the federal government. However, once she had children she decided to become a stay-at-home mom. She was fifteen years old and in grade ten during 9/11.

SOCIETAL PERCEPTIONS OF ISLAM

During the interview process I asked the female student participants to tell me how they felt Islam and Muslims were perceived by Quebec society at large in addition to their experiences in secondary schools. I felt it necessary to hear their thoughts on how they believed society perceived them because my assumptions in doing this study were that schools are a microcosm of society and the types of perceptions that people have of Muslims in society may resonate with the way they were perceived in a school setting. As I contend in Chapter Three, a number of state policies and institutions in Quebec have anti-Muslim biases. The interview process sought to understand if these biases were perceived by participants in Quebec society as well as in their secondary schools. All female participants felt that there were some levels of racism towards Muslims within Quebec. Based on their experiences, some felt racism was much less apparent in their daily lives than others. Noor, for example, felt that some of the anti-Muslim racism in society was exaggerated by the media:

> I think some people are ok with Muslims, some people are not, but most of the people I meet are nice. But I know there are people who don't like Muslims, but mostly we see that in the media and I don't see that much. But I did when I was in Montreal in the metro and those things. Yeah, there you felt bad.

Noor described how her interactions with people in Quebec did not seem negative. However, she still acknowledged that anti-Muslim sentiments existed in Quebec society. It may be possible that Noor felt she had experienced less discrimination than the other participants who believed that anti-Muslim racism clearly existed in Quebec society, as Noor was a white French Quebecois convert to Islam. What was interesting about Noor's comments was that despite feeling that racism towards Muslims was not too bad, she had personally been targeted by people in Quebec for her Muslim appearance while taking public transportation. Noor went on to explain these incidents that took place in the subway in more detail:

> *Noor:*   They would sometimes insult you and say *'go back to your country'* and stuff like that. Like, I could have answered, I am in my country, but I didn't used to answer anything when things like that happened. But it wasn't nice I didn't like to take the subway but I used to take it all the time.
>
> *Naved:*   so in some parts when you were living in Montreal you felt that there was some kind of negative impression of Muslims?
>
> *Noor:*   *Yeah*, yeah, for sure. Once someone started throwing *eggs at me* from a window in an apartment building.

Though Noor did not feel that she was discriminated against openly in her secondary school setting, she was clearly being discriminated against when taking public transportation to get to school. Despite Noor's Quebecoise origins, she had been verbally abused with taunts telling her to "go back to your country", which was indicative of how wearing Muslim symbols like the *hijab* placed her outside of her culture of birth and signified her as 'Other' to some members of Quebec society. Abo-Zena, Sahli, & Tobias-Nahi (2009) have noted that Muslim women who wear the *hijab* often "experience marginalization caused by hate speech such as being told to 'go back to your country'" (p. 13). In this instance, the nationalist subject envisioned themselves in a position of spatial power in which they possessed the right to determine what belonged within the norms of society and what needed to be expelled. Islamic symbols such as the *hijab* in the case of Noor, despite her Quebecoise ancestry, brought about a situation in which she was marked as contaminating the nationalist space and was told to leave. This episode was an example of race thinking, as Noor's Islamic faith was racialized and thus disqualified her from occupying the status of an exalted nationalist subject. Noor never experienced this type of verbal abuse prior to wearing the *hijab*. Therefore, Noor's experiences indicated that her perceived belongingness to Quebec society was contingent upon her conformity to the majoritarian culture. Once she veered away from Quebec societal norms, she was told to "go back to your country", casting her in the realm of 'Otherness'. In addition to facing verbal taunts, Noor also experienced instances of being physically abused when she had eggs thrown at her. The graduation from verbal taunts to physical forms of abuse and violence such as throwing objects at a person for their appearance and perceived beliefs is an example of nationalist subjects feeling they are entitled to manage the space of the nation. As such, they are raising their hands against the 'Other' believing that they are nationally empowered to do so (Hage, 2000). One can draw parallels between these experiences described by Noor and events in Quebec history such as the RA debates and the proposed Bill 60. These events also demonstrated how some members of the majority culture in Quebec felt as though they were in a position to define what did and did not belong within the nationalist space. Noor's experience with physical assault was not an experience shared by the other participants.

Ayesha never received taunts and verbal abuse in face-to-face encounters in Quebec. However, she did experience Islamophobia indirectly through online forums:

> People in Quebec tend to be more secretive about these things [negative perceptions of Muslims] so on the surface it looks like everybody is really happy but then, you know that there's a lot of wrong messages in peoples' heads. For example, when I was in university classes we would have these discussion forums online and sometimes they would be anonymous or even not anonymous. People in class would not speak out but then all of a sudden their Islamophobic tendencies came out of these [online forums] because they are hiding behind a screen, so they don't feel that they're putting themselves too much out there.

Ayesha described how people in Quebec had Islamophobic views and beliefs but would not express them in face-to-face encounters. However, when an opportunity presented itself to voice these beliefs in an indirect manner, Islamophobic discourses emerged. This incident was an example of a type of dormant Islamophobia, which was a common theme with a number of participants. Dormant Islamophobia occurs when Muslims feel or believe that people in their everyday interactions have certain animosities, biases, and preconceived notions towards Islam and Muslims. However; they do not readily express these animosities openly. These Islamophobic perceptions emerge when circumstances facilitate anti-Muslim discourse and actions, such as "hiding behind a screen" through an online forum. Being able to express these views in an indirect manner was far less confrontational than in a classroom setting where students would be required to defend their positions. Hence dormant Islamophobia graduated into explicit forms when a facilitating agent, like the discussion forums, was present.

Other participants described how dormant Islamophobia took on explicit forms when events portraying Muslims in a negative light occupied public and media discourses. Hence, events like the RA debates, discussions over the Charter of Values, and terrorist attacks committed by Muslim extremists facilitated overt or explicit expressions of Islamophobia in the lived experiences of participants. These incidents occurred at the hands of members of society, who, prior to these events, did not display such tendencies towards the participants. Some participants discussed how the Quebec Charter of Values enabled dormant Islamophobia to emerge in explicit forms. In my interview with Ayesha, she briefly commented about the Charter of Values, and suggested that it became an issue of public debate in Quebec because of perceptions that secularism was at odds with people practicing their faith. Ayesha alluded to how Islam was perceived as a threat to Quebec's secularism, perpetuating the notion that Islam is threatening to the core values of Quebec society. Maryam, however; viewed discourses surrounding the charter in a more positive light within the Montreal region:

> I think in Montreal because of the whole *Charte* thing (reference to charter of values)...I think people still respect us, I think that respect is growing. I think especially after the whole *Charte* thing...it's created a platform for people to learn more about Islam and *who these 'Muslims'* are, especially after 9/11.

Maryam, the university undergraduate student, felt that discussions about the charter have created a space where Muslims can voice their views about issues in Quebec, and consequently Quebec society at large can learn more about Muslims. In other words, Muslims have been able to capitalize on this issue and through the debates and discussions about the charter have been able to exercise agency. Consequently, Muslims were being respected more, as people were sympathizing with the plight of Muslim women who would have been negatively impacted by the charter. Maryam believed that the 9/11 terror attacks had cast the Muslim community in Quebec in a negative light and the discussions and the debates over the Charter of Values helped Muslims in Quebec improve their public image, possibly because they were being perceived as victims of injustice, as opposed to the usual depiction of Muslims being violent aggressors. Maryam's comments implied that, notwithstanding the negative sentiments whipped up by media and political elites, people were critical of discriminatory actions and proposed legislations. In general, the female Muslim student participants felt that biases towards Muslims existed in Quebec. Some believed that these biases were more implicit. Others experienced them in explicit forms through taunts and verbal and physical abuse. Similar types of incidents occurred with Muslim women participants in educational settings.

EXPERIENCES IN SECONDARY SCHOOLS

Some female participants experienced overt forms of racism and bias, while others did not feel they were openly discriminated against in secondary school. All of them generally described their experiences in secondary school in a positive manner, while still facing occasional challenges related to how they were perceived because of their faith. As the *hijab* is often a signifier of the 'imperilled Muslim women' archetype in media and public discourses in Quebec society, having a generally positive experience throughout high school was a refreshing surprise to some of the participants:

> Well in general, I would say I had a pretty good high school experience. I was the only girl in my school to wear the *hijab* and to be a *real* visible minority. I mean there were minority cultural groups at my high school but no one really stood out other than myself and I think I was the first one to ever even wear one [*hijab*]. I looked at graduation photographs from previous years and I never saw anyone wearing a *hijab*, so I would say I was the *real* first *visible* minority in my high school. But overall I had a pretty good experience, I didn't feel like I was singled out.

Amina felt it important to emphasize that despite her visible difference, not only at her grade level but within her school's history, that she had a generally positive experience in secondary school. Amina's emphasis on the *hijab* within her school setting was indicative that she felt that she stood out within her student body, yet this was not a major setback for her attending secondary school. Other participants had varying degrees of positive experiences, which is not to say that within the overall positive atmosphere there were not instances of discomfort.

Ayesha attended a high school that she described as being very multicultural with a number of Muslim students. However, she felt that without a visible signifier indicating her religious/cultural identity she blended into the majoritarian culture in her secondary school, which is something she wanted to change:

> I only had one friend that actually wore the *hijab* in my grade, and I wore the *hijab* when I was in grade nine in the middle of the year because I was just sick of not being identified as Arab [i.e. students thought she was of European descent].

Ayesha was able to pass as a white Canadian student despite having an Arabic name. She felt at odds with the notion of passing, discussed in Chapter One, and wanted to assert her Arab identity. For Ayesha, the *hijab* was a visible signifier that gave access to her Arab identity within the secondary school system. This raises an interesting point—based on Ayesha's experiences, the *hijab* is what signified Arabness in her school culture. In other words, a student in her school was not recognized as an Arab unless they were displaying a conspicuous religious/cultural symbol like the *hijab*. Ayesha's donning of the *hijab* also suggested that in some ways she was entangling her religious and ethnic identities, as not all Arabs are Muslim and the *hijab* is an Islamic garment. Some scholars have discussed how Arabs and Muslims are rarely differentiated in media representations of Islam (Salaita, 2006; Shaheen, 2008), however these are reductionist and over-simplified representations. It would seem that Ayesha in some ways was complicit with these reductive stereotypes as she affiliated this religious signifier with her Arab identity. This experience also relates to the racialization of the Islamic faith as Ayesha equated religious symbols with ethnic affiliations. Hence, Ayesha's comments revealed some of the complexities and interrelations between ethnic and religious affiliations. It would appear that through a process of racialization, Ayesha may have been exercising some form of agency as she wanted to be acknowledged as Arab through this religious signifier. Upon wearing the *hijab,* Ayesha experienced unintended consequences where she felt she had to be a spokesperson for Islam:

> You know, when you're a teenager you feel the world is always staring at you. And you know there were random things that happened here and there but overall it was smooth, except for the fact that I felt that I had to be a spokesperson for the *entire* Muslim *ummah* of the world. Like every time there would be a debate that would happen in class everyone would just sort of look to me and I was 14, I was supposed to justify everything!

Wearing the *hijab* brought about some instances of stares and other uncomfortable situations within Ayesha's school setting but nothing that was unbearable for her. The only issue which Ayesha seemed to be annoyed with was that she had to be the Muslim representative voice whenever there were discussions about Islam or Muslims in her classes. Though it may seem that Ayesha was viewing all Muslims to be homogeneous as she makes reference to the "Muslim *ummah*" (i.e. the Muslim community), however this term can be used to describe the Muslim community in a general sense taking into consideration the differences of cultures and ethnicities of Muslims around the world. Rather, I believe Ayesha's comments suggested how others assume homogeneity amongst Muslims worldwide. Such perceptions enabled her to be a representative voice, which came about through a visual signifier, associating *her* with *them.* This was not the case for Ayesha prior to wearing the *hijab*. These comments revealed a subtle irony relating to the intersection of Ayesha's multiple identities. Ayesha used veiling to identify herself as Arab, essentially exercising agency through racializing her faith, while expressing distaste for being

'Othered' when she sarcastically reflected on having to be the spokesperson for the international Muslim community when she started wearing the *hijab*. The anxieties described by Ayesha were possibly exacerbated as the invasions of Afghanistan and Iraq took place while she was still in high school. The situation described by Ayesha is what some have termed "spotlighting", which refers to when "students of minority religious, ethnic, or cultural groups…[are] spotlighted to speak for or otherwise justify what "their group" thinks or what members of their group do" (Abo-Zena, Sahli, & Tobias-Nahi, 2009, p. 8). In subtle ways spotlighting reproduces the myth that Islam and Muslims are monolithic and that there is not a diverse range of views within the Islamic faith regarding world affairs and conflicts. This is hardly surprising given that Ayesha could not even be identified as a Muslim until she visibly wore an Islamic symbol which has often been associated with notions of misogyny and the oppression of Muslim women. In essence, spotlighting asks Muslim students to explain why other Muslims engage in acts of terror assuming that they understand the motivations of terrorists or that they could speak on their behalf. This may result in feelings of guilt by association as spotlighting with regards to the 9/11 attacks assumes that the reasoning for them is somehow explained through the common faith shared by the students and the perpetrators. Ayesha felt a great sense of discomfort when class discussions and debates relating to Islam and Muslims would focus attention on her, because as an adolescent she felt the need to "justify everything" (i.e. the actions of Muslim extremists) even though she did not agree with these actions.

In one instance described by Ayesha she mentioned how one of her teachers through a class discussion reproduced notions of 'culture talk':

> I remember people were talking about Iraq and what not. It was the Iraq—the US had just invaded Iraq and the teacher was trying to be real open minded and she was a very nice person but she still said *'I think we need to understand the Arab mind'* and then the whole class looked at me. And I was like supposed to explain the Arab mind. So there was always that pressure to represent everybody at the same time and I still didn't know who I was.

Ayesha's teacher felt that there was a certain essence or characteristics that were essential to being Arab. Logically then, if there was an "Arab mind" Ayesha was qualified to speak about it because she was one of *them*. Clearly this was troubling for Ayesha because she was still trying to understand who she was. She did not identify with the notions of Arabness as understood by her teacher and classmates, yet she was signified as one of *them*. In this instance, Ayesha's teacher reinforced the perception that Muslims are a monolithic group, all of whom are suitable representatives and authorities of their religion. The unintended actions of Ayesha's teacher—reinforcing notions of Muslims being a monolithic group in which all Muslims, or in the case of Ayesha, all Arabs, are painted with a broad brush possessing innate qualities or a common mindset—can be traumatizing to Muslim students in a secondary setting and can result in teasing, bullying, and possibly even discord within the family unit. Statements and actions by teachers in which there are subtle forms of racism or prejudice are not always based on an intent to paint a negative image of the 'Other' in a classroom setting. Often these incidents occur out of a genuine misunderstanding, as their knowledge of conflicts or other cultures may be misinformed. This can be damaging, as Kincheloe (2005) observes: "[w]ithout an understanding of these specific dynamics, teachers are too often unable…to protect students from the radioactive fallout of hidden structures of racism, class bias, patriarchy, homophobia, colonialism and religious prejudice" (p. 35). Consequently, teachers who are misinformed may be disseminating stereotypes to their students. In relation to discussing conflicts such as the War on Terror, as Ayesha's teacher did, this will inevitably taint students' perceptions of their Muslim classmates even if they are their friends.

When Maryam started wearing the *hijab,* she experienced a similar type of phenomenon, where she suddenly became the gatekeeper of knowledge of Muslims and Islam in her secondary school:

> I didn't really have that many weird experiences in high school but after I started wearing *hijab* in grade eight, mostly people were still respectful but there were a lot of questions that were asked. So I think it was a very *big* shock for me… they would ask me a lot about all those stereotypical things in our religion. So they always needed clarifications. That happens even now.

Maryam experienced a similar type of situation as Ayesha when she started wearing the *hijab,* as her relationship with her peers and teachers changed. Instead of just being a regular student, she had to become a spokesperson for the Islamic faith and for Muslims. Some studies suggest that often questions faced by Muslim women in educational settings are "in the context of epithets propagated by the media" (Abo-Zena, Sahli, & Tobias-Nahi, 2009, p. 15). In other words, the assumption of 'Otherness' underlies these questions. This was the case with Maryam as she described the types of questions that she was asked as originating from stereotypes associated with Islam. These stereotypes, according to Maryam, included questions relating to *sharia,* beheadings, and forced marriages, all of which are tropes in the dominant Western discourse about Islam, as seen in our discussion of Hérouxville in Chapter Three. Hence this was an example of dormant Islamophobia manifesting and becoming explicit. A number of Maryam's peers had biased and contrived notions of Muslims and Islam. Once Maryam began wearing the *hijab* she fit the description of the 'imperilled Muslim woman' in Quebec society, which clearly was not the case before when she was a regular *hijab*less student unqualified to answer questions. Wearing the *hijab* provided her with the credentials to discuss 'Islam', or rather the students' stereotypical views of Islam because she now fit the stereotypical mould. In addition to having to answer questions relating to stereotypes associated with Islam, Maryam also faced taunts and teasing about wearing the *hijab*:

Some of the students, I think back then they would call me—just to make fun of me…that was actually *pretty rough*, they would call me Saddam. So stupid things like that, like Kaddafi, so stupid things like that, but as a joke, I never took it seriously.

Though Maryam did not take the taunts of other students very seriously, it was still indicative of how the *hijab* became a means to change how she was perceived by her peers. Upon donning the *hijab* she had nicknames thrown at her of two violent tyrannical leaders of Muslim countries. Similarly, a study by Michelle Byng (2010) found that media coverage of Muslim women's clothing, particularly the veil, constructed Muslim women as different and having sympathies towards violence against the West. Maryam's wearing of the *hijab* in the eyes of some students indicated affiliations to radicalism and violence. Hence, media discourses linking the *hijab* with violence and terror resonated with perceptions held by students at Maryam's secondary school. In Maryam's experiences, students were not the only ones who held stereotypes of Muslim women who wore the *hijab,* since teachers also had prejudices.

Maryam recounts how she had a history teacher who would make a number of false presumptions about Maryam based on her physical appearance:

I remember in grade 11 or grade 10 at the beginning of the school year, I remember I had a professor, he was our history teacher. And I remember one of my first experiences with him, I think he didn't have too many *hijabis* in his class before and he had this preconceived notion that we were out to get him or something. So once I was like dozing off in his class or something, he came up to me and he kind of accused me of not paying attention and thought that I had headphones under my *hijab.* And he made this whole fiasco in front of the class and I was like what are you talking about. And it was really interesting to see and I kind of told him off too. I was like, that's kind of *rude*, first of all you accuse me like that and I don't know where you're getting these notions from.

Maryam's early encounters with this teacher were not very positive, as she felt he was biased towards her because she wore the *hijab*. She believed the teacher felt that women wearing the *hijab* "were out to get him". His prejudices surfaced when Maryam was daydreaming in class. Instead of telling her to pay attention, he accused her of hiding headphones in her *hijab*. Maryam felt this accusation was unwarranted and disrespectful as she was being accused of something without any evidence to support the accusations. The actions of Maryam's teacher implied a distaste of her wearing the *hijab*. In most instances within a secondary school setting, wearing headphones and listening to music, especially during a teacher's lesson, violates rules and protocols of the school. In doing so, he implied that Maryam was using her *hijab* to 'break the rules'. The nationalist subject, in this instance, the high school teacher, perceived the *hijab* as an aberration that was used to break the rules and therefore had no place in his classroom. He envisioned himself in a position to be able to determine what was and was not acceptable within a state institution. Similar to opinions expressed by Claude Pineault in the Charter of Values consultations, discussed in Chapter Three, the teacher viewed the *hijab* as a type of disguise that was being used to dupe the nationalist subject.

Shaza Khan (2009) has noted that in circumstances where teachers have concerns with students who wear visible religious signifiers like the *hijab*, it is best to address these concerns privately with the student. Students may be offended and feel marginalized in a classroom environment in which the teacher makes a spectacle of the *hijab* in front of the whole class. When discussed privately, many of these tensions can be alleviated. In the case of Maryam, this episode marked a confrontational relationship with her teacher which could have very easily been avoided by speaking privately with the student. Maryam's relationship with this teacher evolved over the course of the year and she felt that as the teacher got to know her better through personal contact, his perceptions changed. So much so that she felt a number of his misconceptions of Islam were clarified through their interactions. Ayesha echoes a similar sentiment as she believed in order for perceptions surrounding Muslims in secondary schools to change, Muslims themselves need to take some initiative:

> I think that Muslims need to slightly get out of their comfort zone and reach out to people because as a Muslim community I think we just wait for people to understand us without trying to make ourselves understood.

Ayesha felt that Muslims needed to proactively engage in dialogue with the school community and society at large in order to be understood. This is similar to findings in studies which suggest that knowing and having interactions with Muslims can bring about a positive shift in perceptions of Muslims and Islam (Esposito & Mogahed, 2007). Ayesha's comments implied passiveness amongst Muslims in secondary school and Quebec society, in which Muslims were the object of others' interpretations. This could be problematic, given that media and political discourses have contributed to casting Muslims in a negative light, as seen in previous chapters. However, Ayesha's comment suggested that she believed Muslims were in a position to counter the dominant discourse about Muslims. In order for perceptions to change, she believed Muslims needed to exercise some degree of agency.

A number of the Muslim female participants discussed how 9/11 impacted their experiences in Quebec secondary schools. As mentioned earlier, three of the five participants attended secondary school during the 9/11 attacks. Despite the fact that this tragic event took place on US soil, its reverberations were felt by some of the participants in a direct manner in Quebec secondary schools. Some of the effects of the 9/11 attacks included losing friends, being bullied, and concerns for safety. Amina discussed how these events affected her relationship with a close friend in secondary school:

There was one incident where after 9/11 that I recall very strongly. There was this guy that I was pretty good friends with. We used to take the bus together and pretty much right after, the day after [the 9/11 attacks], he just completely stopped talking to me. He actually posted something *really* derogatory [about Islam] in his locker and a teacher had reprimanded him for that and had him remove it. And after that he never spoke to me, after 9/11, and before that we used to take the bus to and from the school together and we were pretty good friends.

9/11 changed the way Amina was perceived amongst her friends. Some have noted that events like 9/11 can cause "students who feel pain or threat, particularly over something out of their direct control… to experience frustration and resentment towards the social groups they blame for their feelings" (Liese, 2004, p. 65). As Amina described it, her friendship with a good friend effectively ended because of 9/11, as if the student was trying to punish Amina for these attacks. The assumptions embedded in this student's response were that these actions committed by a fringe group of Muslims were representative of the religion of Islam as a whole. As previously discussed, a number of stereotypes relating to the experiences of Muslim women in secondary schools revolved around the idea that all Muslims held homogeneous understandings and beliefs. According to this logic, the ideology of the Muslim terrorists who committed these acts would be shared by all Muslims. Amina being rejected by her friend in the aftermath of the terror attacks for no apparent explanation was indicative that he believed sharing a common religion with the perpetrators of the 9/11 attacks in some way signaled her acceptance of these acts. It could be said that Amina's friend categorized her as a 'bad Muslim' whose values were incompatible with his. Amina experienced a type of guilt by association which inevitably resulted from this friend's monolithic understanding of Muslims and Islam. Amina also described how understanding Muslims and Islam as homogeneous affected her brother who attended the same school as her during the 9/11 attacks:

It was very closely after 9/11, and me and my brother we took the bus together to and from school. And after school some of the older kids had started picking on him and calling him Bin Laden's son and asking him, *where's your father?* Pretty much they just kind of used the same joke. I guess they were trying to bug him asking him where his father was and saying he's Bin Laden's son.

In this instance Amina's brother was being bullied because of his supposed affiliation with Osama Bin Laden. There was no reason to assume that Bin Laden was in any way related to Amina's brother. However, once again, there was an assumption operating within these taunts. All Muslims, whether they were terrorists or innocent high school kids were held to share the same beliefs, views, and in the case of Amina's brother, were biologically connected. His Islamic faith was categorized as a race, as the taunts implied that he and Bin Laden were somehow related by virtue of both being Muslim. This incident was also indicative of the existence of dormant Islamophobia. Amina's brother, prior to this incident, was never picked on by these boys on the bus. Their targeting of him only came about because of their racist associations of terrorism with Islam. These students knew Amina's brother, they knew about his religious affiliations, yet their racist tendencies only manifested when an opportunity (i.e. terror attacks) presented itself.

In the case of Amina, it was not clear if her head veil was what elicited views of guilt by association. However, Ayesha clearly did feel that the *hijab* was a symbol which was indicative of affiliation with terrorism and the 9/11 attacks:

> One of my friends, she was the only *hijabi* in the grade, the only Arab besides me, so people just started surrounding her. And they weren't trying to bully her, but they were just very curious, right, because they saw *her* people—she's Lebanese—but they saw *hijabis* on TV and they said, you know, did your people do the 9/11? And she's like, those weren't Arabs, those were Afghans. She was in grade seven so she just, she automatically, like swallowed what the news said as well but she like carefully pinpointed it to Afghans. She didn't mention anything about it being Muslims or non-Muslims.

Ayesha at this time was not wearing the *hijab* but her friend in grade seven was. Consequently, students immediately came to Ayesha's friend to understand more about 9/11. As Ayesha's friend wore the *hijab* and the news media was inundated with images of *hijab* clad Muslim women after the attacks—some of whom were being depicted as celebrating the attacks (Kincheloe, 2004)—students came to her wanting to understand the motivations of these acts. Logically, some of the students thought, if they (i.e. Muslims on the news after attacks) wear the *hijab*, and Ayesha's friend wears the *hijab*, they must be the same people. Hence, the students questioned if it was "your people" behind these attacks. In other words, these students assumed Islam was a race. Ayesha's friend perceived the events differently. She believed it was Afghans and not Arabs who were behind the attacks. So she did not make any mention of Muslims or the Islamic faith. She understood, based on media reports, that Afghanis were in some way involved in these events and she identified the supposed terrorists according to ethnicity and not religion. This episode demonstrated how there was a clear distinction in how a Muslim student perceived these attacks and the supposed perpetrators and how non-Muslim students reacted to the same events. The Muslim student perceived the perpetrators according to ethnicity because she was a Muslim and her belief system was apparently incompatible with the acts of terrorism on September 11. Hence she clarified that it was not 'her people', which in her view refers to ethnic affiliation. The perception from the non-Muslim students was quite different. They saw certain Islamic symbols, like the *hijab*, and understood these symbols as representative of ideologies and actions related to the terrorists and the 'Islamic race'.

Noor described how her parents and those of some of her Muslim friends who wore the *hijab* had serious concerns for their daughters' safety at school in the aftermath of these attacks:

Noor: I have a friend who stopped going to school for some time because her parents were scared for her safety when she takes the bus going to school. So she stopped. A few of them stopped I think. But because they didn't want to take off their *hijab*, so they just stayed home. My parents told me to take off my *hijab* right after 9/11 but as soon as I got out of the house I would wear it without them knowing. So I did wear it to school but I don't remember anything that happened.

Naved: So there were a lot of concerns for safety?

Noor: *Yeah*, the parents, mostly the parents were scared for their kids. You did hear about things that happened in the subway. Some people had their *hijab* taken off by other people, stuff like that.

According to Noor, parents of Muslim girls who wore the head veil had serious concerns for their daughters' safety after 9/11. The concerns, as expressed by Noor, were specifically over their daughters wearing the *hijab*. It would seem that these parents understood that the *hijab* was an Islamic symbol in the eyes of the public that signified sympathies or affiliations with terrorism. This occurrence, like Amina's, resonates with Mamdani's (2004) theories relating to 'good Muslims' and 'bad Muslims'. Bad Muslims are those who are perceived to be anti-modern and "refuse the westernization of their bodies and minds" (Thobani, 2007, p. 238). Bad Muslims are those on whom the War on Terror was being waged. By continuing to wear the *hijab* immediately after the 9/11 attacks, parents were concerned that their daughters would be perceived as the 'bad Muslims'. While Noor said she did not experience any problems; parents' safety concerns were warranted, as she pointed out some women were having their *hijab*'s pulled off in the subway.

The act of pulling off the *hijab* in the context of a supposedly multicultural nation and what it entails has been discussed at length by Hage (2000). According to him, the nationalist subject expresses belonging to the nation in two different ways; 'passive belonging' and 'governmental belonging'. Passive belonging is the expectation of benefiting from the nation by virtue of being a part of the nation, whereas governmental belonging involves being in a position to manage the nation so that it remains uncorrupted. Consequently, Hage describes the act of tearing off a woman's *hijab* as nationalist violence rather than racist violence because it is an act of preserving the nationalist space. As we have previously discussed when commenting on participants' experiences wearing the *hijab* while attending secondary schools, the *hijab* after the 9/11 attacks has been perceived as a symbol of affiliation with violence and terror. When people believe their nation is being contaminated by people who share a similar ideology as the perpetrators of 9/11 (i.e. women wearing the *hijab*), nationalist subjects will sometimes take it upon themselves to enact their privilege of governmental belonging and purify the nationalist space by pulling off the *hijab*.

EFFECTS OF MEDIA ON MUSLIM FEMALE PARTICIPANTS

Muslim female student participants believed that the media played an important role in constructing knowledge of Muslims in Quebec society, as well as in Quebec schools. When questioned about how the media impacted perceptions in Quebec society, Sarah discussed how it could "brainwash" people:

Naved: Do you think popular culture, so things like movies, TV, and news media, do you think that that affects how people perceive different groups in society?

Sarah: Yeah, because everyone is like kind of brainwashed by it all because it's everywhere, you can't get away from it.

Naved: Have you ever seen any forms of media, either TV programs, movies, or news stories or anything like that that had Muslims in them?

Sarah: Yeah, but usually it's in a negative way.

Naved: And how were they depicted negatively?

Sarah: Well they're usually bad guys, or the person they're [protagonist] after is them [Muslims].

Naved: What are the types of images you see in that type of medium, like if they are the bad guys how are they the bad guys, are they just mean people?

Sarah: No, they're like bombers and explosions and all that.

Naved: So generally they're represented as terrorists and stuff like that.

Sarah: yeah.

Sarah mentioned how the media could have a "brainwashing" effect because of its pervasiveness in society. With regards to how the media portrays Muslims, Sarah described how the media perpetuated the 'dangerous Muslim man' archetype. She believed that the way Muslims were represented in the media influenced how Muslims were perceived in educational settings. Sarah stated these types of representations can lead to distrust and that students may go as far as thinking that Muslim students may commit acts of violence like blowing up the school. Concerning stereotypes of Muslims perpetuated by the media, Tahir Abbas (2011) argues that "[t]he managed reality that is depicted by the media is transferred on society. When interacting with Muslims, Westerners will automatically perceive them as the stereotypes formulated by the media regardless of the way Muslim people actually are" (p. 71). In other words, the media is instrumental in forming perceptions of Muslims, even if this contradicts the actual beliefs and actions of the vast majority of Muslims. Like Sarah, Amina believed the impact of popular cultural mediums, such as TV and movies cannot be understated:

That's something that kids in secondary school are most exposed to; TV, movies, you know, these are the type of things that they watch. Especially like movies, that's where, you know, a lot of kids spend a lot of their extra free time, watching movies and their ideas do come from this type of medium. It's not just something they're reading about, it's something they're seeing. It's a visual clip. Kind of a snapshot of what Muslims are.

Amina believed that the visual nature of film and television had a major impact on how Muslims were understood. Media representations of Muslims can have a particularly strong impact in a high school setting because according to Amina's experiences, much of students' spare time was spent watching television and movies. Since Muslims are a minority in Quebec, students may not be overly exposed to Muslims and Islamic beliefs. As such, television and films could possibly be important sites of knowledge production for students with regards to how they understand Muslims, because according to Amina they provide a "snapshot of what Muslims are". Stuart Hall (2011) has made similar claims through his examination of issues relating to race representation in the media. He believes that "media are especially important sites for the production, reproduction and transformation of ideologies" (p. 82). Ideologies, according to Hall (2004) refer to "images, concepts and premises which provide the frameworks through which we represent, interpret, understand, and 'make sense' of some aspect of social existence" (p. 271). In other words, media can influence how we construct our knowledge of various aspects of our lives. This is not to say that there is only one conception of race in the media which reproduces the dominant ruling class interpretation of the 'Other'. Rather, there are varying degrees of racist constructions which are reproduced through different mediums such as films, television shows, or news media. Racist portrayals in the media can be *overt* and at times more subtle through *inferential* racism. *Overt* racism in the media is when openly racist views are given legitimacy by people who are in the business of advocating a racist agenda. *Inferential* racism is a type of unconscious racism that stems from certain unquestioned assumptions imbedded within media (Hall, 2011). Both these types of racism are operational in representations of Muslims in the media. However, one must exercise caution in over-emphasizing the influence of media in knowledge production of Muslims, as people are not just passive receivers of whatever messages are disseminated through popular cultural media. Jiwani (2010), in her examination of representations of Muslim women in Canadian media, warns against viewing these representations in an over-deterministic fashion, assuming audiences lack agency. Nonetheless, she believes that negative representations of Muslims in the media "legitimize certain actions and inactions, authorize particular ways of seeing the world, and lend credibility to specific interlocutors" (Jiwani, 2010, p. 64).

Media representations of Muslims according to all of the participants tended to be one dimensional characterizations that revolved around the archetypes of the 'imperilled Muslim woman' and 'dangerous Muslim man', as Maryam stated:

They're pretty much type cast [i.e. Muslims in the media]. I don't really see them in American media besides things like terrorist plots or movies about terrorism. So they're represented very one dimensionally. And I never see Muslim families in everyday life going to school or things like that.

Maryam lamented how Muslims were rarely ever portrayed in the media as regular people doing normal activities in everyday life and being contributing members of society. This can be problematic as Hall (2004) argues that our understanding of race and the meanings that race carries are particularly constructed through the media. Hence, perpetuating these negative stereotypes could possibly impact how people in society and schools think of Muslims. Maryam did not articulate in great detail the stereotypes of Muslims in the media besides mentioning the prototypical Muslim male terrorist. However, others have documented that typecasts of Muslims in the media disseminate a number of different tropes relating to race, gender, and class (Alsultany, 2012; Kincheloe, Steinberg, & Stonebanks, 2010; Shaheen, 2001, 2008).

None of the Muslim female student participants pinpointed a specific media outlet that had influenced perceptions of Muslims and Islam in Canadian and Quebec society or secondary schools; rather they mentioned various forms of popular cultural media in a general sense. However, some participants did mention specific instances or events that were highly publicized by the media, which helped fuel anti-Muslim racism in Quebec society:

Like for example, reasonable accommodation. You know, halaal meat comes up anything that they [media] can pick on they'll just start picking on it and as I said, for me that's where I see it [anti-Muslim bias] the most; in the media. When I'm outside going places I don't feel anything wrong so it feels like I'm in a different world. Because when I'm reading the comments under the news [articles] on the internet it's all crazy stuff, they're all against Muslims but when I meet people they're all nice.

Noor mentioned how the RA debates, and issues raised in these, like meat slaughtered in accordance with Islam, were used by the media to "pick on" Muslims. Noor also alluded to how dormant Islamophobia took on a more explicit character through comment postings on online news articles. Noor expressed how news articles, when they negatively portrayed Muslims through events like the reasonable accommodation debates, fanned the flames of Islamophobia. Noor felt shock over this because when she met people face-to-face she did not have such negative experiences. Noor described a paradoxical situation where despite people being nice to her in face-to-face interactions, she still experienced sentiments of discrimination and hatred towards her faith. Noor also mentioned in her interview how a local Imam of a mosque was misquoted by a francophone Quebec newspaper, claiming that he advocated the implementation of the *sharia*. According to Noor, the story was concocted and purposely misquoted the Imam to frame him as a 'dangerous Muslim man' who wanted to apply the *sharia*, which has been equated with oppression, lapidating, and the severing of limbs in Quebec. Having completed my discussion of female Muslim students' experiences, I turn now to consider those of Muslim male students and teachers. These categories of participants described a number of issues relating to anti-Muslim racism which share some commonalities with the experiences discussed in this chapter.

MENACING AND MANIACAL MUSLIMS

Experiences of Muslim Male Students and Teachers

MUSLIM MEN'S EXPERIENCES IN SECONDARY SCHOOLS IN QUEBEC

The participants. There were seven Muslim male student participants, only one of which was a high school student at the time of the interview. All of them attended high school in the Greater Montreal region and like the female interviewees, all came from middle-class socio-economic backgrounds. Three of the males attended English public schools, three attended public French schools, while one attended a private French school. All identified themselves as practicing Muslim men while they were in high school. As previously mentioned, the names used for the Muslim male student participants were Yusuf, Malik, Ismail, Ahmad, Adam, Zaid, and Ali. Yusuf, Malik, and Ismail were interviewed individually, while the other four participants were interviewed together in a group discussion. Ahmad, Adam, Zaid, and Ali were given the choice to do the interviews individually but they felt more comfortable to do so through a group discussion format. In the group discussion, some participants were less vocal than others, however all members participated in the interview and responded to issues that they felt comfortable answering. During the time of the interview, Yusuf was in his second year of Collège d'enseignement général et professionnel (CEGEP), which is a post-secondary educational level in Quebec, where students are required to obtain credits before they are eligible for universities. Yusuf was the sole participant who had attended a private school throughout his secondary education, which had only a few Muslim students. Malik was a third year CEGEP student at the time of his interview. He was one of the only Muslims in his entire secondary school. Malik felt that he was very visibly Muslim while he attended secondary school as he had a Muslim sounding name and a "big beard" which he felt visibly identified him as Muslim. Ismail was a first year CEGEP student at the time of his interview. Like Malik, he attended a school where there were very few Muslims. So he felt he was clearly identifiable as a Muslim in his school. Ahmad was completing his final year of high school during the group discussion and he attended a school that had many different minority groups including a number of Arabs and Muslims. Adam and Ali were both completing their final year of CEGEP and Zaid was an undergraduate student during the time of the group discussion. All three of them attended high schools that had a number of Muslim students. Upon completing the discussion of Muslim male experiences in secondary schools, this chapter will also discuss comments from teacher participants to learn how they have experienced and perceived Islamophobia in the schools that they have worked at.

Societal perceptions of Islam. As was the case with the Muslim female student participants, I also questioned the Muslim male student participants about how they felt Muslims and Islam were perceived by society before delving into their high school experiences. Some of the participants in the group discussion felt that there were very negative and biased views towards Muslims in Quebec society:

Ahmad: They think Muslims are like a *monster*, or some *bacteria*. The way they see Muslims in Quebec in general, they don't like outside cultures. They're too into North American culture. They're closed. They're not interested in other cultures to find out what is Islam, what is Christianity, what is Judaism, particularly with Islam because the media negatively promotes Islam. For example, if there's an American or a Quebecois who beats their kid 42 times there's some kind of mental sickness associated with that person, but when it's an Arab who kills someone he's a terrorist. When it's a Muslim he's a terrorist when it's a white person, a Christian, it's a mental disorder. But if it has something to do with a Muslim or a Muslim country in general, it's automatically labeled terrorism. It's [Islam] something really bad, untreatable, needs to be expelled. People are very misinformed here in Quebec.

Adam: I think we tend to generalize, just like how they generalize *us*, obviously there's people who understand us. Some people go out of their way. In schools the pure hard core Quebecois usually are more understanding of our different ways, from my experience. You can't just generalize on them like how they generalize on us.

Ahmad: that's right there are nice people out there, most my friends are Quebecois because they understand Islam, but in general, I'm generalizing here, but the majority I find they have a negative view of Islam.

The comments by Ahmad indicated that he felt strongly that there were biases against Muslims in Quebec society. He felt that Islam was perceived as a type of threat to the majoritarian culture which needed to be expelled. He used language that described Islam as a "bacteria", implying the faith was perceived as a contaminant that could infect society. Consequently, being Muslim or adhering to Islam was likened to a sickness which was "untreatable" and therefore "needs to be expelled". Ahmad's response suggested that he felt Quebec society engaged in culture talk by assuming a certain biological essence which predisposed Muslims to violent behaviour. Therefore, if a Muslim committed an act of violence, there was no analysis seeking to understand why these acts were committed. Rather, they were understood to be manifestations of inherent tendencies towards violence which would be labeled as terrorism. According to Ahmad, similar types of violent actions were constructed as aberrations and exceptions when committed by members of the dominant culture. Hence, such behaviour would be explained away through mental illness because actions of violence and abuse were not viewed as essential to the make-up of the white majority. Ahmad's comments also related to the notion of exaltation, as he alluded to a certain set of imagined qualities present in the nationalist subject. Because Muslims were perceived as 'Other' and outside the nationalist imaginary, when Muslims engaged in violence it could not be understood to arise from mental illness. Such acts were believed to be a natural consequence of *their* culture, excluding them as nationalist subjects. A similar situation to what Ahmad described occurred in Quebec in the murder trial of Guy Turcotte. Turcotte was a cardiologist from Quebec who murdered his two children aged three and five years old, in February 2009. Turcotte, a member of the white Quebecois majority obtained the sympathies of a jury who were unable to find him guilty of mercilessly killing his own children. His violent behaviour could only be understood as a result of a mental lapse or deficiency (CBC News, 2014).

Of all the members in the group discussion, Ahmad felt most strongly that Islam was negatively constructed and understood in Quebec. Some other members seemed to agree with Ahmad's comments through non-verbal cues such as nodding their heads in approval of his statements. However, Adam felt that he was making generalizations. This, according to Adam was unfair because it engaged in a similar type of essentializing discourse which was often targeted at Muslims. However, despite Adam's views that Ahmad was generalizing, he did not voice disagreement over what was being said. There was a type of implicit acknowledgement that there was truth in what Ahmad was saying as Adam himself mentioned how "they generalize on us". In other words, Adam did acknowledge that there were generalizing stereotypes of Muslims. He felt that Ahmad's statements should have been clarified, not implicating all Quebecois with such views. Some participants discussed concrete examples of discrimination that they faced in Quebec due to their 'Islamic' appearance.

For the Muslim female participants, it was clear that visible signifiers such as the *hijab* identified them as 'Other' within Quebec. For some of the male participants, having brown skin and a beard brought about a similar type of 'Othering', as described by Malik:

> I was in McDonalds once and this old lady came up to me, and back then I had the *big beard*, and she came up to me and she said you should shave that beard, it reminds us of what happened at 9/11. And I'm thinking to myself, how do *you* know they have big beards? Most of the time when you see the pictures [of 9/11 terrorists] most of them don't have big beards, they have small beards, but why is *big beards* attached to terrorism, you know?

This experience had some similarities with those of Noor who mentioned how Muslim women were having their *hijab's* pulled off shortly after 9/11. Malik described how a large beard worn by a brown skinned man had a similar effect of a nationalist subject wanting to exercise a perceived sense of spatial power by defining what did and did not belong in Quebec society. Malik's experience was arguably the closest equivalent to having a *hijab* pulled off that a Muslim male could experience. However, the question arises, what makes the beard so threatening? When non-Muslim men have large beards does it garner such a response? Malik found this instance troubling and confusing, as he pointed out that the 9/11 terrorists were for the most part either clean shaven or had small beards. Malik was the only male participant who mentioned having a beard throughout secondary school, which was a means of identifying him as a Muslim. Malik's experiences suggested that similar to how the symbol of the *hijab* came to signify oppression and the plight of the 'imperilled Muslim woman', a "big beard" signified radicalism and the 'dangerous Muslim man' archetype to some in Quebec who felt that his beard reminded them of what happened on 9/11.

Ismail also felt that there were a number of reductive stereotypes in Quebec society that associated Muslims and Islam to violence:

> Well because of the media and everything that's always being portrayed towards Muslims, like, we're seen as – like I don't really know how to explain this but you know that whole *terrorist* scenario/stereotype sort of thing. That's what comes into my mind. Because at school that's the jokes that would come upon me and people of my kind. That's all I see how people see us. They see us as something like...how can I explain this, more like people just wanting to murder and kill and that whole concept of jihad. It's basically a portrayal which is actually not true and wrong in many ways.

Ismail, like Ahmad, felt that Muslims in Quebec were perceived as villainous. Ismail suggested that the dominant frame of Muslims was that of the 'dangerous Muslim man' who was out to harm the Westerner. Ismail believed that the identity of his "kind" was reduced to the singular figure of the Muslim terrorist as he exclaimed "that's all I see how people see us". Ismail's comments painted an image of an almost inescapable characterization of Muslims. They were perceived as people who just wanted to engage in indiscriminate violence and murder. Ismail alluded to how these stereotypes trickled into his experiences in secondary school. Ismail discussed how the taunts that he came across in secondary school exclusively revolved around affiliations to terrorism because of his religious background. Similar to Amina's accounts of her brother, Ismail suggested that his classmates in secondary school were categorizing him as one of the 'bad Muslims' because of an assumed biological affiliation with terrorism and terrorists, as his faith was perceived as a race. In some ways it would seem that Ismail himself racialized his Islamic faith as he referred to his co-religionists as "people of his kind". Arun Kundnani (2014) observes that "since all racisms are socially and politically constructed rather than reliant on the reality of any biological race, it is perfectly possible for cultural markers associated with Muslimness (forms of dress, rituals, languages, etc.) to be turned into racial signifiers" (p. 11). It would seem that facing a constant racialization of the Islamic faith through his experiences, Ismail himself had begun to view his religion as a race. Other participants discussed similar challenges in their experiences throughout secondary school.

Experiences in secondary school. Most of the male participants, like the females, generally felt that their overall experience in high school was positive. However, all the participants felt that there were some levels of racism against Muslims in their secondary schools. Yusuf, like Ayesha and Maryam, felt tremendous pressure to represent Islam when he was a secondary student:

> Well going to school—I went to a private French high school—I have to say, we weren't *just* a minority, there were barely any Muslims in that school. The thing, going to such a French school, people don't really know a lot about Muslims. So as a Muslim over there, a teenager, you feel obliged to represent your religion and sometimes it's kind of hard because you're at that age where you're not only trying to find out who you are but you're trying to fit in as well. So sometimes you leave out some of the things of Islam so that you could just tell people what they want to hear maybe, and not necessarily show the right image of Islam. And that's mainly it for the students, but I mean like for the teachers, a lot of times they're going to show videos and stuff that might not necessarily be for [Islam], but you don't have any choice but to accept it. Like one of the videos I had seen in my high school it had to do with Muslim sisters praying behind men, and that was just one mosque that they used in the video but they kind of made a general image of how women are inferior to men in Islam, which isn't the case. But at that age, like, you don't really know how to say your thoughts, how to be against it. So you're better off just keeping your mouth shut.

Yusuf described how being a high school student was a time of self-exploration. This was difficult for him because of certain assumptions associated with Muslims and Islam in his secondary school, which he did not ascribed to. Yusuf was cognisant of his 'Otherness' in his high school setting as well as the types of understandings people had of Muslims and Islam. Hence, he would feel the need to try and "fit in", suggesting that being an accepted member of the student body was not a taken-for-granted situation for him. Rather, he needed to make efforts to be perceived as 'normal' even if this meant telling students "what they want to hear" at the expense of misrepresenting his faith. Some studies have shown that within educational institutions, students have been able to assert their Muslim identity through participation with Muslim student groups formed within the school, as these help ease tensions relating to peer pressure and prevent marginalization (Khan, 2009; Zine, 2001). Unfortunately in Yusuf's school such an organization did not exist.

The challenges of being a Muslim minority in school were compounded with further difficulties when teachers would show materials casting Muslims in a negative light. Yusuf's comments suggested that he would be at odds with the types of media portrayals of Muslims presented by his teacher, as he described a video that was shown to his classmates gave off a "general image of how women are inferior to men in Islam". Such imagery of Muslim women in the Canadian context have been documented in depth by Jiwani (2010), who contends that "[t]he tendency within the news media and current affairs programming has been to project representations of the veiled woman as essentially an abject and victimized Muslim figure" (p. 65). Yusuf felt that in his classroom setting he had no "choice but to accept" the types of portrayals of Islam that were disseminated to the students despite the fact that he felt such information was casting his faith in a negative light. Instead of the classroom being a space where Yusuf felt comfortable to express himself, his identity, and his beliefs, he described feelings of alienation, 'Otherness', and was forced to accept prejudicial discourses about his faith. Yusuf described how the archetype of the 'imperilled Muslim woman' was perpetuated through media presented to his class. Despite disagreeing with these portrayals, he felt the need to regulate his views and beliefs about the issue. Perhaps he did not want to engage in a confrontation with his teacher, as doing so would potentially draw more attention to his Islamic faith and in such a situation could further create feelings of alienation with his peers. Abo-Zena, Sahli, and Tobias-Nahi (2009) observe that children in educational settings often have fears and anxieties over being disliked because of their religious affiliations. Such a situation not only inhibits social adjustment and causes marginalization, but can also affect school performance. The tensions described by Yusuf were similar to those described by other participants.

Participants from the group discussion mentioned that school curricula in Quebec, as well as teachers in some instances, facilitated anti-Muslim biases:

Zaid: The only problem that would come up, especially in Ethics class or religion class, where debates would come over different religions and then people had their opinions and what not. Other than that high school was ok.

Naved: And what kind of things would come up in those discussions that you can recall?

Zaid: Well we'd compare other religions like Christianity to Islam and all the other religions and then there would be discussions to that. So there would be people who would agree and disagree and that would cause debates and *even* fights. I remember once we were talking about Islam and comparing it to Judaism and there were a few people who got offended and there was a Muslim and a Jew and they began to fight in class. And they started fighting after class as well. But it got better afterwards. But it shows that this religion class caused more tension.

Ali: I think they want politically correct answers as well. Like a lot of times if you say what you want, what you believe in, you won't get the full marks. They want you to say what the media says.

Adam: The most *secular* response.

Ali: Yeah, exactly.

Ahmad: The school I went to, some kids had problems with other religions, because it was a school where the Quebecois were a minority maybe 20%. Everyone else was Arabs, Chinese, Afghan, and all other cultures. It wasn't the students that had issues; I found it was the teachers. For example, once in physics class I was balancing a book on my head and the teacher said, *Ahmad, stop praying*. He thought it was funny and a good joke, but I didn't appreciate that and the students understood that. Or for example, just because I would pray at school, when I go to school I observe the afternoon prayer. I pray outside. But I've never encountered a student—they will ask me questions, but never in a negative way, but the way the teachers view it, when you talk about your religion [in a positive way], they're against that. It's like you said before, you won't get full grades if you're not 'with the teacher'. For example, my Ethics teacher, he's not educating people he's *mis*-educating people by not giving information that is precise and neutral. When it comes to Christianity, Judaism it's fine but with Islam he chooses information against Islam and he presents this to students as if it's normal but it's not something that's normal.

Zaid discussed how his Ethics and Religious Culture class at times would be a source of tension in his high school, particularly when religions were discussed. These tensions involved debates within the classroom and on one occasion even escalated to a violent confrontation outside of the class. Zaid did not specifically imply that his teacher was responsible for the confrontation. However, other participants in the group discussion felt that teachers facilitated tensions towards Muslims and Islam.

Ali's comments suggested that teachers wanted students to regurgitate dominant media discourses even if these contradicted their own beliefs and understandings of issues. Therefore, Ali's understanding of what "politically correct" implied arose from what was being said in the media. Adam added to these comments and stated, "the most secular response", to which Ali agreed. This was an example of how the students were identifying how the state policy of French secularism, as discussed in Chapter Three, infused media discourses. These comments also demonstrated how a state institution, like a secondary school, reproduced dominant Quebec media discourses and state policies, as teachers seemingly wanted students to mimic these if they were to receive "full marks". Not conforming to state policies and media discourses carried the penalty of not getting "full marks". These comments suggested that some of the participants perceived their classrooms as apparatuses of state indoctrination, as they felt obliged to give "the most secular response" even if this was at odds with their Islamic beliefs. As was the case with Yusuf, other participants also felt the need to regulate their speech with regards to their beliefs within a classroom setting. A similar pattern has been noted by Sunaina Maira (2014) in her study of Arab, South Asian, and Afghan communities in the US. In this study it was found that Muslim youth felt their right to free speech was restricted in the context of the War on Terror because they believed they were under constant surveillance. It would appear that in the post-9/11 context some Canadian Muslim youth also feared reprisals for their beliefs because they perceived them as contravening state policies of secularism and thus regulated their speech.

In Ahmad's experiences some teachers not only expected students to accept state policies and media discourses but also engaged in the process of misinforming their students about Islam and Muslims. Ahmad described how one of his teachers singled him out as on object of ridicule because he was an observant Muslim student who prayed the afternoon prayer in school. Ahmad described how students around him did not bother him when he would observe prayers, and would ask questions which he did not perceive as demeaning. However, he felt a sense of conflict and tension towards his teachers when he would speak about his religion in a way that contradicted state policies and media discourses. Ahmad felt a strong bias from his Ethics and Religious Culture teacher when discussing Islam. He felt that his teacher would pick and choose what to present about Islam, thus creating a distorted picture of his faith. Ahmad described how his Ethics and Religious Culture course facilitated constructing his Islamic faith as 'Other'. Ahmad specifically identified his teacher as being the cause of these tensions through presenting the Islamic faith with his own bias. He felt that his faith was being unfairly presented and if he wanted to get "full grades" he would have to be "with the teacher". In other words, he was indirectly being forced to accept dominant media and state discourses about Muslims within his Ethics and Religious Culture class. If he did not do so, he felt that he would be penalized.

An important reoccurring theme that came up with Muslim male participants when recounting their high school experiences was the archetype of 'dangerous Muslim men' which would regularly appear in different forms within their secondary school settings. As mentioned previously, Muslim male students would sometimes have taunts thrown at them relating to violence and terrorism. Some of these stereotypical views towards Muslim men manifested within the school culture during dress-up days like Hallowe'en:

> *Zaid*: Well, in high school, especially around grade ten and eleven, we had two classes one of them was Ethics and we were talking mainly about Islam, Christianity, Judaism, Buddhism, and that stuff and also in our Contemporary World class, we were talking about the war between Palestine and Israel. So the topic of Islam was *pretty* popular in grades ten and eleven. So one Hallowe'en, I guess you can say there was a Hallowe'en party or Hallowe'en day at school, and a few people—a group came dressed up as the so called 'Muslim' with the turban and beard and what not. So they came to school like that, and as people saw they also took their gym clothes and made a turban and found,

I don't know paper or what not, and made a beard and that was their costume for the day.

Naved: And why would they dress up as Muslims for Hallowe'en, what were they trying to show by wearing the turban?

Zaid: I guess they were trying to be unique but they weren't. I don't think they were trying to offend us. I guess mostly the purpose of Hallowe'en costumes is to look *scary*, so I guess they were trying to show that as being terrorists or Muslims.

Zaid discussed how the topic of Muslims and Islam came up in some of his courses, namely the grade eleven Contemporary World class and the Ethics and Religious Culture course, as he attended secondary school during the height of the War on Terror. Though Zaid did not directly indicate that these courses negatively depicted Muslims, his comments did suggest that through these courses students in his school received exposure to Muslims and the Islamic faith. Hence, "the topic of Islam was pretty popular" in the senior levels of the school that Zaid attended. So on Hallowe'en, a group of students thought it would be a good idea to come to school dressed up as Muslims. Zaid's comments link the instruction in his Contemporary World and Ethics and Religious Culture classes with this incident. This suggested that the information that students obtained about Muslims and Islam in these courses was consistent with media and state discourses which consistently reproduce the image of the 'dangerous Muslim man'. This archetype employs a number of visual signifiers including the beard and clothing items such as the turban (Gottschalk & Greenberg, 2008), which is what students wore to embody this archetype. Zaid mentioned how in his Ethics and Religious Culture class other faiths were also discussed, specifically mentioning Christianity, Judaism, and Buddhism. However, of the faiths discussed, only Islam and Muslims were identified as threatening figures worthy of imitating on Hallowe'en.

The presence of the 'dangerous Muslim man' archetype is further confirmed when Zaid discussed why he thought non-Muslim students would think that dressing up as Muslims on Hallowe'en would be an appropriate costume: "the purpose of Hallowe'en costumes is to look scary". Therefore, it would be logical to assume that if students were dressing up as Muslims on Hallowe'en it was because they perceived a certain type of 'Otherness' in the Muslim faith which was threatening and dangerous, much like how students wear costumes depicting vicious killers, monsters, or other intimidating figures on Hallowe'en. Zaid's description of this episode was very telling. He mentioned that a group of students came dressed up as the "so called Muslim". Zaid did not state that the students came dressed as violent terrorists. The students came dressed as the 'Muslim', or at least how the figure of the 'Muslim' has come to be known in Western discourse. Zaid mentioned how he felt that the intent of students was not malicious, indicating that the students wearing these costumes did not feel that such a depiction was in any way offensive.

Rather, this incident demonstrated the students' understanding of what it meant to be 'Muslim'. According to Zaid, their understanding of 'being Muslim' on Hallowe'en embodied the tropes of violence and intimidation, as the purpose of the attire was to "look scary". Like discourses and practices relating to culture talk, this incident revealed how there were certain taken-for-granted characteristics associated with Muslimness, as if they are biological or inherent traits which define their essence. A number of the incidents described by the participants above alluded to how media representations of Muslims impacted how they were perceived in secondary schools.

Effects of media on Muslim male participants. All of the Muslim male student participants felt there were biases in how Muslims were represented in popular cultural mediums such as television programs, Hollywood films and the news media:

> I think the media of our time, things like La Presse, TVA, FOX News, CBC all these media never give neutral information. They never just give the news as it is, nothing more, nothing less. It is always opinionated and this has an effect on people's perceptions with Muslims. I can recall when I was in high school, every morning I would come in between 7:50 and 8:50. One day I came around 8:20 and I was having a coffee with some of my friends and some Quebecois and we'd always get into arguments because they would always say things against Muslims that they were getting from the media. If we look at acts of terrorism, 94% of them are committed by non-Muslims. *Only 6%* are committed by Muslims, but we never hear about the *other 94%*. We only hear about acts of terrorism by Muslims. And when people keep on hearing the same message over and over again through the media it will eventually have an impact on how they view Muslims.

Ahmad was the most forthright of all the participants in his belief that media negatively depicted Muslims and about how this affected perceptions of Muslims by the general Quebecois population. Ahmad discussed how in his secondary school experiences he would routinely confront Quebecois students with stereotypes that come from the media. These students were his friends and he therefore felt comfortable discussing their perceptions of his faith. Ahmad specifically discussed how Quebecois students felt there was a connection between terrorism and Muslims. Ahmad's comments implied that in his discussions with these students, there was an assumption that all acts of terrorism were committed by Muslims, whereas the groups that committed the majority of terrorist acts were never discussed. Ahmad did not specifically mention where he got this information from, but a report published by the Federal Bureau of Investigation (FBI) confirmed his statements. This report documented all terrorist acts committed in the US from 1980 to 2005. According to the FBI's database the vast majority of crimes in the US that were considered to be acts of terrorism were committed by Latinos and extreme left wing groups. Acts of terrorism committed by Muslims accounted for only 6% (FBI, 2005).

Ahmad believed that the disproportionate media coverage of Muslims who committed acts of terrorism created an erroneous understanding of Islam amongst the

Quebecois students that he associated with in secondary school. Their understanding of Islam was constructed through the media archetype of 'dangerous Muslim men', which Ahmad felt was illogical as most acts of terrorism were committed by other groups in society. Ahmad's comments infer that media biases from Quebec, the US, and Canada as a whole portray similar types of messages, which negatively depict Muslims and perpetuate stereotypes of 'dangerous Muslim men'. Similarly, Muslim male participants who mentioned specific popular cultural mediums that negatively depicted Muslims often mentioned Hollywood films and US televisions shows, which were easily accessible in Quebec.

Another participant discussed how biased media representations of Muslims were shown in his school and how non-Muslim students linked these representations to Muslims in his classes:

> There was a funny [incident] in class. We were watching a movie and I don't remember what movie it was but in the first scene there was this white man, he was in jail and he was making a movie. So he starts off, hi my name is this and he stutters and he closes the camera, then he starts again, starts recording again and says, hi my name is…closes again. And he does it three times and he closes. And then at the end he goes in the name of Allah the Most Merciful and the he says my name is, and he says a Muslim name and I'm a terrorist and then the movie starts. And it's funny because like only two Muslims in the class and *everybody* looked at us laughing.

Zaid described how a film which depicted Muslim terrorist stereotypes was shown to his class. Zaid did not recall the name of the film, although what he described resonates with a Hollywood film called *Unthinkable* (2010) directed by Gregor Jordan and starring Samuel L. Jackson and Michael Sheen. In the opening scene of *Unthinkable*, similar to what Zaid described, the viewers are presented with a white male who is making a video tape describing how he has placed three nuclear bombs in US cities and that he will detonate them if his demands are not met. The opening scene of this film is very telling as it shows a man, Steven Younger, struggling to speak about his terrorist plot. After attempting numerous times to describe his plot unsuccessfully, he finally begins his message by asserting his Muslim identity starting with the common phrase uttered by Muslims whenever beginning an act of worship, "In the name of Allah". Instead of introducing himself as Steven Younger, as he previously did, he now introduces himself through his Muslim persona of Yusuf Atta Muhammad. Unsurprisingly, the character is now able to discuss his plans without any difficulties as he has openly abandoned his non-Muslim identity, which was the only thing holding him back from describing his violent mission against the West.

Zaid discussed how his non-Muslim classmates automatically linked this scene with the two Muslims in the class. Once again, this episode demonstrated how the racialization of Muslims is a seemingly normal experience for Muslim students in secondary schools in Quebec. The terrorist in the opening scene of the film was a white male and yet simply because of his affiliation with the Islamic faith, students watching the film automatically made a connection between the terrorist and the Muslim students, who aside from their faith, had nothing in common with the character. Zaid's comments suggested that the racialization of Muslims was not perceived as something abnormal, as he was not offended by this association and felt that it was a funny incident. Similarly, other participants who regularly faced taunts and jokes associating them with terrorism did not take much offence to such distasteful actions:

> You know at first when I came into high school, I had the joke, oh, when are you going to *blow up* the school? Or, how about you bomb that person. Just those jokes which refer to terrorism because that's how we're seen as because that's how we're portrayed as in the media. And for me, I would just take them as jokes. I'm like, well ok that doesn't really bother me—go ahead, you know. And what I would do is, I would go along with the joke, and eventually—which that's something they didn't expect—and eventually they stopped making any jokes at all.

Ismail would regularly have taunts and jokes relating to terrorism thrown at him because of his faith. Similar to what was described by Sarah, students would ask Ismail "when are you going to blow up the school?" Ismail felt that stereotypes associating his faith with violence and terrorism were a result of media representations of Muslims, as he mentioned "that's how we're seen as because that's how we're portrayed as in the media". Ismail described how he coped with these taunts by telling his peers "that doesn't really bother me—go ahead". Luckily for Ismail this behaviour from his peers eventually stopped. But for other students that is not always the case.

J'Lein Liese (2004) discusses how there are levels of discrimination that occur in educational settings. The first level of discrimination relates to slurs based on stereotypes. Often slurs can be used to "*dehumanise* another person or social group to justify a violent act" (p. 67). In other words, racial slurs directed at students can eventually escalate into forms of physical violence. In the context of the War on Terror, racial slurs such as 'terrorist' have been employed to "justify retaliatory actions post 9/11" (Liese, 2004, p. 67). This has occurred through the wars in Afghanistan and Iraq, as these nations were described as supporting terror and were a part of a supposed 'Axis of Evil'. Hence the term 'terrorist' is synonymous with groups of people who are enemies of the state in the War on Terror and warrant violent policing. If students are being labelled as 'terrorists' in secondary schools, it should not simply be taken as a joke and should be seriously addressed by teachers and by the school.

Ismail did not mention that any teachers or administrators within his school came to his defence when he was ridiculed in this manner; rather he simply treated these incidents as a joke and did not let these taunts get to him. This type of reaction is similar to Noor's responses, where she felt that racism against Muslims was more of a perception manufactured by the media, even though she had repeatedly experienced racist incidents on her commute to school. Zaid was also seemingly untroubled by how a film which depicted a Muslim terrorist was immediately linked to him and another Muslim student in his class. In all three cases, the Muslim students did not feel that the racism they were experiencing was troubling or something that needed to be seriously addressed.

When considering Muslim female and male student responses along with Chapters Two and Three, which theorized Islamophobia and examined anti-Muslim racism in Quebec, a clearer understanding emerges of how state practices and policies, combined with political and media discourses have enabled manifestations of Islamophobia. French secularism as well as interculturalism have facilitated the construction of an exalted nationalist subject in Quebec. Muslims have been excluded from this status as 'Muslimness' carries with it associations with a religion (i.e. the Islamic faith) as well as presumptions of misogynistic treatment and oppression of women. These perceptions associated with Muslims and Islam oppose the 'core values' of secularism and gender equality in Quebec society. This related to experiences of participants who discussed how they were expected to give the "most secular response" to issues in their class discussions. Students described how they would be penalized for non-conformity to these norms, even if it contravened their faith. Muslim women wearing the *hijab* became visibly marked as 'Other' and were racialized and discriminated against as the *hijab* carries with it assumptions of backwardness and oppression in Quebec society. The 'Otherness' associated with Islam in Quebec political and media discourses as seen in the RA debates and the proposed Bill 60 also resonated with participants' experiences. Some participants discussed how they were told to "go back to your country" or that their beard had no place in Quebec society. These instances, like the RA debates and discussions over the proposed Bill 60 involved exalted nationalist subjects who felt empowered to exclude Muslims from the nationalist space. Teacher participants also noted a number of racist incidents in Quebec secondary schools against Muslims.

TEACHERS' PERCEPTIONS OF ISLAMOPHOBIA IN QUEBEC SECONDARY SCHOOLS

I drew from six teacher participants in this study, three of whom were Muslim and three non-Muslim. All of these teachers were interviewed individually and worked in the Greater Montreal region. Muslim teacher participants had insights on anti-Muslim racism from two perspectives; racism that they had observed towards Muslim students within their secondary schools and racism which they themselves had experienced as Muslim teachers.

Muslim teachers' experiences with racism. Of the three Muslim teacher participants, two were male and one was female, Hamza, Ibrahim, and Alia. Hamza had been teaching in secondary school for eight years at the time of the interview. He was a Social Studies teacher and identified himself as a practicing Muslim man. Ibrahim was in his third year of teaching secondary school at the time of his interview. Ibrahim was a Mathematics and Technology teacher and like Hamza, identified himself as a practicing Muslim. Alia was on maternity leave at the time of the interview. She had worked in the secondary school system for seven years and was planning on returning to teaching upon completing her maternity leave, resuming her position as a Science teacher. Throughout Alia's experiences as a secondary school teacher, she was visibly identifiable as a Muslim as she wore the *hijab* while at work. In addition to providing insights about Islamophobia faced by Muslim students in secondary schools, these participants also discussed how they were perceived by their students. Ibrahim felt that he experienced prejudice from his students because of his faith:

> The event that happened last year, with one of the kids taking a picture of me and posting it on his Facebook page and putting a picture of an airport, the map of an airport, right next to it as if I was planning to blow it up. That was *totally racist* and judgmental. He took a picture of me teaching in class and he said 'terrorist Math teacher?' was the comment that he put there. So that was something *very* racist that happened. Other than that, in the same class, one of the students who was later expelled from the school because of bullying, he used to make planes in the class and throw the planes and he would say, 'sir are you going to destroy that plane' something like that. And I would say, no I won't, I don't believe in that but still he kept on bullying me. But they [other students] were quite impressed they were really surprised how I didn't used to get mad at them and just laughed off their stupidities. They were expecting me to get completely angry, but I told them what you are perceiving is completely false.

Ibrahim described how a student targeted him as an object of ridicule by taking his picture and posting it on his Facebook page and linked his image to terrorism. As was the case with student participants, there was no basis to assume that Ibrahim was going to commit an act of violence or terrorism. However, Ibrahim was associated with such acts by a student by virtue of his faith. Similarly, another student indirectly associated terrorism with Ibrahim by asking him if he was going to "destroy that plane". Ibrahim's comments suggested that he felt the student was trying to make a joke linking him to terrorists who blew up planes, as was the case with the 9/11 terrorist attacks. This student, as described by Ibrahim was a bully. However; his bullying was not limited to students and was also directed towards Ibrahim. The bullying experienced by Ibrahim involved linking him to the trope of the Muslim terrorist. In both examples mentioned by Ibrahim, his students felt empowered to "bully" and ridicule him because of the perceived 'Otherness' associated with his faith.

Ibrahim mentioned how his other students expressed amazement that he was not angered by the student who would throw paper airplanes in his class. Ibrahim suggested that his students who did not openly hurl taunts and engage in racist acts towards him still made assumptions about him. Those assumptions entailed predisposition to anger. Ibrahim mentioned that his students were expecting him to "get completely angry", but that was not the case. Ibrahim's comments suggested that he felt his students had preconceived notions of him and harboured dormant forms of Islamophobia. When discussing this account with Ibrahim in detail, it was clear that he believed that his students felt he was pre-disposed to anger. According to Ibrahim "they were all on board" with regards to the assumptions they had of Ibrahim as a 'dangerous Muslim man'. Ibrahim's accounts described a range of students expressing Islamophobic tendencies. Some students expressed their perceptions of Ibrahim explicitly through bullying or unlawfully taking his picture and ridiculing him on the Internet, while other students engaged in microaggressions with Ibrahim. Microaggressions can be understood as regular exchanges between people that send racist or condescending messages to individuals because of their ethnic, racial, religious, or cultural affiliations (Paludi, 2012). In another instance, Ibrahim described how two female students claimed that Ibrahim unfairly sided with male students over them in a class dispute. Ibrahim stated how these girls openly claimed he was being "sexist". Ibrahim believed that these claims of sexism were rooted in the perception that Muslim men are misogynistic and unfair to women. Hence, these microaggressions assumed Ibrahim was a 'bad Muslim' pre-disposed to anger and oppressive towards women.

Alia described similar experiences of being bullied by students because she wore the *hijab* while teaching. Alia also experienced bullying by other members of her secondary school community:

> At another school there was a teacher that was basically bullying me. She would bring up things like, *oh, your religion allows men to beat other women.* She would bring up these random things, and I'd be like, *are you kidding me?* And finally one day she basically—I was sitting at my desk and she was standing over me pointing her finger in my face and yelling at me things like, *if you claim Muslims are so misunderstood why aren't Imams going on national television speaking up for your religion.* And I remember thinking—obviously when you're being verbally attacked your brain turns off—after I remember thinking, *what TV do you watch?* There's people on the TV all the time and she was trying to allude to the fact that she felt 'you people need to change yourselves when you come to Canada'.

Alia, like Ibrahim, described that she was being "bullied", but in this incident the perpetrator was a teacher. The incident that Alia was discussing took place while the invasions and occupations of Iraq and Afghanistan were ongoing throughout 2006. The type of bullying that Alia experienced involved the archetype of 'imperilled Muslim women', which was regularly employed in media and political discourses throughout the War on Terror, as her colleague clearly felt that Muslim men were enacting violence on Muslim women. Alia would regularly try and explain how Muslims were misunderstood and misrepresented in the media. However, her

115

attempts to change this teacher's perceptions fell on deaf ears as she continued to harass her while she worked at that particular school. Alia felt that this colleague who was bullying her was implying that she did not fit into Canadian society. Her statements were troubling for Alia, as she was born and raised in Canada. Hence, Alia's beliefs and appearance signaled a type of 'Otherness' which excluded her from membership of the nation. This incident was an example of a nationalist subject reaching her threshold of tolerance, as Alia's perceived 'Otherness' could no longer continue without her voicing opposition to it. Alia mentioned how this particular colleague had friends from other ethnic groups such as an East Asian friend. However, Alia's difference was deemed unacceptable to tolerate, as her 'Otherness' was irreconcilable with this colleague's conceptions of nation. In other words, Alia needed to change herself because she was not welcome in *her* country. As was the case with student participants, Alia was being confronted with a member of the majoritarian culture who felt she possessed a sense of spatial power permitting her to determine who belonged and who did not.

Hamza's experiences as a secondary school teacher did not involve any incidents of being bullied by students or staff members. However, he did feel that in the post 9/11 context, Muslim students have experienced challenges relating to how they have been perceived by other students:

> I think with some young kids it's a *lot* for them to deal with when all their friends aren't Muslim and sometimes it's hard to stand up and say I am Muslim and they get a bit more timid. One story that comes to mind was once there were two Muslims in our school and one of them asked the other if he was Muslim because he wasn't sure. But the other one was with a bunch of friends and he kind of denied it and said, no I'm not. And later when we saw the two of them together, one of the students asked the other, well you said you weren't Muslim before and he [the other student who denied being Muslim previously] kind of mentioned that sometimes when he's around his non-Muslim friends he didn't want to admit that.

At the school that Hamza was working at, there were very few Muslim students. Hamza noticed that the few Muslim students he interacted with faced challenges. Hamza mentioned how one of the Muslim students at his school was conflicted with his Muslim identity when he was around his non-Muslim friends, so much so that he denied being a Muslim around them. This student was selectively expressing his Muslim identity. Around Muslims, in the confines of a secure space he would acknowledge his Islamic identity. Presumably this student felt that being identified as Muslim would cause him some type of social marginalization or to lose his friends. Abo-Zena, Sahli, and Tobias-Nahi (2009) discuss how Muslim students may engage in such behaviour "in order to minimize the apparent differences between themselves and their non-Muslim peers. Muslim youth may feel pressured to keep secret, deny or even abandon their Muslim faith in an attempt to blend in" (p. 9). This may have been the case with the student described by Hamza, as Hamza mentioned this student felt "shame" or was possibly even "embarrassed" to acknowledge his Islamic identity and what would result from that.

Later on in the interview, Hamza recounted how a Muslim female student was verbally and physically harassed by another student in his school who tried to pull off her *hijab*. Within a secondary school setting, the action of pulling off a woman's *hijab* is usually preceded by less abrasive forms of abuse over an extended period of time and does not usually occur as an isolated incident (Liese, 2009). Hence it would be conceivable that this student may have faced repeated lesser forms of abuse from students related to her appearance prior to this incident. Hamza discussed how wearing the *hijab* in his secondary school posed a major challenge for Muslim women who may have been inclined to do so. Some Muslim female students would come to the school wearing the *hijab* and at some point later in the year stopped wearing it. Hamza associated these events with the social pressures and anxieties that arise from wearing the *hijab* as a signifier of the 'Other' within his secondary school. He mentioned how the *hijab* makes a Muslim student "*very very* visible" which resulted in becoming an "automatic target". Hamza believed that students who wore the *hijab* were perceived as 'Other', which resulted in stereotypical understandings of them. Not wearing the *hijab* or choosing to stop wearing it could possibly prevent this categorization. Hamza also briefly mentioned how some students may pick up stereotypes through media representations of Muslims. As discussed earlier, media representations of Muslims often employ tropes of oppression and backwardness through visible religious signifiers like the *hijab*. Hamza's comments were consistent with student responses suggesting that media discourses about Islam may have some influence in how Muslims in Quebec secondary schools were perceived.

Hamza also expressed how some of his non-Muslim students felt conflicted between their perceptions of Muslims through their interactions with Muslim teachers, and how that contradicted discourses surrounding Muslims that they were accustomed to:

I guess the average teenage kid who is exposed to news bits throughout the day, or news flashes, or whatever information they get from mum, dad, from brothers and sisters is only those few little bits about Muslims committing violent acts, being wars in their countries, news items coming from there about various actions of people in those countries. So that becomes what their exposure is to Muslims and I think it was made evident to me recently because…a student asked me just the other day, because he knew that there were some Muslim teachers in the school and he wanted to know if I was one of them. And he had said that he was speaking to his grandma—who was, I guess, a Francophone Quebecoise—mentioned that Muslims are bad, not contributing much to society, kind of feeding into some of those things [stereotypes]. And he had mentioned to her, I have one or two Muslim teachers in my school that I've had and they've been very positive, very good interactions, and very positive experiences. I think that kind of illustrates that this student is wrestling with

117

what maybe people are telling him, what the media is telling him, and what his real life interactions are and he's finding a difference between reality and perception.

Hamza discussed how a typical student is inundated with negative perceptions of Muslims and Islam through media, family, and society. For one of Hamza's students, there was a disparity between the messages that he received about Islam from a family member and his personal experiences with Muslims who were his teachers. Hamza felt that the perceptions that were held by this student's grandmother were based on stereotypes in Quebec society. Hamza described how the student felt confused by this because the teachers who he knew were Muslims did not fit into the mould described by his grandmother. This incident described by Hamza revealed how the perceptions of Muslims in a secondary school environment, in some instances, were influenced in a positive manner through positive interactions with Muslims, which did not conform to dominant media and state discourses surrounding Muslims. This was similar to sentiments expressed by Maryam and Ayesha, who both felt that perceptions of Muslims in secondary schools can change when Muslims express agency and counter stereotypes through their interactions with the non-Muslim majority. However, As Hamza described, the student felt somewhat conflicted between his experiences with Muslims and the messages that he had been exposed to about Muslims and Islam. This was indicative that positive experiences with Muslims alone are not enough to change perceptions. As Chris Wilkins (2006) observes, simply having exposure to people of different ethnicities does little to challenge perceptions, and "without an understanding of the social structures which create the individual prejudice through which racism is manifested, teachers are unlikely to play a major part in challenging racism" (pp. 16–17). Positive interactions with Muslims may result in students questioning dominant discourses about Muslims, but more actions are required in order for students to overcome some of the cognitive dissonance that may result from these conflicting experiences.

Non-Muslim teachers' perceptions of anti-Muslim biases. There was one male, Jeff, and two females, Jessica and Laura, in this category of participants. At the time of the interview, Jeff was in his fifteenth year of teaching, and primarily taught Ethics and Religious Culture courses. Jessica was in her sixteenth year of teaching. Most of her work-load consisted of teaching French and Ethics and Religious Culture courses. Laura had been teaching for almost twenty years, primarily in the Arts department of her school. Laura felt that the association of Muslim men and terrorism was a common stereotype that manifested in her school. In some instances this was perpetuated by Muslim students themselves in her drama class:

Even here I see the Indian [Muslim] kids being called a terrorist and they laugh it off. I mean it's for jokes right? But is it? I guess they play along [Muslim kids], and the good ones, the *really* good ones, the popular kids who can handle it, they play along, I mean they do play along... I can't say that the brown skinned kids that I've taught haven't enjoyed playing the terrorist, *they have.*

They enjoy it, they laugh about it, they have their whole costume and they'll go full tilt. They'll bring in like strapped bombs and stuff, it's for comedy and there's a purpose and we'll all laugh, you know. The black kid will be the rapper with the grill, and in comedy you're encouraged to use your physical type as a part of your comedy. The fat kid will, you know, come in with the Doritos and it makes me happy that they're using their body type in a way that I'm ok with. I'm ok with this. But in a classroom, in an *English* classroom or a *French* classroom and, you know, someone says *'give this to the terrorist over there'* well that's a whole different ball game and it's happened, I've heard it's happened, I've heard that it happens.

In Laura's experiences as a teacher she had observed how students used terms such as "terrorist" as a joke with Muslim students. Often the response, similar to those discussed earlier, involved the Muslim students themselves laughing off the comments. However, Laura suggested that such comments were not really jokes and promoted subtle forms of racism. Laura discussed how the "popular kids" could handle these types of incidents. Her comments implied that using such terms towards Muslim students can potentially be marginalizing and offensive. If a student is "popular" or has a lot of friends in the school, they can "handle it" because there is less fear of being socially marginalized. However, Laura's comments suggested that this type of behaviour could be damaging to a student who is not as socially adjusted.

Laura distinguished how students using the Muslim stereotype of 'terrorist' could potentially be productive in an educational setting. She alluded to how Muslim students used their physical appearance in her drama classes as a type of satirical device and would act out the 'dangerous Muslim man' archetype. Muslim comedians in the post 9/11 context have used similar techniques to demonstrate the existence of racism towards Muslims in society by embedding their comedy routines with their "experience of exclusion and victimization" (Morey & Yaqin, 2011, p. 198). The overall intent is to entertain the audience, while simultaneously getting the message across that certain groups in society are stereotyped and experience racism and bias. By employing the archetypal image of the Muslim terrorist, Laura believed that the students may have been trying to portray images in their drama routines that had a broader appeal to the class. Some, like Laura, may argue that this is an example of how Muslim students are exercising forms of agency within their school setting as opposed to passively being victims of abuse and taunts that associate their faith with violence and terror. Hall (1996) disagrees with this line of thinking. According to Hall (1996), using racial jokes within one's own racial community is unlikely to denigrate a race, as these jokes form a part of the self-consciousness of that community. However, using racial jokes across racial lines "reinforces the *difference* and reproduces the unequal relations because, in those situations, the point of the joke depends on the existence of racism" (p. 166). Thus, this approach may not have had as beneficial an outcome as Laura intended in her drama class. Nonetheless, Laura's comments suggested that she felt there was a fine line between perpetuating stereotypes and exercising agency. Using a derogatory slur like "terrorist" in an English class, where such a stereotype is not serving any type of satirical purpose, is a blatant form of racism.

Jeff and Laura both felt that media representations of Muslims, especially after 9/11, had been extremely negative and contributed towards creating negative perceptions of Muslim students. Both believed that anti-Muslim sentiments in their secondary schools manifested in subtle forms more often than overtly:

Jeff: I don't know many Muslims students here, I've just heard through hearsay that a couple of students here were harassed because they were wearing *hijabs* and comments were thrown their way. But, and I'm assuming here, you know I wonder even though they [non-Muslim students] may not say anything because you know in our school it's not politically correct to say anything—you know you will be reprimanded for it—but how many times have they [Muslim students] been looked at in a negative way just because of what we're seeing in the news. Recently with the law passed in Quebec where kids can't wear a *hijab* while playing soccer. And how many kids agree with that. We had a discussion in class and they look at an Arab person here, a Muslim person here thinking *eh, you know*…looking down on them because this law was passed in Quebec. So what is *said* and what is *thought* could be two different things. I don't necessarily see it too often in terms of outwardly things being done to the [Muslim] kids besides what little I hear about comments being passed at their expense but I don't hear much of it.

Naved: So if there is racism towards Muslim students you feel that it's more implicit as opposed to explicit?

Jeff: Yeah, for sure. Just by their [non-Muslim students] comments that we hear in class. *Even the jokes.* Kids don't realize that racist jokes *are racism* and how many jokes are at the expense of Muslims, you know?

Jeff's comments inferred that a lack of racist incidents in his school did not necessarily mean that students did not hold racist views towards Muslims. Jeff described how students often harboured negative views towards Muslims which manifested in subtle ways such as "being looked at in a negative way". Jeff suggested that there was dormant Islamophobia present in his school, where students perceive Muslims negatively, primarily through representations of Muslims in the news. As previously discussed, dormant Islamophobia often evolves into explicit and more overt forms of Islamophobia when a situation presents itself.

Jeff's comments also suggested how media and political discourses have reinforced negative views towards Muslims in his class. Jeff referred to highly publicized incidents in Quebec relating to how Muslim girls who wore the *hijab* were prevented from playing soccer, citing concerns relating to safety. The topic of religious headgear being permitted in soccer matches has occupied media and political discourses in Quebec's recent past. The issue came up again in the summer of 2013 when the Quebec Soccer Federation announced a ban on the Sikh turban, which was supported by Pauline Marois, the Quebec Premier at the time (Peritz, 2013). Jeff felt that incidents in Quebec which related to the banning of religious symbols facilitated negative views and comments towards Muslims. Hence, enabling Islamophobia to emerge in the realm of perceptions (dormant Islamophobia) and in actions (explicit Islamophobia). His comments suggested that state policies policing religious minorities, whether intended or not, reinforced negative perceptions of those groups in an educational setting. This was similar to comments discussed in the previous sections where Muslim students and teachers discussed how state and media discourses were perpetuated in educational settings. In both instances, state policies and practices along with negative depictions of Muslims in political and media discourses were reinforced in educational settings through teachers exhibiting anti-Muslim bias or through course content.

Teachers' views on challenging Islamophobia in Quebec schools. On a number of occasions throughout the interview process Muslim and non-Muslim teachers alluded to or provided insights as to how the officially government mandated Quebec Education Program (QEP) could potentially challenge Islamophobia in secondary schools in Quebec. All of the teacher participants believed that there were a variety of courses that could include content to challenge dominant discourses surrounding Muslims. Overwhelmingly, teacher participants felt that the Ethics and Religious Culture (ERC) course could potentially be used as a tool towards this end.

The QEP consists of a number of subject areas such as English, Math, History, and the ERC program, which have each been elaborated on "with reference to common overarching objectives, a set of cross-curricular competencies, and what the Ministry [has] referred to as 'broad areas of learning'" (Morris, 2011, p. 191). The broad areas of learning "deal with major contemporary issues...[and] contribute to the development of a broader world-view" (MELS, 2008, p. 465). They include health and well-being, career planning and entrepreneurship, environmental awareness and consumer rights and responsibilities, media literacy, and citizenship and community life (MELS, 2008). The QEP employs a competency-based approach to learning and defines a competency as "a set of behaviours based on the effective mobilization and use of a range of resources" (MELS, 2001). Therefore, students are expected to acquire the knowledge and skills necessary to effectively address salient social issues. In addition to the competencies of each of the subject areas, the QEP also has cross-curricular competencies which cut across subjects and go beyond the limitations of the subject areas. The cross-curricular competencies "are rooted in specific learning contexts, which are usually related to the subjects [in the QEP]" (MELS, 2008, p. 466). They include the following: uses information, solves problems, exercises critical judgment, uses creativity, adopts effective work methods, uses information and communications technology, achieves his/her potential, cooperates with others, and communicates appropriately (MELS, 2008). The QEP is mandated by the Quebec Ministry of Education and is taught across public and publically-subsidized private schools across Quebec. Students are required to take ERC courses in four out of five of their secondary school years (MELS, 2008). The main objectives of the ERC program are: "the recognition of others" and "the pursuit of the common good" (MELS, 2008, p. 2). The objectives of this program are rooted in a number of principles, which includes fostering living in harmony with others (MELS, 2005). These objectives form the backdrop of the three competencies of the program: reflects on ethical questions, demonstrates an understanding of the phenomenon of religion, and engages in dialogue (MELS, 2008).

Ibrahim cautioned that in order for Quebec educational curriculum to challenge negative perceptions of Islam, certain courses need to be given more emphasis:

Naved: Do you feel that the Quebec Education Program can be used as a tool to engage students in discussion about Islamophobia?

Ibrahim: Yes it can, but it has to be given its proper perspective. I mean like, the Ethics and Religious Culture course is not given much importance, which the idea is good, it's dialogue. That's the basis behind it. But it should be given *more* importance. Even teachers who talk about Ethics, it's like *oh I'm teaching Ethics*, as if they're not an important teacher, as opposed to science and math, which are considered important subjects. I personally think things like ethics would go far in a person's life to make them better humans, compared to math which won't. So those subjects should be given more importance, people should take it more seriously. The Ethics course is a *very* marginal course, and the vast response from the Quebec society has been negative teaching their kids these things.

Ibrahim's comments suggested that the potential to question dominant discourses surrounding Muslims existed within the QEP through courses like the ERC program. However, the effectiveness of these courses was limited because they were not given much importance and teachers teaching these courses had negative attitudes towards them. Other teacher participants described similar beliefs about the possibility of challenging anti-Muslim racism in Quebec secondary schools. Jessica, an ERC and French teacher mentioned her experiences:

Naved: do you feel that the QEP can be used as a tool to engage students in discussions about issues of race, Islamophobia? Do you feel there's a space within the QEP to engage in these discussions?

Jessica: I do it *all the time*. All the time. I'm constantly using current events bringing them in my class addressing different issues about whether it be Muslims, or the separation of Quebec, or the perception of the body, or whatever. I actually thrive on teaching like that because it makes it much more real for the kids and it gives me the opportunity to show them the other side of the story which often they don't see.

Naved: And you're able to use the framework of the QEP to be able to do that in your class?

Jessica: I teach French and Ethics and both disciplines are *really really* easy, it's easy for me to integrate it in those two subjects. Yeah.

Jessica believed that engaging in conversations relating to Islamophobia created a charged environment in her classroom, which made the learning experiences "more real" for her students. Furthermore, she felt that she customarily engaged in such conversations in her classes. Hamza described how various courses within the QEP could potentially discuss issues related to stereotypes and racism in Quebec secondary schools:

> If anything, in the curriculum which is taught, there are opportunities I guess in different subject areas to give a fair and balanced approach or to speak to some of these misconceptions that exist. And I guess it depends on the subject area and I guess the main thing is that as teachers and educators we need to inform ourselves because it's difficult for me to talk about Sikhism if I don't know about it or about Judaism, or about Christianity, or about any other group that I may have a limited knowledge about. So I need to be cautious about what I say and think. With Islam and Muslims, those issues come up in current events classes. Come up in any class basically when there's some literature being read or whatever and a lot of the current contexts refer to maybe parts of the world where Muslims live or some of the novels the kids are reading. So I think it's important that kids get a fair exposure to it. And if we, as educators, don't know, we have to inform ourselves. And maybe that's the role of a Muslim teacher in helping to form the narrative that is discussed about us accurately in classrooms from a pedagogical standpoint.

Hamza believed that within the QEP there was space to engage in anti-racism education. A superficial understanding of various ethnic and religious groups is not sufficient. According to Hamza, detailed knowledge of ethnic and religious minority groups in Quebec society is necessary. This needs to be combined with a deeper understanding of the social processes that create and reinforce racism in a school setting.

Teacher participants discussed in this section strongly felt that Quebec educational curricula, in particular the ERC program could be used as a potential tool to counteract Islamophobia in Quebec secondary schools. Yet, this is not without its contradictions since a number of Muslim student participants described how anti-Muslim racism was perpetuated through their ERC courses. Some Muslim student participants alluded to how teachers used this course as a means to misinform students about Islam. Educational and curriculum theorists have discussed how school curricula can be used to maintain and perpetuate dominant ideologies and subordination in schools. For example, Michael Apple (2000) has argued that schools are sites in which both explicit and hidden curricula are disseminated. The explicit curriculum is what is formally being taught in schools through the various courses and programs that are offered. The hidden curriculum refers to societal imbalances perpetuated through the process of schooling when teachers are uncritically teaching the curriculum. As Tarra Yosso (2010) observes, "[c]urriculum then has multiple layers, including structures, processes, and discourses, each of which combine to present knowledge that align with formal (overt) or informal (hidden) outcomes" (p. 94). Hidden curricula exist because of power imbalances within educational structures. These power imbalances or 'unequal power', as referred to by Apple (1991), afford privilege to some members in society to define what knowledge is accepted as 'official' and worth disseminating, and what forms of knowing are to be ignored and deemed irrelevant. Without altered power relations, critical and responsive educational curricula are unattainable.

Critical race theorists have similarly argued that addressing systemic and structural inequities through educational curricula are ineffectual as these are underscored by devices aimed to preserve cultural privilege and dominance. Hence, there is an inability for traditional educational curricula to be transformative. As Michelle Jay (2010) notes, transformative educational curricula threaten "those dominant groups in our society who have a vested interest in the perpetuation of the mainstream academic knowledge that supports the maintenance of dominant structures, long-present inequities, and the current power arrangements…to subordinate racial minorities" (p. 5). Some have described the process of using educational curricula to maintain cultural privilege and dominance over subordinated groups as a form of hegemony. Hegemony, as described by Gramsci (1971), is a power relationship in which dominant groups are able to maintain dominance over subordinated groups. Hegemony is preserved by universalizing consensus that the dominant group's interests coincide with society's interests. Hence, domination is undetected and therefore perpetuated through consent of the subordinated groups. Within educational contexts, Hall (1986) has argued that the state does not perpetuate the superiority of dominant groups forcefully. Rather, this is achieved through ongoing negotiations and the granting of concessions to subordinate groups to maintain their acquiescence. This can occur through allowances such as 'multiculturalism days', 'international days', and other events which momentarily encourage superficial cultural exchange and dialogue, while masking structural inequalities. Such allowances are exercises in developing 'tolerance' rather than taking concrete actions towards racial equality.

Despite criticisms of educational curricula maintaining and perpetuating white supremacy, some critical race theorists have suggested ways to challenge and engage students in fruitful discussions about racism within educational institutions (Helms, 1992; Leonardo, 2009; Tatum, 2009). One such approach that I believe can facilitate critical discussions about Islamophobia in Quebec secondary schools is by working towards a critical race curriculum. Yosso (2010) has discussed incorporating critical race theory concepts within educational curricula to challenge racial subordination and inequalities within schools, which she terms critical race curriculum (CRC). CRC has five central tenets, which I contend provide useful insights that can inform critical discussions about anti-Muslim racism within schools. These include the following: (1) acknowledging the central and intersecting roles of racism, sexism, classism, and other forms of subordination present within curricular structures and discourses; (2) challenging dominant social and cultural assumptions in relation to the 'Other'; (3) directing the formal curriculum toward goals of social justice and critical consciousness; (4) developing counter discourses through storytelling, narratives, chronicles, family histories, scenarios, and biographies, which draw on the lived experiences racialized students in the classroom; and (5) drawing on historical and contemporary analysis to explicate the connections between educational and societal inequality. Although these principles are intended as a foundation for an educational curriculum centred on social justice and anti-racism, I believe they can also be useful for providing a framework for teachers wishing to express agency within existing educational structures and curricula to challenge racism.

CONCLUSION

We've Jihad *Enough*

Chapter Two of this book discussed how Islamophobia since 9/11 is structured and organized in North American societies through the social relations of race, gender, and class, and has been mediated through the War on Terror. The purpose of discussing these social relations was to provide a theoretical framework for thinking through anti-Muslim racism in this book. Since the archetypes of the 'dangerous Muslim man' and the 'imperilled Muslim woman' regularly surfaced in participants' experiences it would be fair to say that the War on Terror has fundamentally affected the experiences of Muslims in Quebec secondary schools, as the War on Terror has been justified through these archetypes. These archetypes have been further reinforced and given meaning through anti-Muslim racism in Quebec relating to sexularist discourses, state policies of secularism and interculturalism, as well as anti-immigrant/Muslim sentiments expressed in political and media discourses. While one can situate participants' experiences within the broader context of the post-9/11 age and the War on Terror, quite importantly, their experiences resonated particularly with racism and discrimination prevalent in Quebec political and media discourses. Synthesizing the global meta-narrative of anti-Muslim racism within the local context of these participants provides a more nuanced and salient understanding of their experiences. Hence, the challenges of racism experienced by these participants must be directed at the broader post-9/11 culture of fear, but also as importantly directed at the local Quebec and Canadian contexts. Participants' comments suggested a consistent racialization of the Islamic faith, which presumed innate qualities or characteristics associated with 'Muslimness'. Male participants' comments suggested that racialization of Islam associated Muslim men with violence and terrorism. Racialization for Muslim women occurred through the presence of a visual signifier, the *hijab,* identifying these women as 'Other'. Hence an appreciation for the relations of race and gender were essential in examining Islamophobia experienced by the participants, as male and female participants experienced racialization differently based on their gender.

SIMILARITIES BETWEEN PARTICIPANTS AND PARTICIPANT CATEGORIES

A number of common themes and issues emerged from the data analysis of the interviews. The most obvious of these trends was that most participants experienced, directly or indirectly, some form of anti-Muslim racism and prejudice in Quebec society and in their secondary schools. However, there was a wide range in how participants interpreted the racism that they experienced. For example, Noor described how she felt that Islamophobia existed in the realm of media representations of Muslims and not necessarily something that manifested in Quebec society. She held these views despite the fact that she experienced a number of instances which demonstrated that Islamophobia was very real in Quebec, as she was told "go back to your country" and even had eggs thrown at her because of her 'Islamic' appearance. There was a similar type of perception amongst male participants like Zaid and Ismail who both described racist incidents, in which their classmates associated them with terrorism, as not being a very serious issue. Zaid and Ismail described these incidents as "funny" or as "jokes". It is my contention that this attitude exemplified by some participants demonstrated how racism was seemingly normalized in the day-to-day experiences of some of the participants. These participants were not attuned to how they were experiencing racism, as they were not offended and seriously concerned over these issues. In a way, it would seem that they had unconsciously accepted this type of treatment and categorizations. This may have been caused by the negative representations and perceptions prevalent in state policies and practices—as alluded to by participants—as well as political and media discourses in Quebec.

Most participants described how the archetype of 'dangerous Muslim man' as represented by the figure of the Muslim terrorist was regularly perpetuated through the media. Participants also described how they encountered this affiliation to terrorism in Quebec society as well as in secondary schools. Muslim women were confronted with the 'imperilled Muslim woman' archetype. However, some female participants alluded to how the type of racism they experienced was through associations or affiliations with terror as well. This occurred with Amina, when she discussed how she lost a good friend the day after 9/11 because her friend associated her 'Muslimness' with this event. Hence, Muslim women described how they were susceptible to Islamophobia in multiple ways. In some instances wearing a visual signifier like the *hijab* created feelings of 'Otherness' or reinforced the trope of 'imperilled Muslim woman'. However, in the aftermath of 9/11, the *hijab* has also been a symbol associated with violence and terrorism in the experience of some of the participants.

Maryam and Ayesha also noted that once they started wearing the *hijab,* their relationships with their classmates changed. Ayesha felt that the *hijab* put her in the spotlight and consequently she had to be the "spokesperson for the entire Muslim *ummah*", which she found very challenging as she was trying to carve out her own identity and did not feel she fit the archetypal mould of the 'Muslim woman' that was associated with the *hijab*. Maryam was inundated with stereotypical questions relating to 'imperilled Muslim women' once she started wearing the *hijab*, because this symbol signaled her 'Muslimness' to her peers, which was not the case before she wore the *hijab*. Wearing the *hijab* and being recognized as 'Muslim' entailed that Maryam was one of *them* and could now answer questions about (their perceptions of) Islam. The questions Maryam was asked were filled with distortions, yet her peers felt comfortable asking her these questions because she fit the description of 'Muslim woman' and could now speak authoritatively about 'Islam'. The closest thing male participants described as visually signifying their 'Muslimness' was a big beard. For Malik, being brown skinned and having a big beard brought about unwanted attention and falsely signaled his affiliation with terrorism in the eyes of some members of society. Like the *hijab*, Malik's big beard was deemed incompatible with Quebec values by some people. Hence, perceptions of some participants were constructed through visual signifiers of 'Muslimness'.

Muslim teachers, like Muslim students experienced similar types of racist incidents within their secondary schools. Ibrahim encountered explicit and implicit forms of racism from his students. One student went as far as posting an image of him on his Facebook page with the caption "terrorist math teacher?" Alia also experienced racism from students. But her most severe encounter with racism came from another teacher. This teacher regularly "bullied" Alia and associated the archetype of 'imperilled Muslim woman' with Alia and her faith. Therefore, like Muslim student participants, Muslim teachers also faced racism from students and teachers. I believe this was indicative of the pervasiveness of Islamophobia in the schools of the student and teacher participants.

DIFFERENCES

One of the key differences that I noted while analyzing the interviews was that Muslim men did not face a barrage of questions associated with their faith, whereas some of the women described how questioning was central to their experiences as a Muslim in secondary school. This occurred when Muslim female participants started wearing the *hijab* in their schools. This finding was similar to those of Nawell Mossalli (2009) in her study of Muslim teens in the US, where she observed "Muslim boys...in comparison to their female counterparts...were rarely asked questions related to their religion" (p. 57). Maryam alluded to how being asked a lot of questions was empowering, as she was a gatekeeper of knowledge of her faith. Hence, one can argue that wearing the *hijab* gave her an opportunity to teach her peers about Islam. I believe Maryam's experience runs counter to discourses of Muslim women being passive and oppressed, and that perhaps it reveals that some Muslim women have the potential to challenge stereotypes about Muslims and Islam in Quebec secondary schools.

Another important difference between Muslim male and female participants that I encountered was the differences in the types of racisms that these groups faced in secondary schools. Muslim male participants often described concrete instances of racism in which they or their faith were ridiculed or "joked" about. Some of the male participants discussed how they faced taunts and racial slurs associating them with terrorism and violence in their schools. They also described how at times they felt the need to regulate their speech in a classroom setting fearing reprisals for their beliefs. Muslim female participants also discussed concrete forms of racism in the form of verbal and physical abuse. However, these instances usually occurred in their interactions outside of their secondary schools. The types of racism described by most Muslim female student participants in secondary schools involved how they were perceived by their peers. They often described subtle or more implicit forms of Islamophobia. This manifested in how Muslim female students would be asked questions relating to "stereotypes" when they started wearing the *hijab*. This also occurred when there were class discussions about 9/11 and the War on Terror and teachers and students focused undue attention on these students. The underlying assumption here was that these students were privy to 'insider information' as the *hijab* visually marked them as 'Other' and was a symbol associated with a monolithic Islamic entity.

Some of the Muslim female student participants discussed the impacts of 9/11 in their experiences as secondary students, whereas Muslim male students did not mention that this event directly affected their high school experiences. I believe the main reason for this disparity is because three of the Muslim female participants were students in secondary school during the 9/11 attacks, whereas none of the Muslim male participants were in secondary school during that time. From this I have inferred that major events which occupy state and media discourses impacted the experiences of Muslim students in secondary schools. When 9/11 occurred, Muslim students who were in secondary school at the time described how their educational experiences were affected by this event. Throughout the War on Terror, Muslim students' responses alluded to how the invasions and occupations in Afghanistan and Iraq affected their experiences in secondary school. This occurred through class discussions relating to terrorism and "understanding the Arab mind" as well as facing verbal taunts and name calling. Hence, major events that involved Muslims and occupied media and state discourses had influenced the experiences of the participants in this study.

UNDERSTANDING THE CAUSES OF RACISM

In doing this study it became evident that there were a number of factors which impacted the experiences of Muslims as students in schools, as well as in Quebec society after 9/11. The factors alluded to by participants as bringing about and facilitating racist attitudes and behaviours related to state practices and policies, as well as media and political discourses surrounding Muslims and Islam in Quebec within the context of the War on Terror. Drawing from van Dijk (1989), Wong (2011) contends that in racist and nationalist contexts the mass media reproduces ethnic ideologies, which frame ethnic relations in an *us* versus *them* dialectic. As such, "the convergence of the media with other institutions such as the state and, by extension, political parties, can create a powerful force in the public sphere" (p. 156). In my analysis of experiences of Muslim students in secondary schools, the convergence of state practices and policies combined with political and media discourses formed a web of relations through which racist attitudes and actions manifested.

As discussed in Chapter Three, central to Quebec's core values are the notions of secularism and gender equality. These values and official state policies have been used to frame Muslims in Quebec as 'Other'. Participants described how this 'Othering' manifested in their secondary schools, while at the same time implicating media representations as a means of perpetuating Islamophobic perceptions. Muslim student participants described how they were confronted with the archetypes of the 'dangerous Muslim man', the 'imperilled Muslim woman', and Islam as a monolithic entity by both their classmates and teachers, which regularly occur in state and media discourses surrounding Muslims. Muslim male students expressed how they felt the need to regurgitate secular discourses or they would be penalized by not receiving "full marks" in their classes. Muslim female students discussed how their teachers and classmates understood them as 'Other' and being outside of the nationalist space.

Muslim student participants often explicitly mentioned how they felt media representations of Muslims impacted how they were perceived in their secondary schools. They were less explicit in mentioning state practices and policies influencing perceptions of Muslims in secondary schools. It is my contention that to simply point the finger at the media as being responsible for bringing about stereotypes in the experiences of participants does not fully account for the phenomenon of Islamophobia in their secondary schools. Media representations of Muslims in popular culture mediums such as films, television programs, and news media have been given a more impactful influence in Quebec society due to official state policies and discourses surrounding Muslims. North American popular cultural mediums have been inundated with archetypal portrayals of Muslim terrorists and oppressed Muslim women. These representations have been reinforced through state policies and political discourses emanating from the RA debates, the proposed Charter of Values, and sexularism, which have portrayed Muslims as 'Other' and threatening to Quebec society and values.

I found that Islamophobia experienced by participants in this study was a multifaceted phenomenon organized by political, social, and historical processes and relations. Additionally, Islamophobia described by the participants was influenced by both local and global factors. On a global/international level, this study described how participants experienced Islamophobia through discourses and national policies relating to the global War on Terror. Participants also described how Islamophobia occurred through domestic state practices and policies specific to Quebec. This would imply that anti-Muslim racism can be experienced in multiple ways. For example, Islamophobia can arise through tensions, political discourses, and legislations relating to international conflicts, which includes the 'clash of civilizations' thesis. It can also occur through localized narratives, such as notions of Islam and Muslims threatening traditional Quebecois values. In some instances, anti-Muslim racism includes a combination of both domestic and international factors. This could involve the archetypal depictions of the 'dangerous Muslim man' and 'imperilled Muslim woman' who are perpetrators and victims of honour-based violence—a practice which is whitewashed from the collective memories of Quebecers and North Americans in general.

CHALLENGING ISLAMOPHOBIA

Muslim and non-Muslim teacher participants felt that there was space within educational curricula to challenge Islamophobic perceptions and engage in anti-racism education. However, student participants' comments in Chapters Five and Six suggested otherwise. Muslim student participants in this study described how their classes and teachers in secondary schools did very little to challenge stereotypes and often reinforced negative perceptions of Muslims and Islam. I believe this disparity can be explained by the extent to which teachers are willing to express agency to challenge discriminatory and racist views within their classrooms. As a Quebec secondary school teacher, I have found ways of engaging in fruitful class discussions in which perceptions and preconceived notions surrounding religious and ethnic groups have been challenged. Through courses like the ERC program I have been able to teach students how to be critical of media representations of gender, religion, and race. I have used this program to question the legitimacies of conflicts around the world as well as to question dominant discourse about them. Other teachers and researchers have also described varying levels of success in helping to promote mutual understanding and acceptance of various groups in Quebec society through this program. For example, Eric Van der Wee (2011), a pioneer in implementing the ERC program in Quebec English schools discusses how he experienced positive results through this program. Van der Wee (2011) explains his success through developing "a space where the student is free to express him or herself without fear of judgment, where constructive dialogue can take place, and where the instructor is a neutral facilitator for such a process" (p. 246). By taking such steps, he described how he used the ERC program to challenge perceptions of Muslims in the immediate aftermath of the 9/11 attacks. Recounting this, he mentions:

> Shortly after the World Trade Center destruction on September 11th, many news broadcasts showed Palestinians dancing in the streets, rejoicing over what was seen as a decisive blow against an enemy. Many students reacted angrily to this, publicly espousing racial epithets against Muslims everywhere. They were using their "individual voices." Although disturbing, it was, in a sense, fortunate that they felt they could do so, because a great discussion ensued, with the end result being the "group voice" challenging and finally correcting the individual voices. The students became more critical of how the media can easily distort an event, especially when it comes to religion. (p. 246)

Through creating a respectful environment where students felt they could share their views, the students were able to exercise their individual voices. As differing views emerged through the class discussion the facilitator helped in pointing out the logical fallacies in some of the individual arguments, thus allowing for a group voice to emerge challenging erroneous or simplistic perceptions. The process of fostering students' individual voices which are respected and discussed also creates opportunities for Muslim students to share their views and perceptions.

As Ann-Marie De Silva (2011) mentions based on her experiences, "students who follow minority religions in Québec, such as Islam or Hinduism … [have] an opportunity to validate and share a piece of their religious identity that was previously denied by the school curriculum" (Morris, Bouchard, & De Silva, 2011, p. 259). Empowering students to share their individual voices allows for counter discourses to emerge. Such a process gives opportunities for Muslim voices to challenge dominant views from their perspectives, which are seldom heard in media and state discourses in Quebec.

As I conclude, I am reminded of a saying attributed to Malcolm X, "if you don't stand for something, you will fall for anything". In other words, if one does not stand up for one's beliefs and principles, one will accept anything, including subordination, oppression, and social structures that maintain and perpetuate inequities. As an educator, I refuse to passively accept racist attitudes, beliefs, and practices to continue unimpeded in Quebec secondary schools. Through my research, in drawing from, and engaging with existing critical scholarship, I have attempted to stand up for my beliefs, values, and my commitment to social justice. It is my hope that this work will contribute towards social change and equality in Canadian society, as well as inspire educators in various contexts to express agency to challenge racism in their schools.

BIBLIOGRAPHY

Abbas, T. (2006). A question of reflexivity in a qualititative study of South Asians in education: Power, knowledge and shared ethnicity. *Ethnography and Education, 1*(3), 319–332.

Abbas, T. (2011). Islamophobia in the United Kingdom: Historical and contemporary political and media discourses in the framing of 21st-century anti-Muslim racism. In J. Esposito & I. Kalin (Eds.), *Islamophobia: The challenges of pluralism in the 21st century* (pp. 63–76). New York, NY: Oxford University Press.

Abo-Zena, M., Sahli, B., & Tobias-Nahi, C. (2009). Testing the courage of their convictions: Muslim youth respond to stereotyping, hostility, and discrimination. In O. Sensoy & C. Stonebanks (Eds.), *Muslim voices in school: Narratives of identity and pluralism* (pp. 3–26). Rotterdam: Sense Publishers.

Abukhattala, I. (2004). The new bogeyman under the bed: Image formation of Islam the western school curriculum and media. In J. Kincheloe & S. Steinberg (Eds.), *The miseducation of the West: How schools and the media distort our understanding of the Islamic world* (pp. 153–170). Westport, CT: Praeger.

Abu-Lughod, L. (2003, Spring). Saving Muslim women or standing with them? *Insaniyaat*, p. 1.

Ahmed, A. (1999). *Islam today: A short introduction to the Muslim world.* New York, NY: I.B. Tauris.

Ahmed, S. (2000). *Strange encounters: Embodied others in post-coloniality.* London: Routledge.

Ali, M. (2013). Representation of Muslim characters linving in the West in Ontario's language textbooks. *Intercultural Education, 24*(5), 417–429.

Allen, C. (2010). *Islamophobia.* Surrey: Ashgate Publishing.

Al-Saji, A. (2010). The racialization of muslim veils: A philosophical analysis. *Philosophy and Social Criticism, 36*(8), 875–902.

Alsultany, E. (2012). *Arabs and muslims in the media: Race and representation after 9/11.* New York, NY: New York University Press.

Anderson, C., & Denis, C. (2011). Urban native communities and the nation: Before and after the royal commission on aboriginal peoples. In M. Cannon & L. Sunseri (Eds.), *Racism, colonialism, and indigeneity in Canada: A reader* (pp. 59–67). New York, NY: Oxford University Press.

Angus Reid. (2013). *Canadians view non-Christian religions with uncertainty, dislike.* Vancouver, BC: Angus Reid Global.

ANQ. (2010). *Assemblee National Quebec: Bills.* Retrieved September 19, 2011, from Assemblee National Quebec Web site: www.assnat.qc.ca/en/travaux-parlementaires/projets-loi/projet-loi-94-39-1.html

ANQ. (2013). *Assembly National Quebec: Parlimentary proceedings.* Retrieved July 14, 2014, from Assembly National Quebec: http://www.assnat.qc.ca/en/travaux-parlementaires/projets-loi/projet-loi-60-40-1.html

Apple, M. (1991). The politics of curriculum and teaching. *The Realities of Urban Education, 75*(532), 39–51.

Apple, M. (2000). Between neoliberalism and neoconservatism: Education and conservatism in the global context. In N. Burbules & C. Torres (Eds.), *Globalization and education: Critical perspectives* (pp. 57–77). New York, NY: Routledge.

Arendt, H. (1944). Race-thinking before racism. *The Review of Politics, 6*(1), 36–73.

Arendt, H. (1973). *The origins of totalitarianism.* New York, NY: Harcourt.

Asad, T. (2003). *Formations of the secular: Christianity, Islam, modernity.* Stanford, CA: Stanford University Press.

Auger, W., & Rich, S. (2007). *Curriculum theory and methods: Perspectives on learning and teaching.* Mississauga, ON: John Wiley & Sons Canada.

Auld, A., & Tutton, M. (2015, February 14). *National post: Politics.* Retrieved from National Post Web site: http://news.nationalpost.com/2015/02/14/halifax-plot-was-not-culturally-motivated-and-therefore-not-linked-to-terrorism-says-peter-mackay/

Banerjee, S. (2011, May 9). *CTV News.* Retrieved April 10, 2014, from CTV News website: http://montreal.ctvnews.ca/dr-guy-turcotte-begins-telling-his-story-on-witness-stand-1.641656

Bannerji, H. (2000). *The dark side of the nation: Essays on multiculturalism, nationalism, and gender.* Toronto: Canadian Scholars' Press.

Bannerji, H. (2005). Building from Marx: Reflections on class and race. *Social Justice, 32*(4), 144–160.

Barnes, M., Chemerinsky, E., & Jones, T. (2010). A post-race equal protection? *Georgetown Law Journal, 98*, 967–1004.

Baubérot, J. (2012). *La Laicité falsifiée.* Paris: La Découverte.

Bayoumi, M. (2015). *This Muslim American life: Dispatches from the war on terror.* New York, NY: New York University Press.

BBC. (2008, November 4). *BBC News: Middle East.* Retrieved November 23, 2010, from BBC Web site: http://news.bbc.co.uk/2/hi/middle_east/7708670.stm

BBC. (2010, May 3). *BBC News.* Retrieved November 3, 2010, from BBC Web site: http://news.bbc.co.uk/2/hi/americas/8658604.stm

BBC News. (2008, December 7). *BBC News: In pictures.* Retrieved January 29, 2011, from BBC Web site: http://news.bbc.co.uk/2/hi/7769689.stm

Begg, M. (2006). *Enemy combatant: A British Muslim's journey to Guantanamo and back.* London: Free Press.

Bell, D. (1980). Brown and the interest-convergence dilemma. In D. Bell (Ed.), *Shades of brown: New perspectives on school desegregation* (pp. 90–106). New York, NY: Teachers College Press.

Bell, D. (1990). Racial realism–After we're gone: Prudent speculations on America in a post-racial epoch. *St. Louis Law Journal, 34*, 393–402.

Bell, D. (2009). Who's afraid of critical race theory. In E. Taylor, D. Gillborn, & G. Ladson-Billings (Eds.), *Foundations of critical race theory in education* (pp. 37–50). New York, NY: Routledge.

Bilge, S. (2010). Beyond subordination vs. resistance: An intersectional approach to the agency of veiled Muslim women. *Journal of Intercultural Studies, 31*(1), 9–28.

Bilge, S. (2012). Mapping Quebecois sexual nationalism in times of 'crisis of reasonable accommodations'. *Journal of Intercultural Studies, 33*(3), 303–318.

Bilge, S. (2013). Reading the racial subtext of the Quebecois accommodation contraversy: An analytics of racialized governmentality. *Politikon: South African Journal of Political Studies, 40*(1), 157–181.

Blatchford, A. (2014, January 20). *CTV News.* Retrieved February 28, 2014, from CTV News website: http://www.ctvnews.ca/canada/daughter-defends-quebec-couple-s-controversial-testimony-on-values-charter-1.1647679

Bouchard, G., & Taylor, C. (2008). *Building the future: A time for reconciliation.* Quebec, QC: Gouvernment Du Quebec.

Boudreau, S. (2011). From confessional to cultural: Religious education in the schools of Quebec. *Religion and Education, 38*(3), 212–223.

Brean, J. (2013, September 10). *National post: Politics.* Retrieved February 28, 2014, from National Post website: http://news.nationalpost.com/2013/09/10/controversial-quebec-charter-exemptions-based-on-idea-that-some-religious-symbols-have-become-purely-secular/

Budd, J. (2008). Critical theory. In L. Given (Ed.), *The sage encyclopedia of qualitative research methods* (pp. 174–179). Thousand Oaks, CA: Sage Publications.

Byng, M. (2010). Symbolically Muslim: Media, hijab, and the West. *Critical Sociology, 36*(1), 109–129.

CAIR-CAN. (2008, September 20). *CAIR-CAN press releases.* Retrieved September 5, 2011, from CAIR-CAN Web site: http://www.cair-can.ca/itn_more.php?id=P3003_0_2_0-C

Campbell, M., & Gregor, F. (2008). *Mapping social relations: A primer in doing institutional ethnography.* Toronto, ON: University of Toronto Press.

Campbell, M., & Manicom, A. (1995). Introduction. In M. Campbell & A. Manicom (Eds.), *Knowledge, experience, and ruling relations: Studies in the social organization of knowledge* (pp. 3–17). Toronto: University of Toronto Press.

Canadian Women's Foundation. (2012, January). *CWF: Facts about violence against women.* Retrieved February 25, 2014, from CWF website: http://www.canadianwomen.org/facts-about-violence#CAUSES

Carspecken, P. (1996). *Critical ethnography in educational research.* New York, NY: Routledge.

CBC. (2009, September 18). *CBC News.* Retrieved September 5, 2011, from CBC Web site: http://www.cbc.ca/news/canada/montreal/story/2009/09/18/dorval-mosque-vandalized.html

CBC. (2010, March 24). *CBC News.* Retrieved September 5, 2011, from CBC Web site: http://www.cbc.ca/news/canada/montreal/story/2010/03/24/quebec-reasonable-accommodation-law.html

CBC News. (2010, March 12). *CBC News: Montreal.* Retrieved March 17, 2014, from CBC News website: http://www.cbc.ca/news/canada/montreal/charkaoui-to-sue-ottawa-for-24-million-1.881023

CBC News. (2012, September 9). *CBC News: Toronto.* Retrieved March 17, 2014, from CBC News website: http://www.cbc.ca/news/canada/toronto/hassan-almrei-wants-speedy-lawsuit-judgment-1.1227881

CBC News. (2013, September 02). *CBC News: Canada.* Retrieved July 14, 2014, from CBC News website: http://www.cbc.ca/news/canada/montreal/quebec-mosque-vandalized-with-possible-pig-blood-1.1395867

CBC News. (2013, October 30). *CBC News: Montreal.* Retrieved February 25, 2014, from CBC News website: http://www.cbc.ca/news/canada/montreal/quebec-women-s-council-unveils-7-steps-to-stop-honour-crimes-1.2288389

CBC News. (2014, January 10). *CBC News.* Retrieved April 10, 2014, from CBC website: http://www.cbc.ca/montreal/features/guy-turcotte/

CBC News. (2014, November 10). *CBC News.* Retrieved from CBC web site: http://www.cbc.ca/news/canada/montreal/quebec-city-st-jean-sur-richelieu-mosques-vandalized-1.2829698

Center for Human Rights and Global Justice. (2011). *Targeted and entrapped: Manufacturing the "Homegrown Threat" in the United States.* New York, NY: Center for Human Rights and Global Justice.

Cesari, J. (2011). Islamophobia in the West: A comparison between Europe and the United States. In J. Esposito & I. Kalin (Eds.), *Islamophobia: The challenge of Pluralism in the 21st century* (pp. 21–43). New York, NY: Oxford University Press.

Cicourel, A. (1964). *Method and measurement in sociology.* New York, NY: Free Press.

CJC. (2008, May 27). *CJC Media Center.* Retrieved September 5, 2011, from CJC Web site: http://www.cjc.ca/2008/05/27/cjc-qr-condemns-recent-vandalism-at-the-makkah-al-mukarramah-mosque-and-expresses-concern-and-empathy-to-the-muslim-community/

Cobb, C. (2014, July 07). *Ottawa citizen: Local news.* Retrieved July 18, 2014, from Ottawa Citizen website: http://ottawacitizen.com/news/local-news/crown-has-failed-to-prove-its-case-ahmed-lawyer-tells-terrorist-trial

Collet, B. (2007). Islam, national identity and public secondary education: Perspectives from the Somali diaspora in Toronto, Canada. *Race, Ethnicity and Education, 10*(2), 131–153.

Colvin, R. (2009, May 8). *Reuters: Politics.* Retrieved from Reuters Website: http://www.reuters.com/article/2009/05/08/us-obama-muslims-idUSTRE54754920090508?feedType=RSS&feedName=ObamaEconomy&virtualBrandChannel=10441

Commission des Droits de la Personne et des Droits de la Jeunesse. (2011). *Racial profiling and systemic discrimination of racialized youth.* Quebec: Commission des Droits de la Personne et des Droits de la Jeunesse.

Cook, K. (2008). Critical ethnography. In L. Given (Ed.), *The Sage encyclopedia of qualitative research methods* (pp. 148–151). Thousand Oaks, CA: Sage Publications.

Cottle, S. (2006). *Mediatized conflict: Developments in media and conflict studies.* Berkshire: Open University Press.

Corsoro, W. C. (1997). *The sociology of childhood.* Thousand Oaks, CA: Pine Forge.

Cour Superieure du Quebec. (2010). *Loyola High School et John Zucchi Demandeurs c.* Michelle Courchesne, En Sa Qualite De Ministre De L'Education, Du Loisir et Du Sport. Quebec, Canada.

Crenshaw, K., Gotanda, N., Peller, G., & Thomas, K. (1995). Introduction. In K. Crenshaw, N. Gotanda, G. Peller, & K. Thomas (Eds.), *Critical race theory: The key writings that formed the movement* (pp. xiii–xxxii). New York, NY: The New Press.

CTV. (2006, February 9). *CTV News.* Retrieved September 5, 2011, from CTV Web site: http://www.ctv.ca/CTVNews/Canada/20060209/Montreal_mosques_060209/

CTV News. (2013, September 10). *CTV News: Canada.* Retrieved September 9, 2014, from CTV News web site: http://www.ctvnews.ca/canada/new-online-poll-claims-66-support-in-quebec-for-values-charter-1.1448791

CTV News. (2014, February 19). *The globe and mail: News.* Retrieved March 2, 2014, from The Globe and Mail website: http://www.theglobeandmail.com/news/news-video/video-quebec-survey-points-to-rise-in-attacks-on-muslim-women/article16986420/?utm_source=Media+Watch+2%2F28%2F2014&utm_campaign=MW_20-12-2013&utm_medium=email

Curran, P. (2010, August 28). *Montreal Gazette: Sports.* Retrieved November 11, 2010, from http://www.montrealgazette.com/sports/2010wintergames/Montreal+m%C3%A9tro+Parliament+Hill+reported+terror+targets/3448645/story.html

Dalton, M. (2012, January 29). *CBC News: Montreal.* Retrieved February 25, 2014, from CBC News website: http://www.cbc.ca/news/canada/montreal/shafia-jury-finds-all-guilty-of-1st-degree-murder-1.1150023

Dar, J. (2010). Holy Islamophobia, Batman! Demonization of Muslims and Arabs in mainstream American comic books. In J. Kincheloe, S. Steinberg, & C. Stonebanks (Eds.), *Teaching against Islamophobia* (pp. 99–110). New York, NY: Peter Lang Publishing.

Daulatzai, S. (2012). *Black star crescent moon: The Muslim international and Black freedom beyond America.* Minneapolis, MN: University of Minnesota Press.

Davis, N., & Starn, R. (1989). Introduction. *Representations, 26,* 1–6.

De Genova, N. (2002). Migrant 'illegality' and deportability in everyday life. *Annual Review of Anthropology, 31,* 419–447.

Delgado, R. (1989). Symposium: Legal storytelling. *Michigan Law Reivew, 87,* 2073.

Delgado, R. (Eds.). (1995). *Critical race theory: The cutting edge.* Philidelphia, PA: Temple University Press.

Delgado, R., & Stefancic, J. (1994). Critical race theory: An annotated bibliography 1993, a year of transition. *University of Colorado Law Review, 66,* 159–193.

Derfel, A. (2014, October 23). *Montreal Gazette: Local news.* Retrieved from Montreal Gazette web site: http://montrealgazette.com/news/local-news/radicalization-and-mental-health-looking-for-answers

DesRoches, S. (2013). Intercultural citizenship education in Québec: (Re)producing the Other in and through historicised colonial patterns and unquestioned power relations. *Educational Research for Social Change, 2*(2), 5–16.

DeVault, M., & McCoy, L. (2002). Institutional Ethnography: Using interviews to investigate ruling relations. In J. Gubrium & J. Holstein (Eds.), *Handbook of interview research: Context and method* (pp. 751–776). Thousand Oaks, CA: Sage Publications.

Diamond, T. (1992). *Making gray gold: Narratives of nursing home care.* Chicago, IL: University of Chicago Press.

Dickonson, J., & Young, B. (2008). *A short history of Quebec: Fourth edition.* Montreal, QC: McGill-Queen's University Press.

DiMaggio, A. (2008). *Mass media, mass propaganda: Examining American news in the "War on Terror".* Lanham, MD: Lexington Books.

DiMaggio, A. (2009, December 4). *Zcommunications.* Retrieved May 6, 2014, from Zcommunications website: http://zcomm.org/znetarticle/fort-hood-fallout-cultural-racism-and-deteriorating-public-discourse-on-islam-by-anthony-dimaggio/

Dinet, E., & Ben Ibrahim, S. (1925). *L'Orient vu de l'Occident.* Paris: Piazza-Geuthner.

Dougherty, K. (2014, January 21). *Montreal Gazette: Home.* Retrieved February 17, 2014, from Montreal Gazette: http://www.montrealgazette.com/news/Liberals+clarify+stance+charter+niqabs+burkas+chadors+authority+figures/9411201/story.html

Dowling, M. (2008). Reflexivity. In L. Given (Ed.), *The Sage encyclopedia of qualitative research methods* (Vol. 2, pp. 747–748). Thousand Oaks, CA: Sage Publications.

Downs, S. (2011). *Victims of America's dirty war: Tactics and reasons from COINTELPRO to the War on Terror.* Albany, NY: Project Salam.

Dudziak, M. (1988). Desegregation as a cold war imperative. *Stanford Law Review, 41*(1), 61–120.

Dunand, F. (1998). Manuels scolaires et religions, une enquete (1991–1998). *Revue Francais de Pedagogie, 125,* 21–28.

Eder, D., & Fingerson, L. (2002). Interviewing children and adolescents. In J. Gubrium & J. Holstein (Eds.), *Handbook of interview research: Context and method* (pp. 181–201). Thousand Oaks, CA: Sage.

Esposito, J. (1999). *The Islamic threat: Myth or reality?* New York, NY: Oxford University Press.

Esposito, J. (2011). Introduction. In J. Esposito & I. Kalin (Eds.), *Islamophobia: The challenge of pluralism in the 21st century* (pp. xxi–xxxv). New York, NY: Oxford University Press.

Esposito, J., & Mogahed, D. (2007). *Who speaks for Islam? What a billion Muslims really think.* New York, NY: Gallup Press.

Fairclough, N. (1995). *Language and power.* London: Longman.

Fairclough, N. (2003). *Analysing discourse: Textual analysis for social research.* London: Routledge.

Fanon, F. (1963). *The wretched of the earch.* New York, NY: Grove Press.

Fanon, F. (1965). Algeria unveiled. In C. Oglesby (Ed.), *The new left reader* (pp. 161–185). New York, NY: Grove Press.

FBI. (2005, December). *FBI: Reports and publications.* Retrieved April 15, 2014, from FBI website: http://www.fbi.gov/stats-services/publications/terrorism-2002-2005/terror02_05#forward

Fine, M. (2000). Working the hyphens: Reinventing self and the other in qualitative research. In N. Denzin & Y. Lincoln (Eds.), *Handbook of qualitative research* (pp. 70–82). Thousand Oaks, CA: Sage.

Fontana, A. (2003). Postmodern trends in interviewing. In J. Gubrium & J. Holstein (Eds.), *Postmodern interviewing* (pp. 51–65). Thousand Oaks, CA: Sage.

Fourest, C., & Venner, F. (2003). Islamophobie?: Islamophobes? Ou simplement Laiques! *Pro Choix.*

Freeze, C. (2009, March 19). *The globe and mail: National.* Retrieved March 17, 2014, from http://www.theglobeandmail.com/news/national/reluctant-judge-orders-terror-suspect-back-to-prison/article1347742/

Freire, P. (2000). *Pedagogy of the oppressed.* New York, NY: Continuum.

Freire, P. (1985). *The politics of education.* Santa Barbara, CA: Greenwood Publishing.

Friscolanti, M. (2008, July 23). *Maclean's: National.* Retrieved February 23, 2013, from Maclean's website: http://www.macleans.ca/canada/national/article.jsp?content=20080723_115512_115512

Gagnon, A., & Iacovino, R. (2005). Interculturalism: Expanding the boundaries of citizenship. In R. Maiz Suarez, & F. Requejo (Eds.), *Democracy, nationalism and multiculturalism* (pp. 25–43). New York, NY: Frank Cass.

Garber, R. (2014, February 23). *The record: News.* Retrieved March 2, 2014, from The Record website: http://www.sherbrookerecord.com/content/veiled-me

Gauvreau, M. (2005). *The catholic origins of Quebec's quiet revolution, 1931–1970.* Montreal, QC: McGill-Queen's University Press.

Giardina, M. (2010). Barack Obama, Islamophobia, and the 2008 U.S. presidential election media spectacle. In J. Kincheloe, S. Steinberg, & C. Stonebanks (Eds.), *Teaching against Islamophobia* (pp. 135–157). New York, NY: Peter Lang Publishing.

Gilbert, N. (2008). *Researching social life: Third edition.* London: Sage.

Gillborn, D. (2009). Education policy as an act of white supremacy: Whiteness, critical race theory, and educational reform. In E. Taylor, D. Gillborn, & G. Ladson-Billings, *Foundations of critical race theory in education* (pp. 51–72). New York, NY: Routledge.

Giroux, H. (1983). Theories of reproduction and resistance in the new sociology of education: A critical analysis. *Harvard Educational Review, 53,* 257–293.

Giroux, H. (1988). *Teachers as intellectuals: Toward a critical pedagogy of learning.* Westport, CT: Bergin & Garvey.

Giroux, H. (1992). Education, pedagogy, and the politics of cultural work. In D. Trend (Eds.), *Cultural pedagogy: Art/education/politics* (pp. vii–x). New York, NY: Bergin & Garvey.

Goldman, A. (2012, October 23). *Toronto star: News; world.* Retrieved February 23, 2013, from Toronto Star website: http://www.thestar.com/news/world/2012/10/23/i_was_paid_by_ny_police_to_bait_muslims_informant_says.html

Gottschalk, P., & Greenberg, G. (2008). *Islamophobia: Making Muslims the enemy.* Lanham, MD: Rowman & Littlefield Publishing Group, Inc.

Governement du Quebec, Conseil superieur de l'education, Comite Catholique. (1987). *La juridiction et les responsabilites du comite Catholique.* Quebec, Canada.

139

Gouvernement Du Quebec, Ministere de L'Education, Loisir et Sport. (1998). *A school for the future: A new direction for success.* Quebec: MELS.

Governement du Quebec, Ministere de l'education. (1999). *Religion in secular schools: A new perspective for Quebec.* Quebec, Canada: Governement du Quebec.

Gouvernment du Quebec, Ministère des Communautés culturelles et de l'Immigration du Québec. (1990). *Au Québec pour bâtir ensemble: Énoncé de politique en matière d'immigration et d'integration.* Quebec, Canada.

Gramsci, A. (1971). *Selections from teh prison notebooks* (Q. Hoare & G. Nowell-Smith, Eds, & Trans.). New York, NY: International Press.

Green, J. (2003). *Jesus and Mohammad: The parallel sayings.* Berkeley, CA: Seastone.

Green, T. (2015). *Fear of Islam: An introduction to Islamophobia in the West.* Minneapolis, MN: Fortress Press.

Greenwald, G. (2010, February 19). *Salon: News.* Retrieved November 3, 2010, from Salon Web site: http://www.salon.com/news/opinion/glenn_greenwald/2010/02/19/terrorism

Gubrium, J., & Holstein, J. (2003). From the individual interview to the interview society. In J. Gubrium, & J. Holstein (Eds.), *Postmodern inteviewing* (pp. 21–49). Thousand Oaks, CA: Sage.

Hage, G. (2000). *White nation: Fantacies of white supremacy in a multicultural society.* New York, NY: Routledge.

Hall, S. (1986). Gramsci's relevance for the study of race and ethnicity. *Journal of Communication Inquiry, 10*(2), 5–27.

Hall, S. (1996). Racist ideologies and the media. In P. Marris, & S. Thornham (Eds.), *Media studies: A reader* (pp. 160–168). Edinbergh: Edinbergh University Press.

Hall, S. (1997). *Representation: Cultural representations and signifying practices.* Thousand Oaks, CA: Sage Publications.

Hall, S. (2004). Racist ideologies and the media. In P. Marris & S. Thornham (Eds.), *Media studies: A reader* (2nd ed, pp. 271–282). New York, NY: New York University Press.

Hall, S. (2011). The whites of their eyes: Racist ideologies and the media. In G. Dines & J. Humez (Eds.), *Gender, race, and class in the media: A critical reader* (pp. 81–84). Thousand Oaks, CA: Sage Publications.

Haque, E. (2012). *Multiculturalism within a bilingual framework: Language, race, and belonging in Canada.* Toronto, ON: University of Toronto Press.

Harris, P. (2012, March 20). *Guardian: World.* Retrieved February 23, 2013, from Guardian: http://www.guardian.co.uk/world/2012/mar/20/fbi-informant

Hawes, S. (1998). Positioning a dialogical reflexivity in the practice of feminist supervision. In B. Bayer, & J. Shotter (Eds.), *Reconstructing the psychological subject: Bodies, practices and technologies* (pp. 94–110). Thousand Oaks, CA: Sage.

Helms, J. (1992). *A race is a nice thing to have: A guide to being a white person or understanding the white persons in your life.* Topeka: Content Communications.

Humphreys, A. (2012, October 26). *National post: Canada.* Retrieved March 1, 2014, from National Post website: http://news.nationalpost.com/2012/10/26/hamed-shafias-promise-to-his-sister-on-her-wedding-night-if-you-leave-with-your-husband-ill-kill-everyone-here/

Hussain, D. (2004). The impact of 9/11 on British Muslim identity. In R. Geaves, T. Gabriel, Y. Haddad, & J. Smith (Eds.), *Islam and the west post 9/11* (pp. 115–129). Hants: Ashgate.

Jabir, H. (2013, November 9). *Toronto Star: Opinion.* Retrieved March 1, 2014, from Toronto Star website: http://www.thestar.com/opinion/commentary/2013/11/09/quebec_must_respect_womens_right_to_choose_the_hijab.html

Jay, M. (2010). Critical race theoy, multicultural education, and the hidden curriculum of hegemony. *Multicultural Perspectives, 5*(4), 3–9.

Jiwani, Y. (1992, August). To be or not to be: South Asians as victims and oppressors. *Vancover Sun, 5*(45), 13–15.

Jiwani, Y. (2006). *Discourses of denial: Mediations of race, gender, and violence.* Vancouver: UBC Press.

Jiwani, Y. (2010). Doubling discourses and the veilded other: Mediations of race and gender in Canadian media. In S. Razack, M. Smith, & S. Thobani (Eds.), *States of race: Critical race feminism for the 21st century* (pp. 59–86). Toronto, ON: Between the Lines.

Jordan, S. (2003). Who stole my methodology: Co-opting PAR. *Globalisation, Societies and Education, 2*(1), 185–200.

Karakasoglu, Y., & Luchtenberg, S. (2004). Islamophobia in German educational settings: Actions and reactions. In B. v. Driel (Eds.), *Confronting Islamophobia in educational practice* (pp. 35–52). Sterling, VA: Trentham.

Karim, K. (2000). *Islamic peril: Media and global violence.* Montreal: Black Rose Books.

Karim, K. (2002). Making sense of the 'Islamic peril': Journalism as cultural practice. In B. Zelizer & S. Allen (Eds.), *Journalism after September 11* (pp. 101–116). New York, NY: Routledge.

Karmis, D. (2004). Pluralism and national identity(ies) in contemporary Québec: Conceptual clarifications, typology, and discourse analysis (Mélanie Maisonneuve, Trans.). In A.-G. Gagnon (Ed.), *Québec: State & society* (pp. 69–96). Peterborough, ON: Broadview Press.

Kashmeri, Z. (1991). *The gulf within: Canadian Arabs, racism and the Gulf War.* Toronto: Lorimer.

Kellner, D. (2004). September 11, terror war, and blowback. In J. Kincheloe & S. Steinberg (Eds.), *The miseducation of the West: How schools and the media distort our understanding of the Islamic world* (pp. 25–42). Westport, CT: Praeger.

Khan, S. (2009). Integrating identities: Muslim American youth confronting challenges and creating change. In O. Sensoy & C. Stonebanks (Eds.), *Muslim voices in school: Narratives of identity and pluralism* (pp. 27–40). Rotterdam: Sense Publishers.

Kincheloe, J. (2004). Introduction. In J. Kincheloe & S. Steinberg (Eds.), *The miseducation of the West: How schools and the media distort our understanding of the Islamic world* (pp. 1–23). Westport, CT: Praeger.

Kincheloe, J. (2005). *Critical pedagogy primer.* New York, NY: Peter Lang.

Kincheloe, J., & Steinberg, S. (1997). *Changing multiculturalism.* Philadelphia, PA: Open University Press.

Kumar, D. (2012). *Islamophobia and the politics of empire.* Chicago, IL: Haymarket Books.

Kundnani, A. (2014). *The Muslims are coming: Islamophobia, extremism, and the domestic war on terror.* New York, NY: Verso.

Labelle, M. (2010). *Racisme et antiracisme au Québec. Discours et déclinaisons.* Quebec: Presses de l'Université du Québec.

Ladson-Billings, G. (2009). Just what is critical race theory and what's it doing in a nice field like education. In E. Taylor, D. Gillborn, & G. Ladson-Billings (Eds.), *Foundations of critical race theory in education* (pp. 17–36). New York, NY: Routledge.

Larochelle-Audet, J., Borri-Anadon, C., & McAndrew, M. (2013). *La formation initiale du personnel scolaire sur la diversite ethnoculturelle, religieuse et linguistique dans les universites quebecoises: Portrait quantitatif et qualitatif.* Montreal: Centre d'études ethnique des universités montréalaises.

Lean, N. (2012). *The Islamophobia industry: How the right manufactures fear of Muslims.* London: PlutoPress.

Leonardo, Z. (2009). The colour of supremacy: Beyond the discourse of 'white privelege'. In E. Taylor, D. Gillborn, & G. Ladson-Billings (Eds.), *Foundations of critical race theory in education* (pp. 261–276). New York, NY: Routledge.

Leroux, D. (2010). Québec nationalism and the production of difference: The Bouchard-Taylor commission, Québec Identity Act, and Québec's immigrant integration Policy. *Quebec Studies, 49,* 107–126.

Leroux, D. (2012). Debating Québec's interculturalism as a response to Canada's multiculturalism: An exercise in normative nationalisms? *Canadian Diversity, 9*(2), 67–71.

Leroux, D. (2013). The many paradoxes of race in Québec: Civilization, laïcité, and gender inequality. In L. Caldwell, D. Leroux, & C. Leung (Eds.), *Critical inquiries: A reader in studies of Canada.* Halifax: Fernwood Publishing.

Lewis, B. (1993). *Islam and the West.* New York, NY: Oxford University Press.

Lewis, P. (1997, October 24). Islamophobia: A challenge to us all. *The Church Times*.

Liese, J. (2004). The subtleties of prejudice: How schools unwittingly facilitate Islamophobia and how to remedy this. In B. V. Driel (Ed.), *Islamophobia in educational practice* (pp. 57–69). Sterling, VA: Trentham.

Lings, M. (1983). *Muhammad: His life based on the earliest sources*. Cambridge: Islamic Texts Society.

Liogier, R. (2012). *Le mythe de l'islamisation: Essai du rune obsession collective*. Paris: Seuil.

Lopez, I. (2004). The social construction of race. In J. Rivkin & M. Ryan (Eds.), *Literary theory: An anthology* (2nd ed, pp. 964–974). Oxford: Blackwell publishing.

MacLeod, I., Nease, K., & Seymour, A. (2010, August 28). *Montreal Gazette: News*. Retrieved November 11, 2010, from Montreal Gazette Web site: http://www.montrealgazette.com/news/Parliament+ Montreal+subway+were+targets+expert/3451550/story.html

Mahmood, S. (2005). *The politics of piety. The Islamic revival and the feminist subject*. Princeton, NJ: Princeton University Press.

Mahrouse, G. (2010). Reasonable accommodation' debates in Quebec: The limits of participation and dialogue. *Race and Class, 52*(1), 85–96.

Maira, S. (2014). Surveillance effects: South Asian, Arab, and Afghan American youth in the war on terror. In S. Perera & S. Razack (Eds.), *At the limits of justice: Women of colour on terror* (pp. 86–106). Toronto, ON: University of Toronto Press.

Maloney, R. (2015, January 07). *Huffington post: Politics*. Retrieved from Huffington Post website: http://www.huffingtonpost.ca/2015/01/07/thomas-mulcair-paris-shootings-ottawa-attack_n_ 6432136.html

Mamdani, M. (2004). *Good muslim, Bad muslim: America, the Cold War, and the roots of terror*. New York, NY: Three Leaves Press.

Margolis, E. (2008). *American Raj: Liberation or domination*. Toronto, ON: Key Porter Books.

Marx, S. (2008). Critical race theory. In L. Given (Ed.), *The Sage encyclopedia of qualitative research methods* (Vol. 1, pp. 163–167). Thousand Oaks, CA: Sage.

Mastracci, D. (2015, February 11). *Huffington Post: Politics*. Retrieved from Huffington Post Web site: http://www.huffingtonpost.ca/davide-mastracci/harper-mosques_b_6649228.html?utm_source= Media+Watch+12%2F02%2F15&utm_campaign=MW_16-06-2014&utm_medium=email

Mazigh, M. (2009). *Hope and despair: My struggle to free my husband, Maher Arar*. New York, NY: Emblem Editions.

McAlister, M. (2001). *Epic encounters: Culture, media, and U.S. interests in the Middle East, 1945– 2000*. Berkeley, CA: University of California Press.

McAndrew, M. (2010). The Muslim community and education in Quebec: Controversies and mutual adaptation. *Intenational Migration and Integration, 11*, 41–58.

McAndrew, M., Oueslati, B., & Helly, D. (2007). L'évolution du traitement de l'islam et des cultures musulmanes dans les manuels scolaires québécois de langue française du secondaire. *Canadian Ethnic Studies, 39*(3), 173–188.

McDonough, K. (2011). "Voluntary and secret choices of the mind": The ERC and liberal-democratic aims of education. *Religion and Education, 38*(3), 224–240.

McLaren, P. (1997). Critical pedagogy. *Teaching Education, 9*(1), 1–1.

McLaren, P. (1998). Revolutionary pedagogy in post-revolutionary times: Rethinking the political economy of critical educatior. *Educational Theory, 48*, 431–462.

McNally, D. (2002). *Another world is possible: Globalization and anti-capitalism*. Winnipeg, MB: Arbeiter Ring Publishing.

Media Education Foundation. (2005). *Media education foundation: Handouts/articles*. Retrieved June 30, 2014, from Media Education Foundation website: www.mediaed.org/wp/handouts-articles

MELS. (2001). *QEP: Introduction*. Retrieved March 4, 2011, from QEP Web site: http://www.mels.gouv.qc.ca/dfgj/dp/programme_de_formation/primaire/pdf/educprg2001/ educprg2001-010.pdf

MELS. (2005). *Establishment of an ethics and religious culture program: Providing future direction for all Quebec youth*. Quebec: MELS.

MELS. (2006). *Value assigned to the professional judgment of teachers: Questions and answers*. Quebec, QC: Gouvernment du Quebec.

MELS. (2008, May). *MELS: Ethics and religious culture*. Retrieved January 23, 2011, from MELS Web site: https://www7.mels.gouv.qc.ca/DC/ECR/pdf/ecr_secondary.pdf

Miller, M. (2008). Otherness. In L. Given (Ed.), *The Sage encyclopedia of qualitative research methods* (Vol. 2, pp. 587–589). Thousand Oaks, CA: Sage Publications.

Ministere de l'Education, du Loisir et du Sport. (2007). *Quebec education program: Secondary cycle two*. Quebec: Gouvernement du Quebec.

Mirza, K., & Bakali, N. (2010). Islam: The fundamentals every teacher should know. In J. Kincheloe, S. Steinberg, & C. Stonebanks (Ed.), *Teaching against Islamophobia* (pp. 49–64). New York, NY: Peter Lang Publishing.

Mirzeoff, N. (2005). *Watching Babylon: The war in Iraq and global visual culture*. New York, NY: Routledge.

Mishler, E. (1997). Representing discourse: The rhetoric of transcription. *Journal of Narrative and Life History, 255–280*.

Mogensen, K. (2007). How U.S. TV journalists talk about objectivity in 9/11 coverage. In T. Pludowski, *How the world's news media reacted to 9/11: Essays from around the globe* (pp. 301–319). Spokane, WA: Marquette Books.

Mohideen, H., & Mohideen, S. (2008). The language of Islamophobia in internet articles. *Intellectual Discourse, 16*(1), 73–87.

Mookerjea, S. (2009). Hérouxville's Afghanistan, or, accumulated violence. *Review of Education, Pedagogy, and Cultural Studies, 31*(2), 177–200.

Morey, P., & Yaqin, A. (2011). *Framing muslims: Stereotyping and representation after 9/11*. Cambridge, MA: Harvard University Press.

Morgalis, E., & Romero, M. (1996). The department is very male, very white, very old, and very conservative": The functioning of the hidden curriculum in graduate sociology departments. *Harvard Education Review, 68*(1), 1–32.

Morris, R. (2011). Cultivating reflection and understanding: Foundations and orientations of Quebec's ethics and religious culture program. *Religion and Education, 38*(3), 188–211.

Morris, R., Bouchard, N., & De Silva, A.-M. (2011). Enthusiasm and ambivalence: Elementary school teacher perspectives on the ethics and religious culture program. *Religion and Education, 38*(3), 257–265.

Mossalli, N. (2009). The voice of a covered Muslim-American teen in a Southern public school. In O. Sensoy & C. Stonebanks (Eds.), *Muslim voices in school: Narratives of identity and pluralism* (pp. 55–69). Rotterdam: Sense Publishers.

Murphy, E., & Dingwall, R. (2001). The ethics of ethnography. In P. Atkinson, A. Coffey, S. Delamont, J. Lofland, & L. Lofland, *The handbook of ethnography* (pp. 339–351). Thousand Oaks, CA: Sage Publication.

Nagata, A. L. (2004). Promoting selfe reflexivity in intercultural education. *Journal of Intercultural Communications, 8*, 139–167.

Nieguth, T., & Lacassagne, A. (2009). Contesting the nation: Reasonable accommodation in rural Quebec. *Canadian Political Science Review, 3*(1), 1–16.

O'Brien, J. (2014, February 12). *IFP Press: News*. Retrieved February 18, 2014, from IFB Press Website: http://www.lfpress.com/2014/02/12/women-arent-coerced-into-wearing-the-head-coverings-according-to-report

Olwan, D. (2013). Gendered violence, cultural otherness, and honour crimes in Canadian national logics. *Canadian Journal of Sociology, 38*(4), 533–555.

O'Toole, E. (2014, October 23). *The Guardian: Comment*. Retrieved from The Guardian web site: http://www.theguardian.com/commentisfree/2014/oct/23/ottawa-shooting-canada-terrorism-draconian-response

Palmer, P. (1997). *The courage to teach: Exploring the inner landscape of a teaher's life*. New York, NY: John Wiley & Sons.

Paludi, M. (2012). *Managing diversity in today's workplace: Strategies for employees and employers.* Santa Barbara, CA: Praeger.

Paperny, A. M. (2016, April 13). *Global news.* Retrieved from Global News: Montreal: http://globalnews.ca/news/2634032/hate-crimes-against-muslim-canadians-more-than-doubled-in-3-years/?utm_source=Media+Watch+-+April+16%2C+2016&utm_campaign=MW_16-06-2014&utm_medium=email

Parker, L. (2010). Race is race ain't': An exploration of the utility of critical race theory in qualitative research in education. *International Journal of Qualitative Studies in Education, 11*(1), 43–55.

Parker, L., & Stovall, D. (2004). Actions following words: Critical race theory connects to critical pedagogy. *Educational Philosophy and Theory, 36*(2), 167–182.

Perigoe, R. (2007). September 11 in Canada: Representation of muslims in the Gazette. In T. Pludowski (Ed.), *How the world's news media reacted to 9/11: Essays from around the globe* (pp. 319–340). Spokane, WA: Marquette Books.

Peritz, I. (2013, August 20). *The globe and mail: Politics.* Retrieved April 23, 2014, from The globe and mail website: http://www.theglobeandmail.com/news/politics/parti-quebecois-under-fire-over-proposal-to-ban-religious-symbols/article13869072/

Perkel, C. (2012, Decemeber 7). *Toronto star: News.* Retrieved March 18, 2014, from Toronto Star website: http://www.thestar.com/news/canada/2012/12/07/canadas_evidence_against_mohamed_mahjoub_tainted_by_torture_lawyer_says.html

Pignatelli, F. (1998). Critical ethnography/poststructuralist concerns: Foucault and the play of memory. *Interchange, 294*, 403–423.

Plucinska, J. (2015, June 24). *Time magazine.* Retrieved from Time: US: http://time.com/3934980/right-wing-extremists-white-terrorism-islamist-jihadi-dangerous/

Potvin, M. (2010). Social and media discourse in the reasonable accommodation debate. *Our Diverse Cities, 7*, 78–83.

Proudfoot, S. (2010, October 31). *Montreal Gazette; life.* Retrieved January 23, 2011, from Montreal Gazette Web site: http://www.montrealgazette.com/life/Growing+foreign+born+population+forge+Canada/2666075/story.html

Prout, A., & James, A. (1997). A new paradigm for the sociology of childhood? Provenance, promise, and problems. In A. Prout & A. James (Eds.), *Constructing and reconstructing childhood: Contemporary issues in the sociological study of childhood* (pp. 7–33). London: Falmer.

Pugliese, D. (2014, November 1). *Ottawa citizen: News.* Retrieved from Ottawa Citizen website: http://ottawacitizen.com/news/national/defence-watch/harper-silent-on-anti-muslim-backlash-over-killings-of-soldiers

Quantz, R. (1992). On critical ethnography (with some postmodernist considerations). In M. LeCompte, W. Millroy, & J. Preissle (Eds.), *The handbook of qualitative research in education* (pp. 447–505). San Diego, CA: Academic Press.

Rahman, S. (2007, December). *Transnational media reception, Islamophobia, and the identity constructions of non-Arab Muslim diasporic community:The experiences of Bangladeshis in the U.S. since 9/11* (PhD dissertation). Southern Illinois university, Carbondale, IL.

Ramachandran, T. (2009). No woman left covered: Unveiling and the politics of liberation in multi/interculuralism. *Canadian Woman Studies, 27*(2,3), 33–39.

Rana, J. (2007). The story of Islamophobia. *Souls: A Critical Journal of Black Politics, Culture, and Society, 9*(2), 148–161.

Rana, J. (2011). *Terrifying muslims: Race and labor in the South Asian diaspora.* Durham, NC & London: Duke University Press.

Raymond, G. (1992). *Basic interview skills.* Itasca, IL: F.E. Peacock.

Razack, S. (1998). *Looking white people in the eye: Gender, race, and culture in courtrooms and classrooms.* Toronto: University of Toronto Press.

Razack, S. (2008). *Casting out: The eviction of Muslims from western law & politics.* Toronto, ON: University of Toronto Press.

Razack, S. (2010). Abandonment and the dance of race and bureaucracy in spaces of exception. In S. Razack, M. Smith, & S. Thobani (Eds.), *States of race: Critical race feminism for the 21st century* (pp. 87–110). Toronto, ON: Between the Lines.

Razack, S. (2014). The manufacture of torture as public truth: The case of Omar Khadr. In S. Perera & S. Razack (Eds.), *At the limits of justice: Women of colour on terror* (pp. 57–85). Toronto: University of Toronto Press.

Rezai-Rashti, G. (2005). The persistence of colonial discourse: Race, gender, and Muslim students in Canadian schools. In V. Zawilski & C. Levine-Rasky (Eds.), *Inequality in Canada: A reader on the intersection of gender, race and class* (pp. 178–187). Don Mills, Ontario: Oxford University Press.

Roberts, M., & Roberts, A. (1996). *Memory: Luba art and the making of history.* New York, NY: The Museum for African Art.

Runnymede Trust. (1997). *Islamophobia a challenge for us all.* London: Runnymede Trust.

Runnymede Trust. (2007, February). *Runnymede trust: Reports.* Retrieved March 1, 2013, from Runnymede Trust website: www.runnymedetrust.org

Russell, G., & Kelly, N. (2002). Research as interacting dialogic processes: Implications for reflexivity. *Forum: Qualitative Social Research, 3*(3), Art. 18.

Rymarz, R. (2012). Teaching ethics and religious culture in Quebec high schools: An overview, contextualization, and some analytic comments. *Religious Education: The Official Journal of the Religious Education Association, 107*(3), 295–310.

Saghaye-Biria, H. (2012). American Muslims as radicals? A critical discourse analysis of the US congressional hearing on 'The Extent of Radicalization in the American Muslim Community and that Community's Response'. *Discourse and Society, 23*(4), 508–524.

Said, E. (1979). *Orientalism.* New York, NY: Vintage Books.

Said, E. (1993). *Culture and imperialism.* New York, NY: Alfred A. Knopf.

Said, E. (1997). *Covering Islam: How the media and the experts determine how we see the rest of the world.* New York, NY: Vintage Books.

Salaita, S. (2006). *Anti-Arab racism in the USA: Where it comes from and what it means for politics today.* Ann Arbor, MI: Pluto Press.

Sammon, B. (2001, September 26). Bush urges Afghans to help oust Taliban. *Washington Times.*

Sandford-Gaebel, K. (2013). Germany, Islam and education: Unveiling the contested meanings of the headscarf. In Z. Gross, L. Davies, & A.-k. Diab (Eds.), *Gender, religion and education in a Chaotic postmodern world* (pp. 185–197). New York, NY: Springer.

Sarwar, G. (2000). *Islam: Beliefs and teachings.* London: The Muslim Educational Trust.

Status of Women Canada. (2003). *Fact sheet: Statistics on violence against women in Canada.* Ottawa: Status of Women Canada.

Schlein, C., & Chan, E. (2010). Supporting Muslim students in secular public schools. *Diaspora, Indigenous, and Minority Education: Studies of Migration, Integration, Equity, and Cultural Survival, 4*(4), 253–267.

Schultze, H. (Ed.). (1994). *Islam in schools of Western Europe. An example of intercultural education and preperation for interreligious understanding.* Cologne: Bahlau.

Securite Publique Quebec. (2009). *Quebec government: Securite publique.* Retrieved February 25, 2014, from Quebec Government website: http://www.securitepublique.gouv.qc.ca/en/police/publications-statistiques-police/statistiques-violence-conjugale/statistiques-violenceconjugale/violence-conjugale-2009/5059.html

Selby, J. (2011). French secularism as a 'guarantor' of women's rights? Muslim women and gender politics in a Parisan banlieue. *Culture and Religion: An Interdisciplinary Journal, 12*(4), 441–462.

Sensoy, O. (2009). Where the heck is the "Muslim world" anyways? In O. Sensoy & C. Stonebanks (Eds.), *Muslim voices in school: Narratives of identity and pluralism* (pp. 71–85). Rotterdam: Sense Publishers.

Sensoy, O. (2010). "Mad man Hassan will buy your carpets!": The bearded curricula of evil Muslims. In J. Kincheloe, S. Steinberg, & C. Stonebanks (Eds.), *Teaching against Islamophobia* (pp. 111–134). New York, NY: Peter Lang Publishing.

Sensoy, O., & Stonebanks, C. (2009). *Muslim voices in school.* Boston, MA: Sense Publishing.

Services Canada. (2012, June). *Sectoral outlook 2012–2014: Quebec region.* Retrieved February 10, 2014, from Services Canada: http://www.servicecanada.gc.ca/eng/qc/sectoral_outlook/so_RegionQuebec.pdf

Shaheen, J. (2001). *Reel bad Arabs: How Hollywood vilifies a people.* New York, NY: Olive Branch Press.

Shaheen, J. (2008). *Guilty: Hollywood's verdict on Arabs after 9/11.* Northampton, MA: Olive Branch Press.

Sheehi, S. (2011). *Islamophobia: The ideological campaign against Muslims.* Atlanta, GA: Clarity Press.

Sherry, M. (2008). Postcolonialism. In L. Given (Ed.), *The Sage encyclopedia of qualitative research methods* (Vol. 2, pp. 650–655). Thousand Oaks, CA: Sage Publications.

Solorzano, D., & Yosso, T. (2009). Critical race methodology: Counter-Storytelling as an analytical framework for education research. In E. Taylor, D. Gillborn, & G. Ladson-Billings (Eds.), *Foundations of critical race theory in education* (pp. 131–147). New York, NY: Routledge.

Spivak, G. C. (1988). *In other worlds: Essays in cultural politics.* New York, NY: Routledge.

Stasi Commission. (2003). *Stasi commission report.* Paris: Gouvernement du France.

Steinberg, S. (2004). Desert minstrels: Hollywood's curriculum of Arabs and Muslims. In J. Kincheloe & S. Steinberg (Eds.), *The miseducation of the West: How schools and the media distort our understanding of the Islamic world* (pp. 171–179). Westport, CT: Praeger.

Steinberg, S. (2010). Islamophobia: The viewed and the viewers. In J. Kincheloe, S. Steinberg, & C. Stonebanks (Eds.), *Teaching against Islamophobia* (pp. 79–97). New York, NY: Peter Lang Publishing.

Stonebanks, C. (2010). The inescapable presence of 'non-existent' Islamophobia. In J. Kincheloe, S. Steinberg, & C. Stonebanks (Eds.), *Teaching against Islamophobia* (pp. 29–48). New York, NY: Peter Lang Publishing.

Sutherland, A. (2014, November 13). *Montreal Gazette: News.* Retrieved from Montreal Gazette website: http://montrealgazette.com/news/local-news/man-pleads-guilty-in-2012-acid-attack-on-ex-girlfriend-tanya-st-arnauld

Swartz, E. (1992). Emancipatory narratives: Rewriting the master script in the school curriculum. *Journal of Negro Education, 61,* 341–355.

Talbani, A. (1993). Intercultural education and minorities: Policy initiatives in Quebec. *McGill Journal of Education, 28*(3), 407–419.

Tammivaara, J., & Enright, D. (1986). On eliciting information: Dialogues with child informants. *Anthropology and Education Quaterly, 17,* 218–238.

Tanner, D., & Tanner, L. (1975). *Curriculum development: Theory into practice.* New York, NY: Merrill.

Tatum, B. (2009). Teaching white students about racism: The search for white allies and the restoration of hope. In E. Taylor, D. Gillborn, & G. Ladson-Billings (Eds.), *Foundations of critical race theory in education* (pp. 277–290). New York, NY: Routledge.

Taylor, C. (2007). *The age of secularism.* Cambridge, MA: Harvard University Press.

Taylor, E. (2009). The foundations of critical race theory in education: An introduction. In E. Taylor, D. Gillborn, & G. Ladson-Billings (Eds.), *Foundations of critical race theory in education* (pp. 1–16). New York, NY: Routledge.

Teotonio, I. (2010, January 11). *Toronto Star: News; GTA.* Retrieved February 23, 2013, from Toronto Star website: http://www.thestar.com/news/gta/2010/01/11/informant_paid_millions_to_infiltrate_toronto_18_testifies.html

Thobani, S. (2007). *Exalted subjects: Studies in the making of race and nation in Canada.* Toronto: University of Toronto Press.

Thobani, S. (2010). White innocence, Western supremacy: The role of Western feminism in the "War on Terror". In S. Razack, M. Smith, & S. Thobani (Eds.), *States of race: Critical race feminism for the 21st century* (pp. 127–146). Toronto, ON: Between the Lines.

Thomas, D. (2006). A general inductive approach for analyzing qualitative evaluation data. *American Journal of Evaluation, 27,* 237–246.

Thomas, R. (2014). Violence and terror in a colonized country: Canada's Indian residential school system. In S. Perera & S. Razack (Eds.), *At the limits of justice: Women of colour on terror* (pp. 23–37). Toronto: University of Toronto Press.

Threadgold, T. (2003). Cultural studies, critical theory and critical discourse analysis: Histories, remembering and futures. *Linguistik Online, 14*(2), 5–37.

Tirri, K. (2009). Ethical dilemmas in conformation school experienced by Finish confirmation schoolteachers. In G. Skeie (Ed.), *Religious diversity and education: Nordic perspectives* (pp. 223–234). Munster, Germany: Waxmann.

Trumpener, B. (2016, July 29). *CBC Website*. Retrieved from CBC News: http://www.cbc.ca/news/canada/british-columbia/crown-seeks-peace-bond-for-john-nuttall-and-amanda-korody-under-fear-of-terrorism-criminal-code-section-1.3701536 .

Turgeon, L. (2004). Interpreting Québec's historical trajectories: Between la société globale and the regional space (S. Lyons, Trans.). In A.-G. Gagnon (Ed.), *Québec: State & society* (pp. 51–61). Peterborough, ON: Broadview Press.

Van der Wee, E. (2011). On the front lines: A teacher's experience with Quebec's ethics and religious culture program. *Religion and Education, 38*(3), 241–256.

van Dijk, T. (1989). Mediating racism: The role of the media in the reproduction of racism. In R. Wodak (Ed.), *Language, power, and ideology: Studies in political discourse* (pp. 199–226). Amsterdam & Philadelphia, PA: John Benjamins.

van Dijk, T. (1994). Critical discourse analysis. *Discourse and Society, 5*(4), 435–436.

Waddington, D., Maxwell, B., McDonough, K., Cormier, A., & Schwimmer, M. (2011). Interculturalism in practice: Québec's new ethics and religious culture curriculum and the Bouchard-Taylor report on reasonable accommodation. In M. Peters, & T. Besley (Eds.), *Interculturalism, education & dialogue.* New York, NY: Peter Lang.

Weller, P., Feldman, A., & Purdam, K. (2001). *Religious discrimination in England and Wales.* London: Home Office Research Study.

Weninger, C. (2008). Critical discourse analysis. In L. Given (Ed.), *Sage encylcopedia of qualitative research methods* (Vol. 1, pp. 145–147). Thousand Oaks, CA: Sage Publications.

Wilkins, C. (2006). Student teachers and attitudes towards 'race': The role of citizenship education in addressing racism through the curriculum. *Westminster Studies in Education, 24*(1), 7–21.

Willaime, J. (2007). Different models for religion and education in Europe. In R. Jackson, S. Miedema, W. Weisse, & J. P. Willaime (Eds.), *Religion and education in Europe: Developments, contexts and debates* (pp. 194–209). Munster, Germany: Waxmann.

Wong, A. (2009). The winter of Our discontent: "Reasonable Accommodation" and the 2007 Québec election. In T. Rahimy (Eds.), *Representation, expression & identity: Interdisciplinary insights on multiculturalism, conflict and belonging* (pp. 137–152). Oxford: Interdisciplinary Press.

Wong, A. (2011). The disquieting revolution: A genealogy of reason and racism in the Québec press. *Global Media, 4*(1), 145–162.

Yosso, T. (2010). Towards a critical race curriculum. *Equity and Excellence in Education, 35*(2), 93–107.

Zine, J. (2001). Muslim youth in Canadian schools: Education and the politics of religious identity. *Anthropology & Education Quarterly, 32*(4), 399–423.

Zine, J. (2006). Between orientalism and fundamentalism: Muslim women and feminist engagement. In K. Hunt & K. Rygiel (Eds.), *(En)gendering the war on terror* (pp. 27–51). Hampshire: Ashgate Publishing.

Zine, J. (2006). Unveiled sentiments: Gendered Islamophobia and experiences of veiling among Muslim girls in a Canadian Islamic school. *Equity & Excellence in Education, 39*(3), 239–252.

Zine, J. (2009). Unsettling the nation: Gender, race and Muslim cultural politics in Canada. *Studies in Ethnicity and Nationalism, 9*(1), 146–163.

147

INDEX

Printed in the United States
By Bookmasters